BITTER CARNIVAL

BITTER CARNIVAL

RESSENTIMENT

AND THE ABJECT HERO

Michael André Bernstein

PRINCETON UNIVERSITY PRESS   PRINCETON, NEW JERSEY

Copyright © 1992 by Princeton University Press
Published by Princeton University Press, 41 William Street,
Princeton, New Jersey 08540
In the United Kingdom: Princeton University Press, Oxford
All Rights Reserved

Library of Congress Cataloging-in-Publication Data
Bernstein, Michael André, 1947–
Bitter Carnival : ressentiment and the abject
hero / Michael André Bernstein.
p.   cm.
Includes index.
ISBN 0-691-06939-5
1. Abjection in literature.   2. Heroes in literature.   3. Cynicism
in literature.   4. Literature—History and criticism.
I. Title.   II. Title: Ressentiment and the abject hero.
PN56.A23B4   1992
809'.93353—dc20   91-25871   CIP

This book has been composed in Linotron Galliard

Princeton University Press books are printed
on acid-free paper and meet the guidelines
for permanence and durability of the Committee
on Production Guidelines for Book Longevity
of the Council on Library Resources

Printed in the United States of America

10 9 8 7 6 5 4 3 2 1

for

ANNA-NORA BERNSTEIN

and

MOSES ELCH BRUGGER

nothing matters but the quality
of the affection

Contents

Acknowledgments ─────────────────────────────

SINCE I began work on this book, I have benefited from the intelligence, time, and generous advice of a circle of close friends and colleagues. To be able to articulate at least a portion of my gratitude to them here is one of the major pleasures of completing the work. Two of these in particular, Alex Zwerdling and Gary Saul Morson, participated in the shaping and reshaping of the entire text, offering encouragement, close scrutiny and exacting criticism with a commitment of time and lucidity that I hope will seem justified by the pages that follow. I was saved from a great many errors and alerted to many fresh possibilities by the instigations of Jeffrey Akeley, Robert Alter, John A. DeWitt, Caryl Emerson, R. Scott Hamilton, Robert Hollander, Leo Lowenthal, Thomas G. Rosenmeyer, the late Jean Seznec, Richard Sieburth, Katharine Streip, and Robert Yarber. The staff at Princeton University Press, especially Beth Gianfagna, production editor; Victoria Wilson-Schwartz, my copy editor; and Robert Brown, literature editor, have my gratitude for their detailed and constructive suggestions. Most important, my wife, Jeanne Wolff Bernstein, helped me in ways that the rhetoric of an acknowledgment could never register.

I want to thank the American Council of Learned Societies, the Koret Foundation, the Committee on Research of the University of California, Berkeley, and the Departments of English and Comparative Literature at the University of California, Berkeley, for granting me the time and the funds to work on this study.

In very different versions, sections of chapters 1, 2, and 6 appeared as three separate articles in *Critical Inquiry*, where Robert von Hallberg has been a consistently helpful and encouraging advocate for my writing. Part of chapter 4 was published in the volume *Rethinking Bakhtin: Extensions and Challenges*, edited by Gary Saul Morson and Caryl Emerson (Evanston: Northwestern University Press, 1989). I am grateful to all the editors involved, both for their valuable suggestions and for permission to reprint portions of these essays here.

For his generous permission to use the painting *Un moment hors du temps*, on the cover of the book, I would like to thank the artist, Gérard Lapagesse. I am very grateful as well for the cooperative support of his gallerist in Paris, Jacques Adolphe Martin, at the Galerie Naïfs du Monde Entier.

BITTER CARNIVAL

Introduction

Murder and the Utopian Moment

you'll never know what obsessive hatred really
smells like [. . .] That's the hatred that kills you.
[. . .] it will ooze out over the earth . . . and
poison it, so nothing will grow but viciousness,
among the dead, among men.
  (Louis-Ferdinand Céline, *Mort à crédit*)

Death is psychosomatic.
  (Charles Manson, *Year of the Fork, Night of
  the Hunter*)

IN JULY 1979, on my way to visit my family in Toronto, I stopped for a few
days in New York. On one of those evenings, at a friend's apartment, I
wanted to see who was playing in some of the clubs I used to visit when I
still lived on the East Coast. My friend passed me a copy of that week's
Village Voice, and I can still remember idly flipping through it before turning back for a moment to glance at the cover. Then I felt the room turn
suddenly quiet, and something that must have been nausea but seemed
utterly unfamiliar constricted my world to a kind of dispersed aching. The
headline read: "Blinded by the Light: The Einhorn-Maddux Murder
Case." The beginning of the article was framed on the left by a photo of a
heavy-set, bearded man called Ira Einhorn above the caption "Philadelphia's favorite hippie son, sought cosmic consciousness and ingenuous
child women he could mold," and on the right by a picture of a young
woman, Holly Maddux, who was described as "shy and self-doubting,
sought a guru. She found him in Einhorn, who today stands charged with
her murder."[1] Although I could not recognize her at first from the harsh,
over-exposed newspaper image—a detail that in itself disturbed me—I immediately realized that the victim was the same woman I had known a
decade earlier when she was a student at Bryn Mawr College. Even though
we had several friends in common, Holly and I were never especially intimate and had lost touch altogether after she temporarily withdrew from
the university. So it was not the news of her death alone that shocked me,
nor even learning about it so accidentally and publicly. It was the story of
her being bludgeoned to death and hidden in a steamer trunk for almost

eighteen months, the brute fact of the murder, that continued to haunt me for a long time.

The details of the killing were unnervingly weird, even for an era and a milieu in which the weird was commonplace. But what gave the story the kind of exemplary significance that prompted the *Village Voice* to devote much of an entire issue to it, and that, a decade later, would lead an investigative journalist to publish a luridly detailed book about the case (*The Unicorn's Secret: Murder in the Age of Aquarius*), was Ira Einhorn's status as a prankster-theoretician, organizer, and hero of Philadelphia's radical and hippie communities. It was Einhorn the murderer, not Holly Maddux his victim, who made the event "newsworthy," and after an initial revulsion at the disparity of concern, I, too, began to let myself follow the vicissitudes of Einhorn's bizarre career. What obviously most impressed the reporters was Einhorn's success in bridging supposedly irreconcilable constituencies. His advice was sought by the "counter-culture" of Philadelphia's hippie enclave, Powelton Village, and by Robert De Witt, the diocese's Episcopal Bishop, who temporarily put Einhorn on his payroll; by the city's underground press and by William S. Cashel, the President of Pennsylvania Bell, who scheduled regular meetings with Einhorn in order to stay better informed about significant social issues; by the advocates of an "alternative university" and by the administrators and students of Harvard's Kennedy School of Government, where Einhorn had been appointed a Fellow for the fall semester just before the discovery of Holly Maddux's body in the locked closet of an enclosed porch overlooking his backyard.[2]

Before his dramatic arrest, Ira Einhorn had placed himself at the center of several highly charged local festivals, including, in April 1967, Philadelphia's first "Be-In," and, three years later, always alert to changing slogans and rallying-cries, the April 1970 nationally televised "Earth Day" in Fairmount Park. Even today, the photographs of those occasions show how immensely popular such celebrations were, ceremonies that in their licensed freedom and joyous suspension of all restraints resembled nothing so much as a contemporary Saturnalia, a re-creation in the modern city parks of the carnivalesque market squares of medieval and Renaissance Europe. The central impulse of a "Be-In" was to mark out a utopian space in which to practice the rites of the coming permanent revolution, rites in which there would be no more distinction between participants and spectators since all roles would be interchangeable and neither script nor director would be necessary. The exuberant revelers massed together to jettison the repressive demands of a society based on hierarchies of value and acts of ordering. In their eyes, the instinctual renunciations exacted by the too well-regulated lives of their parents and teachers served only to nourish a culture of anxiety and frustrated denial. Morse Peckham, who had been Einhorn's professor, as well as friend and mentor, at the University of

Pennsylvania, had coined the phrase "man's rage for chaos," to celebrate the power of "artistic perception . . . to weaken and frustrate the tyrannous drive to order,"[3] and, for a brief time, the promise of an entirely beneficent chaos seemed to be in the process of realization. But like the traditional carnival, that era's Saturnalia also had its dark side, its current of anarchic violence and disdain for constraints of any kind, including ultimately, among its sociopathic visionaries like Ira Einhorn, the prohibition against murder.

"The atrocity of the act carries one above mere contempt,"[4] is how Rameau's Nephew explains his fascination with the aesthetics of evil, and there is a grim sense in which my own response to Einhorn and all that he embodied confirmed some of the most sardonic of Jean-François Rameau's insights into human nature. In other circumstances, Einhorn, the "cosmic consciousness" who fused radical politics, drugs, and paranormal psychic explorations, would have struck me as more ridiculous than sinister, a figure entirely characteristic of his time and defined by the perfect conjunction of his self-representation and the commonplaces of his day. He was exactly what Rameau calls an "espèce" or "type—the most frightening of all epithets because it indicates mediocrity and the ultimate degree of contempt."[5] But no matter how complex and difficult to delineate my response to Ira Einhorn might be, there is no doubt that it went far beyond such contempt. My response, although instinctive and automatic, was also deeply troubling, because it appeared to privilege the very pathology that had helped make possible a character like Einhorn in the first place. I seemed to be acceding to the terms of a dichotomy (the grip of evil, if it is only "original" or ruthless enough, on our imaginations, versus our indifference to pedestrian normalcy) whose actual consequences I found unendurable. And so I began to wonder about the sources of that acceptance, both in order to understand it better, and perhaps, by having done so, to contest more coherently its imaginative force.

I have always written out of the conviction that the narratives on which our imaginations are nourished help script both the fantasies and the actual decisions of our everyday lives. The sway of a powerful literary convention is exercised as effectively in mass culture as in great art, and the entire career of someone like Ira Einhorn was possible only because he succeeded in focusing upon himself all of the identificatory sympathy aroused by the character type he seemed to incarnate. The clearest way to anticipate the larger ambition of this book is to stress that I intend neither to belabor a character like Einhorn nor to take him as symbolic of the "sixties." But I believe that both he and his epoch are characteristic manifestations of a certain utopian anarchism at the heart of the Saturnalian impulse. Whether enacted by men like Ira Einhorn and his followers in the 1960s, or by the "revolutionary millenarians and mystical anarchists of the Middle Ages" whose violent careers Norman Cohn anatomized in *The Pursuit of the Millennium*, when the tropes of a Saturnalian reversal of all values spill over into daily life, they usually do so with a savagery that is the grim underside of their exuberant affirmations. It is precisely the festival's bitter side, the relationship between its celebratory and its rage-filled aspects, that I want to probe.

Without his violence, Einhorn's combination of seductive charm and gaping insecurity, his nimble, improvisatory wit cloaking a chronic incapacity ever to finish a serious project, and his sense of planetary significance coexisting with a fundamental self-doubt about his intellectual/sexual worth might have made him seem like a contemporary and all too human instance of a type I already had defined as "the Abject Hero" in an earlier reading of Diderot's *Le Neveu de Rameau*.[6] But the shock of Holly Maddux's murder brought home to me with stark immediacy how permeable were the frontiers between the literary and theoretical questions with which I was grappling and the moral and cultural landscape I inhabited.

Einhorn, I learned, had boasted openly of his craziness. In a 1970 piece he wrote for the Catholic Art Association, he announced that "Violence is the simplest mode of contact—it allows touch without formality,"[7] and during his famous 1971 campaign for mayor of Philadelphia against Frank Rizzo, he claimed an elective affinity with Charles Manson. Nonetheless, the personal flair on which he relied for his career, and which, in a sense, constituted his sole occupation, survived even the gruesome revelations at his indictment. Einhorn was defended by the city's former District Attorney, Arlen Specter, now a United States Senator from Pennsylvania, and due in large part to his considerable local celebrity, he was released on forty thousand dollars bail. In the event, Einhorn was never brought to trial since he chose to forfeit bail and flee to Europe, where presumably he is still living today.

Einhorn's public role, like his own temperament, had flourished amidst contradictions and gathered energy from occupying seemingly incompatible positions. Like a stock figure whose antics appeared perfectly scripted to play the licensed jester in the drama of a bitterly divided city, Einhorn managed to perform successfully to multiple, and mutually suspicious, audiences. Presenting himself as something between a shaman and a clown, Einhorn spoke to anyone who would listen, but without ever allowing his interlocutors to gauge the proportion of seriousness or mockery in his words. Most winning of all, his mockery extended to himself as often as to others, and he seemed quite ready to join in whatever laughter his pretensions as a "guru" raised.[8] A constantly shifting repertoire of tones, attitudes, and ideas served to keep open the maximum number of opportunities for self-promotion, until finally Einhorn really did move easily between hostile social worlds, becoming a "celebrity rebel" in the vanguard of his supposedly disenfranchised and unheeded peers.

But flaunting one's contempt for the constraints of normative, prosaic life and finding a kind of liberation in the kinship between oneself and a mythologized image of the underground and the outlaw is a thoroughly familiar gambit. Its conventions have been repeated, although with an increasingly derivative shrillness, at least since the beginning of the nineteenth century, as part of the rhetoric by which each generation stakes its claim to a radically fresh perception. Retrospectively, perhaps the most significant aspect of such self-representation during the 1960s was how widely its tropes circulated and how readily they found acceptance, even in circles that might have been expected to cast a colder, more skeptical eye on the self-aggrandizing claims of the day. Often it seemed that the same longings possessed both the hippies of Powelton Village and the perceived guardians of conventional pieties, so that instead of meeting resistance, people like Einhorn were welcomed sympathetically by leaders of the very institutions they despised. Being part of Einhorn's conversational circle conferred a certain status on even the most solidly established of his interlocutors: it served to prove the imaginative flexibility and intellectual range of men whose successful careers appear to have left them feeling curiously vulnerable to charges of philistine mediocrity and "Establishment" privilege. Graduates of the same universities from which people like Einhorn had dropped out, and raised on the same narratives that endowed the rebel with the talismanic glamor of authenticity, the corporate executives, educators, and civic leaders whom Einhorn approached were, at the level of a shared cultural mythology and fantasized desires, already persuaded of his potential significance before any actual dialogue began. It is important to grasp that the people Einhorn fascinated were not, as conventional theory would have it, trying to "co-opt" a revolutionary threat in order to safeguard their privileges. On the contrary, they themselves genuinely believed in much of his message about their own inadequacies, and at the level of wish fulfillment found his lifestyle both more glamorous and more authentic than their own. No doubt, considering the professional choices and daily lives of his interlocutors, they apparently had little hesitation in rejecting the domain whose representative Einhorn claimed to be. But, as we are only beginning to understand with any precision, such rejection is often accompanied, in the words of Peter Stallybrass's and Allon White's *The Politics and Poetics of Transgression*, by "a psychological dependence upon [those who have been] rigorously opposed and excluded at the social level. It is for this reason that what is *socially* peripheral is so frequently *symbolically* central," and that choices and traits that had been "expelled as 'Other,' return as the objects of nostalgia, longing and fascination."[9]

At least since the French Revolution, the figure of the "mad" artist, the uncompromising, single-minded rebel, and the philosopher working at the (appropriately named) "cutting edge" of the unthinkable have been staples of cultural mythology, applauded by the consumers of our culture precisely for the signs of excess that testify to how completely the archetype has been embodied.[10] In effect, what seduced Einhorn's admirers was less a particular individual than a literary/philosophical character by whom they had already been won over numerous times in the books and movies on which they had grown up, a character who could draw on all the resources of a long tradition heroicizing his defiant integrity and refusal to "conform." Einhorn united an apparent readiness for self-mockery with a mastery of what Theodor Adorno had called "The Jargon of Authenticity," and during the time before Holly Maddux's body was discovered, that combination was potent enough to give Einhorn an immediate measure of power over anyone responsive to those cues.

Einhorn's elaborate network of contacts in the academic, political, and business hierarchies indicates the astonishing receptivity of diverse mainstream constituencies and discourses to the rhetoric of the self-declared marginal and powerless. To what extent such receptivity has always functioned as a kind of "containment strategy," a willingness to yield on minor matters in order to preserve intact the integuments of actual power, and to what extent it can also lay bare a real loss of faith in the values and practices of the traditional social institutions on the part of its own leaders, is one of the central questions addressed in this book. But it is a question that needs to be posed anew in different historical contexts and moments of crisis, and any attempt at an answer must be responsive to the specific and distinct pressures of the lived moment.

For the mid-1960s, however, there is abundant evidence that significant sections of both the intelligentsia and the principal voices of popular culture were united in a common eagerness to throw off the authority of inherited intellectual, moral, and political conventions. Crystallized in texts like Norman O. Brown's *Love's Body* (1966), with its academic Dionysianism; R. D. Laing's *The Politics of Experience and The Birds of Paradise* (1967), with its celebration of the schizophrenic as incarnating the truth of a mad society; or Eldridge Cleaver's *Soul on Ice* (1968), with its homophobia and vision of rape as "an insurrectionary act" provoked by white racism, the era was rich in quasi-prophets, who differed in their specific recommendations but shared a contempt for the pedestrian decencies and mutual concessions on which ordinary communal existence depends. The longing for an immediate Apocalypse, for an instantaneous and utter transformation of "the history of all hitherto existing society," was wedded both to a rejection of the practice of intellectual discrimination and a concomitant refusal to recognize any meaningful frontier between madness and sanity.[11]

I will not be concerned in the study that follows to offer another example of the by now rather tired genre of "sixties bashing." But I do want, from the outset, to argue that when we celebrate the carnivalesque and speak so confidently of the utopian longing for a radically open and unfettered relationship, not just toward one another, but toward the conflicting impulses and desires whose interactions shape us, there is a cruel human risk to these idealizations. The viciousness that can be released by the carnival's dissolution of the accumulated prudential understanding of a culture needs to figure in our thinking about the rhetorical strategies and ideological assertions within which utopian theorizing is articulated. And this necessity is all the more compelling because the theorizing so often prides itself upon transcending the historical consequences of its own axioms. The readiness to sacrifice not so much one's own as everyone else's welfare for the sake of a doctrinaire fantasy is *the* archetypal totalitarian impulse and is as traceable in intellectual debates as in political programs.

The *déformation intellectuelle* in our cultural debates is marked by an indecent haste to label, and then evaluate, ideas on the flimsiest and most self-flattering criteria. Any critical analysis of the literary-historical problems posed by the Saturnalia as the embodiment of carnivalesque desire, and any reminder of the immense cost of earlier efforts to give utopian longings a local habitation and a name, must risk directly confronting that *déformation*. But these problems are themselves only an aspect of the broader issues of how we scrutinize the values we champion and/or contest in our interpretations of narratives, and how we struggle to bring into a mutually clarifying perspective our sense of fundamental human hopes and the lived historical experience of specific communities.

What Einhorn made clear to me was how, in the right circumstances, abjection could lead directly to a *ressentiment* embittered enough to erupt into murder. *Ressentiment* like his combines anger, envy, and pride, the three most destructive of the still pertinent medieval catalog of sins, and it is a characteristically modern hypocrisy to cloak such impulses for as long as possible in the language of social compassion. The inescapable reality of the trajectory from abjection to *ressentiment*, and its incarnation, whether in the revolutionary cells whose inscape Dostoevsky traced in *The Possessed*, or in the grotesque fusion of delirious anti-Semitism and abject self-pity of the Vichy Collaborators chronicled in Louis-Ferdinand Céline's World War II trilogy, compelled me to confront a deeper and more anxiety-provoking nexus of historical, moral, and narrative problems than I had envisaged when I began this project. In the process, the nature of my thinking underwent numerous changes, and the book that ensued is, among other things, an attempt to register as lucidly as I can the exigencies of that confrontation.

More specifically, I intend to return to the classical topoi and theories of the Saturnalian dialogue to see how a certain literary mode and its attendant philosophical and rhetorical vision slowly unfolded, following a logic that is partially formal and internal to the genre and partially a response to new historical conditions and crises. From Horace's paradigmatic account of a master-slave encounter during the festival of the Saturnalia, to the emergence of the Abject Hero as a parasite confronted by the fascinated disapproval of an Enlightenment intellectual in Diderot's *Le Neveu de Rameau*, to the violent fusion of abjection and *ressentiment* in Dostoevsky and Céline, my attention will be focused on the literary works in which these problems receive their most provocative articulations. But at the book's conclusion, I want to return to our contemporary situation to see how our most widespread and long-lived myths, together with the conventions of mass culture, supplied the tropes by which a pathological killer could present himself as the accuser of the society he had brutalized. That the murderer, Charles Manson, almost immediately became one of the most potent icons of his era and began to function as a literary myth in subsequent narratives makes clear how pervasive the tropes of abjection and *ressentiment* are in our culture's imagination, and how easily our theoretical fascination with the illicit and the taboo can be marshaled by anyone who has a stake in eliding the differences between murderers and their victims.

My aim, explicitly argued in the final chapter but implicitly present throughout the whole book, will be to test the theoretical judgments and emotional identifications we perform so confidently—and apparently courageously—in our textual interpretations by confronting them with the demands of our daily lives and the prosaic judgments on which our social and cultural habitat depends for its survival. The works on which I will concentrate in this book all proceed by questioning the pieties of their day—including, in their most recent incarnations, the piety that applauds any radical subversion of normative social codes—but they do so in a way that exposes the compromises and subterfuges of every side in the debate: the smugness of the comfortable marshals of order as well as the *ressentiment* of the frustrated local Raskolnikovs, brooding on their thwarted potential in a thousand urban garrets. And if I have followed any one principle in the chapters that follow, it is only to listen as closely as possible to the conflicting voices in the texts I will be analyzing, to those dialogues in which every one of the questions I will be repeating were first broached in all their insistent complexity.

Part I _____

PROBLEMS AND PRECURSORS

. . . so thick bestrown
Abject and lost lay these . . .
  (John Milton, *Paradise Lost*)

One

I Wear Not Motley in My Brain:
Slaves, Fools, and Abject Heroes

A clown, perhaps, but an aspiring clown.
  (Wallace Stevens, "The Comedian as the
  Letter C")

"THERE IS no slander in an allowed fool, though he do nothing but rail."[1]
So Olivia assures Malvolio in Shakespeare's *Twelfth Night*, but, of course,
the very necessity of giving voice to such assurance indicates that offense
has already been given, if only to the prickly steward, "sick of self-love" and
temperamentally hostile to the clown's impertinent playfulness. The crucial
word here is "allowed," as Olivia seeks to show the essential harmlessness
of her fool's raillery, not by disputing the content of his barbs, but rather,
by emphasizing what kind of person has uttered them. Her remark cuts
two ways, since it defines a commonly recognized guild ("allowed fools")
whose speech, as the very condition of its tolerated license, may amuse or
bore, but never wound, their patrons, and another group, whose social
position is sufficiently uncertain and whose vanity sufficiently susceptible
(a steward, for example, with aspirations above his station) to permit even
a fool's words to sting them. Only a genuine fool, in other words, would
take offense at anything said by so inconsequential a creature as a noble-
woman's hired clown. Olivia's reproof is really a miniature lesson in decorum: her definition has all the confidence of an aristocrat's instinctive grasp
of everyone's allotted role in her household and sure knowledge of how
much significance should be granted to their utterances. How fragile such
confidence proves, how vulnerable to the vicissitudes of fortune or desire,
is one of Shakespeare's most persistent themes, central not only to comedies like *Twelfth Night* but to virtually every play in the canon.

Even in this brief exchange, however, Malvolio is not without resources,
and he has anticipated Olivia's words with a lesson of his own:

I protest I take these wise men that
crow so at these set kind of fools
no better than the fool's zanies.

(1.5.82–84)

From the beginning, that is, Malvolio refuses to engage the issue of how much weight ought to be attached to a fool's banter, questioning instead the quality of mind and character able to find amusement in such creatures. Indeed, the annoyance evident in Olivia's rebuke indicates that Malvolio's words have skirted dangerously close to "slander," and her suggestion that the steward is only acting like another kind of fool represents an irritable attempt to neutralize his protest. The entire scene is constructed like an echo chamber, in which folly rings out from character to character: Malvolio and Olivia exchange accusations of foolishness while Feste accuses both of acting like fools, and in the spectator's eyes, all three are correct in their diagnoses. It is as though folly were like a contagion which, once introduced into the world of the play, spreads unstoppably from person to person. One of the chief "tests" of the characters is precisely how they deal with their own folly once its power to govern human behavior has been made manifest. The sympathetic figures accept, as part of their human lot, that they are in some sense fools, while the play's resolution banishes those who reject the lesson entirely and continue to blame others for their own folly.

Thus, in the course of the play, Olivia, too, must pass through her own lesson in the folly of misrecognition; but our sympathies in the dialogue I have quoted are clearly not with Malvolio, and his argument is never given a serious hearing by the other characters. He is too much the archetypal "malcontent" to frame his complaint persuasively, and by splitting the role of clown and embittered social critic into two distinct figures, Shakespeare effectively denies either one an authoritative perspective.[2] But if it seems as though I have made too much of a momentary exchange in *Twelfth Night*, consider this outburst of aggrieved self-defense by Jean-François Rameau, failed composer, failed parasite, and unhappily patronless "allowed fool":

> There is no better role in the company of the great than that of a fool. For a long time there was an official king's fool but never an official king's wise-man. I am Bertin's fool as well as that of many others; right now, perhaps, I am yours, or, perhaps, you are mine. A sage would not keep a fool. Therefore, whoever does have a fool isn't a wise man, and if he is not a wise man, then he must be a fool, and if he is a king, then perhaps he is only his fool's fool.[3]

In Diderot's satire, our sympathies shift bewilderingly from the *philosophe* to the nephew and back again, and we are never able to arrive at a consistent assessment of either speaker's authority. This dizzying series of intellectual and emotional reversals, in which *Moi* and *Lui* alternately seem to triumph, only to have the grounds of their victory suddenly prove inadequate, accounts for much of *Le Neveu de Rameau*'s power to perplex and fascinate its readers. Although never published during its author's lifetime, the dialogue is pivotal in Diderot's career as a writer, as well as in the complex history of the "wise fool" as a central vehicle of satiric negation. All of these aspects will need to be explored in detail when we return to analyze *Le Neveu de Rameau* as a model text in which the literary possibilities of a new kind of Saturnalian ironist, a character I call "the Abject Hero," are first deployed with full self-consciousness. For the moment, though, it is enough to register how closely Jean-François Rameau's argument ("only a fool would keep a fool") echoes Malvolio's splenetic outburst.

Yet, if the intellectual thrust of the two statements is virtually identical, each deriving from a conventionally sanctioned Stoic maxim, the affective resonance is entirely different if the speaker is a Malvolio as opposed to a Rameau. Malvolio is giving voice to an apothegm he believes does not implicate him, whereas Rameau talks from the position of a "licensed fool" who acknowledges his membership in a craft he can no longer either tolerate or abandon, but whose boundaries, he feels, encompass the entire social universe with iron hoops. In the world of *Twelfth Night* it is not Feste who lashes out at the whole institution of fools and their patrons. In the accepted tradition of the licensed fool, Feste is free to demonstrate his mistress's folly and to mock her sentimentality ("Good madonna, give me leave to prove you a fool" [1.5.53]), but his position is too securely embedded in the conventions of his role and the specific dramatic situation to be questioned from within. Only a deluded *arriviste* like Malvolio has reason to feel disgust at "these men that crow so" at the behavior of "set fools," and his gullible self-regard and grotesque behavior vitiates much of the force his criticism would otherwise possess. But when the questioner, like Rameau, is fully aware of how deeply he himself is implicated in the behavior and values he finds ridiculous, a new dimension of painful self-consciousness comes into play, and the entire relationship of the characters to one another, to the positions they defend or contest, and, most importantly, to the reader attempting to make sense of the work, is radically transformed.

Before attempting a more general definition of this transformation, I want to glance at a still earlier text in which the topos that underlies both Malvolio's and Jean-François Rameau's protest is first articulated with lapidary concision:

"imbecillus, iners, si quid vis, adde, popino.
tu cum sis quod ego et fortassis nequior, ultro
insectere velut melior verbisque decoris
obvolvas vitium?" quid, si me stultior ipso
quingentis empto drachmis deprenderis? . . .[4]

["I am weak, lazy, and if you like to add, a glutton. But you, since you are just the same and maybe worse, would you presume to assail me, as though you were a

better man, and would you throw a cloak of seemly words over your own vices?"
What if you are found to be a greater fool than even I, who cost you five hundred
drachmas?]

Horace's Saturnalian dialogue with his slave Davus contains, in its 118
hexameter lines, a remarkable repository of images, character types, and
rhetorical strategies that succeeding generations of writers continue to
draw upon, sometimes implicitly, as in the Renaissance use of a "wise fool"
to mock the folly of kings and masters, and sometimes explicitly, as in *Le
Neveu de Rameau*, where both *Moi* and *Lui* repeatedly cite specific Horatian
verses and arguments. The philosophical issues raised in Horace's Satire
2.7 may be little more than illustrations of standard Stoic paradoxes that
only the philosopher who has conquered his baser wants is free (*Mónos ho
sophòs eleútherhos* [Only the sage is free]), and that irrespective of his official
rank, a fool is always a kind of slave (*Pās áphrhon doũlos* [Every fool is a
slave]).[5] But the skill with which Horace has embedded these paradoxes in
a witty and plausible dialogue and the daring with which he has represented his own well-known characteristics as fitting targets of the satire's
sting give the work its exemplary force. The accusations that Horace endures from his slave and the literary structure within which those charges
are framed reverberate throughout subsequent Western literature, and it is
one of my aims to explore these reverberations as they continue to echo in
the most diverse and unexpected circumstances.

So far in these opening pages I have given three concrete instances of a
textual paradigm flexible enough to be operative in a variety of genres and
languages. Although my examples illustrate particularly striking realizations, it may be helpful now to attempt a more general, even if necessarily
partial, formulation of the Saturnalian dialogue's fundamental structure.

A master and his slave, a monarch and his fool, a philosopher and a
madman: even as the particulars of the role change with the epoch and
text, the underlying configuration seems to remain the same. Irrespective
of the specific work in which such pairings occur, we respond, long before
the details of the argument clearly emerge, to a convention whose power
rests on its promise to subvert our notion of power and convention, and to
a fixed set of characters whose dialogues will undermine our trust in the
existence of stable identities and fixed character traits. At the center of the
agon there is always a moment of absolute reversal when it is the slave, like
Horace's Davus, who calls his master "O totiens servus [O you slave many
times over]" (2.7.70), or Diderot's frustrated sponger, Jean-François Rameau, who proves the *philosophe* no better than the fool of a fool.

Popular wisdom and high literature have long been at one in seeing a
simultaneously haunting and comic parallel in the destinies of monarchs
and their fools. But in Anglo-American criticism it was only with the appearance in 1935 of Enid Welsford's ground-breaking study, *The Fool: His*

Social and Literary History, that scholars from a variety of disciplines became more alert to the significance of the buffoon as a crucial figure in the courts, literature, and popular festivals of medieval and Renaissance Europe, as well as in the character types of Elizabethan drama. In turn, the more recent acceleration of interest in the anarchic world of the carnival is undoubtedly due to the belated translations of Mikhail Bakhtin's writings. It is largely through Bakhtin's influence that we have learned to apply terms like "carnivalization" to the collapse of hierarchic distinctions on which the confrontation I have outlined depends, and it is a major part of Bakhtin's legacy to have taught us better how to value the liberating energy of the carnivalesque. For Bakhtin and his successors, carnival laughter is both a form and a vehicle of popular liberation. They see in the festive license of the Saturnalia, with its carnivalization of all normally inflexible distinctions, the embodiment of a permanent utopian longing, a glimpse of a prelapsarian world free from cast and cant, "opposed to all that was ready-made and completed, to all pretense at immutability."[6]

Yet Bakhtin's description of the carnivalesque has a distinctly melancholy undertone, since it is framed as a largely *post festum* recollection of a tradition whose last full realization he finds in the works of François Rabelais.[7] His typology of laughter is full of richly textured local insights, but it is haunted from its inception by a nostalgic longing for a realm of pure spontaneity, for a rite of universal participation whose essentially affirmative character is guaranteed by its very universality. Characteristic of such a carnival is the ability to absorb every aspect of life into the whorl of its supposedly "regenerating power," and to abolish entirely all distinctions between participant and viewer: "Carnival does not know footlights, in the sense that it does not acknowledge any distinction between actors and spectators. Footlights would destroy a carnival, as the absence of footlights would destroy a theatrical performance. Carnival is not a spectacle seen by the people; they live in it, and everyone participates. . . . While carnival lasts, there is no other life outside it."[8]

But as soon as the question of literary representation arises, the "footlights" that separate actor and spectator, reader and character, come into being, assuring the very divisions the work's carnivalesque rhetoric would deny. Belatedness, the knowledge of coming after the festival has already been fragmented, is thus not limited, as Bakhtin wants us to believe, to a post-Renaissance bourgeois culture; it is itself a condition of every Saturnalian text. What changes throughout history is not the inclusiveness of the carnival per se but the literary consequences of acknowledging that belatedness.[9] It is precisely these consequences that interest me: the ways in which the Saturnalian conventions become increasingly problematic, and the carnivalesque dialogues more shrill and unnerving. I do not want merely to locate a counter-tradition, but rather to isolate a negative and bitter strand at the core of the Saturnalia itself.

There are two conceptually separable concerns in a project like this: the first is the treatment of a specific genre, the Saturnalian dialogue, which includes ancient and Renaissance works as well as modern texts; the second is the analysis of a particular figure, the Abject Hero, who is essentially modern and makes his first full appearance in *Le Neveu de Rameau*. As the proportion of my chapters and the emphases of my individual readings make clear, it is on the second of these two issues that I will focus. But problems that can be divided so cleanly in principle are in practice often vitally, and even messily, intertwined. Of course, neither the classical Saturnalia, nor modern, theoretical constructs like Bakhtin's notion of carnival, privilege abjection. Instead, they emphasize the positive vigor of the briefly dominant underling. But since it is as the antithesis of the Saturnalia's optimistic and celebratory assumptions that the Abject Hero emerges, understanding the figure requires a vision of the tradition within which he arose and whose destructive aspects he continues to incarnate, no matter how much the convention's frontiers and surface characteristics have changed in succeeding eras.

If we return now to consider the initial description of the Saturnalian dialogue's confrontation, a number of questions occur as soon as one begins to endow it with any historical specificity:

1. How are the various roles of master and slave, monarch and fool, etc., defined in a work that sets up a dialogue between the two? Are the determinants exclusively social in conception or do they contain, from the beginning, a moral and psychological dimension? For example, there is no inherent assumption in Roman literature that a master need be either wiser or better than the slave who is his property; the differences in power and personal autonomy are decisive, but, for all their importance, these distinctions carry few implications about the personal qualities of either man. On the other hand, a monarch is conventionally presumed to possess an entire range of attributes in addition to his politico-legal authority, such as wisdom, a knowledge of statecraft, a devotion to principles of order, a sense of justice, etc., all of which his licensed fool presumably lacks. These initial, and purely conventional, expectations are crucial in determining both the points of contention between the speakers and the thrust of the dialogue's irony. Thus, for a Davus to prove that his master is only a slave himself subverts the normative understanding of their respective roles in a more fundamental way than his argument about Horace's laziness or lack of courage. But in order to undermine the claims of a representative Enlightenment sage, a parasite like Jean-François Rameau must direct his aim at the *philosophe*'s pretensions to moral and intellectual superiority, not merely at his social rank and economic prosperity.

2. How much familiarity about the generic roles of his antagonists can the author assume as a kind of literary/cultural *donnée* already known to his

reader, and to what extent must these expectations be explicitly thematized in the work itself? The fundamental model of a master/slave relationship, for instance, is both broader and more clearly codified than that between a *philosophe* and a corrupt sponger. Accordingly, Diderot will need to spend far more time than Horace in establishing the pertinent characteristics of his respective social types and the likely areas of contention between them. A norm can only be contested once it has been recognized as such, and a relationship inverted only after its initial premises are firmly known. The question of the reader's competence to recognize the operative conventions and character types is crucial in determining his expectations. But the audience's competence, its education as consumers of the genre, also guides the author's strategies by giving him a ground bass upon which to improvise his own variations and against which his unexpected dissonances can be heard with maximum force. The more strictly the narrated encounter follows the model in its pure form, the more the experience of previous instances creates a framework of pre-texts with which the new example is aligned and according to which its specific unfolding will be interpreted. The "licensed fool" of the Renaissance courts and Elizabethan drama, for instance, is expected to "demonstrate" his master's folly in an entertaining fashion, and a reader of *Twelfth Night* is already prepared, by a prior knowledge of the convention, to focus on Feste's wit in performing his task, without spending time wondering at the clown's audacity in making light of Olivia's sentiments. But a convention can also be drawn upon in a more disguised fashion, so that part of the text's difficulty may arise from the ways it seeks to delay, and sometimes to thwart entirely, recognition of how it has adapted the topos for its own purposes. This issue becomes particularly acute in works like Dostoevsky's *Notes from Underground* or Céline's World War II trilogy, novels that depend heavily on the battle of wills and wits between a *ressentiment*-riven Abject Hero and his supposed betters. But in these books, the contest has taken so violent and exacerbated a form that there is a risk the reader will fail to identify the convention at all, and thus see the works as deficient in coherence and structure.

3. What measure of self-consciousness about their roles do the characters themselves possess, and with what degree of naturalness or ill-ease do they inhabit the conventional requirements of their parts? It is important to notice that this question is distinct from the earlier one about the *audience's* recognition of the topos; indeed, the two kinds of knowledge, one strictly internal to the text as part of the characters' consciousness and one external as part of the reader's competence, may be set against one another by the author in order to complicate the effects of his fiction. When an "allowed fool" like Feste says "put me into good fooling" (1.5.29), he shows himself capable of standing outside the consciousness of a court fool and must be brought (bribed) into it. But as the trope of being "put into good fooling"

by the master's purse is itself already part of the convention, marking the difference between a hired clown and an actual simpleton, there is no thematic tension between the spectators' recognition of the role and Feste's own brilliant incarnation of its demands. For all Feste's intelligence and quirky pride, on both of which he frequently, perhaps even with suspicious overfrequency, insists in declarations like "I wear not motley in my brain"(1.5.55), there is no disruptive surplus of self-consciousness to interfere with the smooth functioning of his generically determined position in the play. But in *Le Neveu de Rameau*, *Moi*, *Lui*, and the reader engage in an ambiguously complex struggle among various levels of literary foreknowledge, and it is precisely Jean-François Rameau's resentful self-recognition of his role as a "licensed fool" and *Moi*'s growing discomfort at finding himself trapped in the equally stereotyped position of the "fool's" opponent that makes it impossible for anyone to arrive at a superior vantage point from which to judge the speakers with a competence—and hence authority—greater than their own.

4. What temporal structure determines the fictional duration of the dialogue, and how does the temporal framing affect the carnivalesque liberty of the fool or slave? The Roman Saturnalia was celebrated from the seventeenth to the nineteenth of December, and although traditionally it was a time during which slaves were permitted to address their masters with a special measure of license, the certainty that the customary relations would resume almost at once profoundly marks what we know of actual Roman carnival practice as well as the literary versions of Saturnalian dialogues. An analogous sense of strict chronological limits also determines the encounter between *Moi* and *Lui* in *Le Neveu de Rameau*, but it is a limit arbitrarily set by *Moi* alone, and its very imposition betrays a degree of ill-ease more strictly personal and hence more significant thematically than one occasioned by an officially sanctioned festival. By the time of Dostoevsky and Céline, there is no longer any certainty of a return to "normalcy" at all, so the narrative does indeed present a carnivalesque world subject to a permanent inversion of all values, but the consequences are far more lethal and savage than the triumphantly "regenerative" ones envisaged by utopian critics.

These four questions illustrate, in a schematic form, the most prominent variables in the basic pattern, and each of the works I will focus on tends to highlight the consequences of selecting one of the possible configurations as the foundation for its narrative. But the essentially literary decisions about how to determine and then work through a particular variant are also profoundly affected by more elusive cultural pressures, like the conceptions of wisdom and folly, power and servitude, dominant in the society as a whole. The conceptualization of moral and psychological categories is possible only as part of the entire system of beliefs and values by which a culture understands itself, and this conceptualization necessarily affects the ways in which these categories are presented in fictional texts. At issue here is not the simple reflection within a narrative of "external" cultural norms and prejudices. Rather, it is a matter of an author's effective utilization of the codes by which a character can be identified as, say, a buffoon, a madman, or a sage. These codes owe their authority both to an acquired familiarity with literary conventions and to contemporary criteria of judgment absorbed, often unconsciously, from a multiplicity of other public discourses (law, medicine, theology, etc.). A writer may intend to demonstrate the inadequacy or limitations of those criteria, but in order to throw them into doubt, he must first be able to register them accurately enough in his text so the reader recognizes that his own culture's values are implicated in the dialogue. As a result, the most successful realizations of the Saturnalian dialogue demonstrate a complex interaction between the relatively fixed and permanent aspects of the paradigm and the purely contingent, historically changing assumptions of the society in which, and sometimes against which, it is composed.

Consider, for example, William Empson's itemization of the changing fate of the term *fool*, whose meaning has encompassed someone who is: simpleminded; lacking in "common sense"; innocent or inexperienced; duped (as in "made a fool of"); loved or pitied as a dependent; a clown, professional jester, or mocker; a knave, obstinately and viciously stupid; a speaker of the plain truth that no one else utters; and even a man with saint-like qualities (the Pauline "fools for Christ's sake").[10] Analogously, although the word's etymology from the Latin *follis*, a "pair of bellows," makes clear that the heads of fools were pictured as empty husks and their speech as mere "hot air," the same image, re-imagined under different pressures, could be transformed to suggest a gust of wind powerful enough to blow away pretensions or to kindle into fire a spark of truth.

Except in the most self-conscious literary texts, only a small number of these definitions will be intended in the normal public discourse of a community at any given historical moment, while the other meanings are registered, if at all, as a vague penumbra of cultural memory. However, a central feature of the Saturnalian dialogue is not only that, like any acutely sophisticated verbal construct, it can draw on all of the earlier meanings simultaneously and embody them in a convincing character but that it finds in the simultaneity itself a rich source of new literary opportunities. The complexity of a character like Fyodor Karamazov, for example, is due precisely to his incarnating so many of the different senses Empson has traced in the evolution of the idea of the "fool." The father of the four Karamazov brothers is at once a rather clever clown, an obsessive lecher with hysterical symptoms who is both duper and duped in his lust, an affected pseudo-gentleman, and at times even a privileged truth-speaker (as in his arguments with the smugly liberal "Westernizer," Pyotr Alexandrovich Miüsov). Moreover, he is fully aware that his behavior is that of a fool who cannot help exhibiting all of these logically incompatible qualities, and he experiences his condition with the agony of a continual inner laceration. The very longevity of the Saturnalian dialogue has generated a cumulative understanding of its key terms, and, in its modern versions, this understanding is itself part of the fictional characters', as well as of the readers', horizon of expectations.

It is this internalization that gives rise to the Abject Hero. The self-contempt of figures like Jean-François Rameau or the Underground Man is due to their haunted sense of only acting according to "type," of lacking authenticity even in their suffering, where they most need to feel original. But the Saturnalian dialogue's historical duration and widely shared cultural availability, both of which so torment the Abject Heroes, are what make the topos a particularly promising vehicle for a satiric challenge to an era's dominant values. Since the reader recalls previous examples of such challenges, he knows in advance that whoever serves as the text's spokesman for the normative values of the day will no doubt prove himself ridiculous, and more importantly, that even those values that the reader wishes to believe are universal will not escape the relativizing derision of the "licensed fool."

If the strategy and expectations of the fictional characters have been profoundly altered by a learned familiarity with the Saturnalian dialogue's personae and intellectual premises, then so have the reader's by his knowledge of just how unappealing is the role of the "wise fool's" opponent. And it is just at this point that the text's double game becomes particularly tense. It sets the audience's responses as tutored by traditional literary conventions—usually along the supposedly subversive lines of championing the rebelliousness and impertinence of the ironist—against its normal criteria of judgment as expressed in the public discourses of the age. How self-congratulatory such identification with the figures of subversion and anarchy can be is one of my central concerns in this book, and some of the more insidious implications of such flattering identification are emphasized in the concluding chapter. But at its most sophisticated, the Saturnalian dialogue strives to use the reader's own experiences from these twin realms, the social and cultural habitat in which he dwells and the genre memories that mobilize his identificatory sympathy—in order to implicate him directly in the work's mockery. Hence our nervousness when we gradually realize that the voice of a "monster" like the Underground Man or the narrator of Céline's trilogy has placed us, in the very act of judging him a monster, in a position identical to that occupied by *Moi* in his confrontation with Rameau's Nephew. Not to condemn the viciousness of such types would make us their moral accomplices; but to condemn it risks identifying us with a series of increasingly dull and obtusely unimaginative spokesmen for commonplace pieties.

For the reader to have a sound vantage point from which to judge the combatants in a Saturnalian dialogue, he and the author must know and agree upon a standard of ethics and behavior that is outside of, and independent of, the debates in the text. But as soon as that standard is brought directly into the text as a thematic crux, it necessarily loses any absolute authority. Since the values have themselves become part of the debate, they cannot be invoked to settle the contest in the work. The reader is no longer at liberty to rely on a prior code to settle who is right in the dialogue, since it is the validity of that very code that is the bone of contention between the book's antagonists. To do so is merely to occupy the place of one of the fictional combatants, not to resolve their debate with any certainty. The insidious "game" of a novel like *Notes from Underground* or *D'un château l'autre*, a "game" whose moves were first mapped by Diderot's *Le Neveu de Rameau*, is to force the reader to occupy the place of one of the stereotyped antagonists, all the while knowing how untenable such a position really is.

As the licensed fool evolves into the Abject Hero of modern fiction, and then suffers the fusion of his abjection with *ressentiment*, the Saturnalian dialogue turns into a grim trap in which the characters and the readers are equally caught. Undeniably, there is often a distinctly repellent quality in the characteristic "family traits" linking the Abject Heroes we will explore in this study, and yet our encounters can yield some of the exhilaration of any genuine engagement with the most dubious side of our imaginative identifications. From the impertinent slave of Augustan Rome to the unrepentant Collaborator of Vichy France, the voices to which we shall be listening in the following pages remind us, with a mixture of malice, cunning, and rage, that for them the carnival was always marked by bitterness and that the licensed fool whose jests, so we comfort ourselves, contain no slander, may already have shed his clown's motley and begun to rail in earnest. The ensuing Saturnalia will indeed inaugurate Bakhtin's "carnival without footlights," but it will be experienced as a communal catastrophe of devastating proportion. The carnivalesque marketplace depicted in modern literature will be far different from the idealized image of a boisterous medieval fair or even from the safe confines of Diderot's Café de la Régence. Instead, the reader will follow an itinerary through a continent in ruins, in which insane murderers and shell-shocked victims stagger from one bombed-out castle to another. The most fitting slogan for this apocalyptic carnival is Céline's outcry toward the end of *Rigodon*: "that's what man has come to with all his immense, ecumenical, superatomic progress: everybody's in the arena and not a single spectator is left in the stands."[11]

> What is a monster? A being whose survival is
> incompatible with the existing order.
>   (Denis Diderot, *Eléments de physiologie*)

When Diderot proposes his famous definition of the monster, he immediately qualifies it by reminding us that "the existing order is ceaselessly changing; how, then, in the midst of such vicissitudes, could any species survive unchanged?"[12] In the moral realm, as well as in the world of nature, Diderot recognized that monstrosity is a relative, temporally defined term, not a transcendent category that can be grasped *sub specie aeternitatis*. What we regard as monstrous may bear within itself the normative logic of a future dispensation; it may represent an unhappy, isolate survivor of a time in which it was once daily custom; or, most troubling of all, the monstrous may tempt us to see it as only the fractured mirror of our own cultural identity, showing forth the instinctual repressions and ideological compromises on which our ideals depend for their very energy and structure.

The speech act by which we designate someone a monster implicates both parties, initiating a tense dialogue in which repudiation can never entirely shut off an element of mutual recognition. Although, in our time, no one has probed the iron network of dependencies linking civilization to its most monstrously alien impulses with more pessimistic lucidity than Sigmund Freud, his work in this domain followed directly the pathmarks laid down by the eighteenth-century rationalists. For example, Jean Starobinski brilliantly describes the reversals through which eighteenth-century thought became increasingly fascinated by the very monstrosities the Enlightenment was supposed to dissipate:

> Reason, conscious of its powers, sure of its prerogatives, welcomed the forces of feeling and passion and looked to them as sources of additional energy. In this way it thought to unify man in the light of good and intellect. . . . But, once having granted desire all its rights, reason found it had acquired elements of darkness and dream that it had hitherto excluded.[13]

Goya's art offers exemplary images of this reversal, most strikingly in the eighty plates of *Los Caprichos* (1799), which includes the epochal "The Dream of Reason Brings Forth Monsters." Here, as Starobinski sees:

> Reason is confronted with something radically different from reason: It knows the secret bonds that link it to these monsters, for they are born of its own demands, or rather of the rejection of its own demands. They represent the

anarchic power of negation, which would not have appeared if the imperative of everyday order had not been proclaimed. This is an encounter fraught with consequences, for reason, seeing in its enemy the inversion of its own reality, the reverse without which reason would not be light, yields to the fascination of a difference it cannot escape.[14]

But whether the examples are from Goya's *Los Caprichos* or from classical texts like Euripides' *Bacchae*, there is no doubt that the most potent icons of aesthetic form have trafficked regularly with forces "incompatible with the existing order"—and not always in order to harness or dissipate them. The urge of a study like this one, an urge itself perhaps already tainted by the monstrous, is to hear as clearly as possible the dispute between a culture and its discontented rejects, and to bring within a single focus the changing ploys by which the inescapable accents of reason and the shrill raillery of abject bitterness have continued to address, spurn, and enthrall one another in an interminable contention.

I have already emphasized how one of the most crucial aspects of this contest is the cunning with which it has compelled its readers to become participants in a debate that is, after all, encountered in the pages of the fictional dialogue. The principled bracketing of normative moral discriminations in the face of a work of art, a bracketing on which aesthetic theory has insisted at least since Kant, carries little persuasion in our response to texts like *Notes from Underground* or *D'un château l'autre*. A critical rhetoric that insists on excluding criteria of judgment whose provenance is as much ethical and social as aesthetic will find itself awkwardly mute in considering texts that explicitly thematize, if only to contest, those very criteria. Like the word *fool* itself, the *monstrous* is a term whose range extends from the natural to the historical realms, and from the domains of ethics and law to that of artistic structuring. Since all of these senses may be at issue in a particular text, none of them can be ruled out of place at the outset without trivializing our encounter with the fictions.

If Diderot, for example, knew how partial and self-serving our concept of the monstrous is, he was equally aware that such knowledge only complicates and chastens specific judgments; it neither eliminates their pertinence nor frees us from the pressures to understand ourselves better by asking on what grounds we are prepared to sanction certain practices and beliefs while pathologizing others. At the level of their form, *Le Neveu de Rameau*, *Notes from Underground*, or Céline's trilogy are, above all else, different quests for the most compelling structure in which to frame precisely these questions, and each of the books strives to deny its readers the option of remaining in the stands, securely watching the combat as neutral observers. Encountering the genuinely monstrous in a literary text (e.g., de Sade's phantasmagoric tableaux or Céline's racist pamphlets), is properly terrifying because it forces us either to repudiate its articulation (thereby acting as one more censorious participant in its fiction) or, by refusing to do so, to become tacit accomplices to the claims of the monstrous.

"Critique," as Walter Benjamin wrote, "is concerned with the truth content of a work of art, the commentary with its subject matter."[15] Any study of works like the ones explored here must move regularly, and, I suspect unfashionably, between a commentary and a critique, and in so doing, insert its own distortions of emphases and presumptions of judgment. But at least it is spared the more common critical presumption of inventing its own problems: the dialogues that we shall be listening to and joining in flourish by eliciting both a commentary and a critique, and explicitly appeal to our sense of social and historical "values" as well as to our pleasure in aesthetic "invention." That such an appeal only makes our status as readers and critics all the more uncomfortable will become amply evident in the course of our investigation.

> And how comfortless is the thought that the
> sickness of the normal does not necessarily imply as
> its opposite the health of the sick, but that the latter
> usually only present, in a different way, the same
> disastrous pattern.
>   (Theodor Adorno, *Minima Moralia*)

To have specified a set of problems with regard to the monstrous is one way to bring us closer to understanding the nature of the Abject Hero, since from the perspective of orthodox values, a common moral blindness and subversive mockery places the monster and Abject Hero in intimate proximity to one another. But the kinship between the two, although close, is not a matter of simple identity. Put crudely, one could say that although the monster need not be an Abject Hero, abjection always contains a strong admixture of the monstrous. The rejection of conventional ethical and social codes that both embody may take the form of daemonic rebellion in the monster whose pride refuses all shackles or restraints (the model of Lucifer's "Non Serviam"); his rebellion scorns questions of safety or even of survival and finds in the very hopelessness of his battle a desperate exhilaration that seems as limitless as the forces it would overthrow. The Abject Hero, on the other hand, has none of this recklessness or pride: he calculates the cost of each repudiation with the obsessive accuracy of a bankrupt accountant and feels himself constantly on the verge of exhaustion or collapse. Instead of Blake's titanic Satan, the Abject Hero's model is the tawdry Devil who visits Ivan Karamazov, clothed not in fire and brimstone but like a poor country cousin coming to sponge a loan. His rage is never far from a whine, and his raillery always contains a furtive supplication.

In our culture a pure monster may possess, as Jean-François Rameau sees with discomforting lucidity, a kind of grandeur-in-evil that compels, if not quite awe, then at least a distinct prestige for the intensity of his passion: "If it is important to be sublime in anything, it is especially so in evil. One spits on a petty thief, but can't withhold a sort of respect from a great criminal. His courage amazes you. His brutality makes you shudder. One admires integrity of character above all."[16] But to be abject is never to have experienced the monster's single-mindedness. Instead, there is a cringing defiance deprived of any trust in one's own power and vitiated by a self-contempt at least equivalent to one's loathing for others. And yet the Abject Hero's defiance is just as intractable, his nature just as "incompatible with the existing order" as that of the most ruthless monster. The Abject Hero often longs to be exactly such a creature; his rare words of praise are reserved for the transcendent villains, and his whole being is a helpless dialogue between the urge to curse and attack without restraint and the anxiety immediately aroused by even the slightest danger. Where the monster is monologic in his self-absorption, the Abject Hero is condemned to dialogue, since his consciousness is an echo chamber of incompatible desires and prohibitions, a sound box in which the voices of the monster, the contentedly successful citizen, the desperately hungry parasite, and the resigned failure exchange insults and advice with bewildering inconsistency. But precisely by being denied the glamor of a Promethean rebel, by occupying the logically impossible space created by the intersection of the satanic and the servile, the Abject Hero is both a more complex and ultimately a more subversive figure than the monster whose self-identity remains inviolate.

Abjection has received so little critical attention primarily because its lack of glamor makes it too distasteful to contemplate at length. But in *ressentiment*, for all its shabbiness and self-loathing, there is a potential for extraordinary violence and a rage whose ferocity has been repeatedly mobilized by political movements. *Ressentiment*'s very efficacy as a historical force has made at least a degree of theoretical scrutiny inescapable, and in Friedrich Nietzsche *ressentiment* found its most brilliant philosophical diagnostician. Nietzsche's analysis will be crucial for our discussions of Dostoevsky, Céline, and contemporary culture in the last three chapters. But because *ressentiment* can be understood best as a malignant modern outgrowth of abjection, a kind of "empowered abjection,"[17] which only begins to receive central literary representation in the nineteenth century, I think it helpful to postpone a detailed analysis of *ressentiment* until after the lineaments of abjection have been coherently traced and shaded.

Abjection and *ressentiment* can be distinguished most readily by their different relationships to temporality and to the urge for vengeance: abjection suffers constantly new, and usually externally imposed, slights and degradation, whereas *ressentiment* is trapped forever in the slights of the past. A lacerated vanity nourishes both abjection and *ressentiment*, but repetition is less crucial to abjection than to *ressentiment*, which experiences its existence as a perpetual recurrence of the same narcissistic injury. Moreover, the man of *ressentiment* is actually "proud" of his abjection, and, as in *Notes from Underground* , he sees in it both his torment and the sign of his higher consciousness. The sufferer from abjection derives no such compensatory pride from his humiliation, but neither does he dwell as obsessively on fantasies of revenge on imaginary enemies. What "empowers" someone afflicted by *ressentiment* is the intensely focused, but impotent, hatred with which he feeds his sense of having been treated unfairly, and his hope of someday forcing others to suffer in his place. Particularly in Céline's novels, characters tend to fluctuate between the two states, exhibiting traits of both abjection and *ressentiment* in the course of the narrative. In Dostoevsky, though, one can schematize the differences in more clear-cut ways, since he presents, along with abject and *ressentiment*-riddled souls like *The Brothers Karamazov*'s Smerdyakov, characters like *The Idiot*'s Lebedyev, who are thoroughly abject but with none of the murderous desires of *ressentiment*.

Criticism has become quite comfortable with the figure of the daemonic rebel, and, at least in its Nietzschean mode, with the man of *ressentiment*, but a certain *frisson* of fallen splendor still seems to be necessary in order to attract the critic's attention. Thus it is not really so surprising that so few works address abjection directly. Among the best known to do so is Julia Kristeva's *Powers of Horror: An Essay on Abjection*. Kristeva has recognized abjection's uncanny grip on human consciousness, and her description does much to bring so recalcitrant a concept into the realm of discursive critical analysis. But although she draws primarily, and often persuasively, on literary representations of abjection for concrete examples, the focus of her book is on the abject as a universal psychological condition, a fissure in the relationship between consciousness and corporality that arises at the most elemental levels of human response to the facts of physical existence itself:

> Food loathing is perhaps the most elementary and most archaic form of abjection. When the eyes see or the lips touch that skin on the surface of milk . . . I experience a gagging sensation and, still farther down, spasms in the stomach, the belly . . . *nausea* makes me balk at that milk cream, separates me from the mother and father who proffer it. "I" want none of that element, sign of their desire; "I" do not want to listen, "I" do not assimilate it, "I" expel it. But since

the food is not an "other" for "me," who am only in their desire, I expel *myself*, I spit *myself* out, I abject *myself* within the same motion through which "I" claim to establish *myself*.[18]

Abjection, in Kristeva's reading, undermines the conventional Freudian distinctions between conscious and unconscious and bridges the supposedly discrete symptom formations charted by psychoanalytic clinical practice. Linked primordially to the body's excretions, the abject "is something rejected from which one does not part," a horror that violates "identity, system, order." For Kristeva "The corpse, seen without God and outside science, is the utmost of abjection. It is death infecting life."[19]

For all its local insights, the sweep of Kristeva's account elides its specificity, so that her abject is hypostatized, functioning as a global concept that, depending on the circumstances, can be regarded as at once a force, a condition, a drive, or a kind of frantic reaction in the face of mortality. As Kristeva recognizes, "He who denies morality is not abject; there can be grandeur in amorality and even in crime that flaunts its disrespect for the law—rebellious, liberating, and suicidal crime. Abjection, on the other hand, is immoral, sinister, scheming and shady." Thus, quite rightly, she sees Dostoevsky and Céline as central chroniclers of abjection. But she is equally ready to consider Sophocles, the Mosaic dietary laws, Lautréamont, and Proust within the same framework, and on the very page as the passage just quoted, Kristeva refers to "the abjection of Nazi crime" made visible in "a heap of children's shoes" piled up "in the dark halls of the museum that is now what remains of Auschwitz."[20]

Yet here, if anywhere, the distinction I made earlier between the monstrous and the abject is most unmistakable, and an analysis of abjection that can move without hesitation from *Oedipus at Colonus* to taboos associated with menstruation, and then to the Holocaust seems to me to abandon, by overextension, the explanatory force of the term.[21]

A crucial difference between Kristeva's account and the ways I regard abjection is that for her its eruption does not require the active intervention of adult discourse. Since the experience of the abject she describes is primordial and universal, grounded in the individual's earliest awareness of his own and his mother's body and in the daily reality of bodily evacuations, physical self-disgust, and separation anxieties, cultural differences may structure the specific associations and loci of abjection, but they do not create it. From my perspective, however, abjection is a social and dialogic category, and its expression is always governed by the mapping of prior literary and cultural models. Abjection is only felt in conversation with another, with a voice, whether internal or external, whose oppressive confidence arises through its articulation of the normative values of society as a whole. The Abject Hero hears this voice as simultaneously more powerful and more tamed than his own; he encounters in it the judgment of a social order he fears and despises in equal measure, but against whose might he knows himself possessed of only the shabbiest ruses and most ignominious strategies.

But perhaps all of these differences are themselves only consequences of a more basic divergence. The Abject Hero whose destiny I will be tracing in this volume evolves directly out of the wise fool of satiric literature and the holy fool of religious parables. Moreover, this evolution is deliberately assumed, consciously thematized at its most challenging moments, by both the author and the fictional character himself, as different historical models and roles are ransacked by the Abject Hero in an attempt to legitimize his sense of impotent superiority. What the Abject Hero seeks to exploit is a double authority deriving from a double ancestry. The first is the freedom of the King's fool, who, as the Abject Hero recalls from his own reading, is always shown by the most respected texts, whether classical or modern, as understanding more in his folly than do the self-servingly rational court-iers. This is a licensed clown, as the Abject Hero also recognizes, whose insights the audience has learned to applaud for their perceptiveness and justice. The second role model is the archetypal "wild man from the desert" whose imprecations and prophecies proved true when all the philosophies professed by the officially sanctioned sages were revealed as hollow. The Biblical model of the "vox clamantis in deserto," although not unique, is Western culture's most powerful instance of this archetype.[22] And indeed, considering how text after text shows us the disastrous consequences of mocking such an inspired visionary, who would still be ready to disregard him without considerable hesitation?

But the Abject Hero is also aware of how potentially ludicrous his invo-cation of such archetypes must appear, and he himself is far from convinced of their pertinence to his condition. The Abject Hero is ready to wear motley, but only in order someday to replace the well-dressed courtiers; and he is willing to thunder against the court's degeneracy, but only in the hope of being invited to share in its delights. His burden is not merely the contempt he senses from society's spokesmen but, more gallingly, his awareness of being a meretricious fraud, usurping without authentic title the oppositional rhetoric invented long before by a host of genuinely for-midable and inspired outsiders.

For the abject consciousness, self-knowledge, instead of providing the relief of a certain distance from one's predicament, only intensifies it, and a lucid irony about one's plight may be the worst torment of all, since it immediately converts into an additional, especially acute symptom of the very state it is intended to diagnose. Here, self-awareness is *not* part of the solution; it is the very core of the problem. In Philip Roth's cruelly accurate account: "Oh, ironic paranoia is the worst. Usually when you're busy with your paranoia at least the irony is gone and you really want to win. But to see your roaring, righteous hatred as a supremely comical act subdues no one but yourself."[23]

> Oh, perhaps all this is only a portrait of a theo-
> retical man. . . . But why is it, though, that these
> theoretical people . . . are capable of such very real
> suffering, and end in such very real tragedy?
> (Fyodor Dostoevsky, *A Raw Youth*)

Imagine, as a momentary illustration, the following, perhaps familiar, situation: two men meet in a bar or bus station and one begins to tell the other of his woes, introducing numerous details of his well-deserved failures in life, his despair, and so forth, always interspersing his story with outbursts of wild self-praise and congratulations. But the listener keeps interrupting, "You know, I've already read that in Diderot and Dostoevsky. Aren't you only imitating Jean-François Rameau and the Underground Man? Isn't all this just the old Karamazov idea: the performance of the self in all its vileness out of the sheer compulsion to perform? Can't you find a more original problem or at least a new story?" And if, indeed, the first speaker is not only familiar with these authors but quite aware that no matter how he tries, his narrative can never emerge except as a variation on their literary paradigms, then, presumably, the last possible claim for his own dignity will have been proved derisive.

Faced with so helpless a predicament, the Abject Hero's most promising option is to attempt to pass himself off as a monster. The very reading that has helped blight his self-esteem has shown him the curious prestige habitually attached to the monster. If he were to succeed in embodying, both for himself and his interlocutor, the role of civilization's daemonic double, the madman who rages forth when all the compromises and repressions of socialization have been shattered, then the Abject Hero might indeed effect a sudden reversal in his wretched position. And so Rameau, the Underground Man, Fyodor Karamazov, and the Célinian narrator keep trying to sound ever more monstrous. But for them, even that tone—one that ought to issue forth as an untamed natural force—is itself as mediated as all of their other attitudes and poses. To mimic the monstrous is still to be only a mimic, and to model one's speech after the mad is still to be dependent upon prior examples. But, paradoxically, to desire such a voice for oneself *is* genuinely monstrous, and to attempt to convince others of its truth is, in its very fraudulence, a distinctly mad enterprise. So the Abject Hero is again doomed to a doubled existence: parodying a role that is, in reality, already his own, and imitating a state that he already inhabits.

Because the Abject Hero exists only in relationship to others, the character of his interlocutor is as crucial in determining his options as any inner impulses. After all, the listener is under no obligation to endure a stream of whining taunts and sarcasms, and a good index of the Abject Hero's skill lies in his ability to seduce someone from a radically different social and moral sphere into a real dialogue. Stefan Collini shrewdly asks, "What mixture of masochism, anxiety, self-criticism or other discontent lies behind the half-acknowledged wish to be arraigned and harangued by licensed lash-wielders?"[24] To this list, richly suggestive as it is, Collini might have added a curious species of vanity, the kind of self-congratulation that rewards someone who permits himself to be openly criticized, thus giving public evidence of his own tolerant sophistication and lack of unseemly self-defensiveness. Of course, such a strategy may also cloak the most acute anxiety, and the readiness to expose oneself to extravagantly absurd criticisms is often just a means to evade accusations that are more threatening, because they lie too close to one's own fears. The shrewdness of the Abject Hero can be gauged by how successfully he takes the measure of his interlocutor, how effectively he can break down his partner's self-assurance and force him to acknowledge that his whole being is at stake in their confrontation.

Linked to the issue of what compels the two fictional speakers to initiate and then sustain their dialogue is the related question of the authors' imaginative investment in their Abject Heroes. The culture's easily mobilizable fascination with the licensed fool and the incendiary as privileged truth-tellers often serves writers as a powerful stimulus, suggesting a narrative pattern and dramatis personae that can be adapted to the circumstances of any era. In straightforward cases, the text's satiric energy is directed largely outward at particular social abuses or immediate enemies, and the voice through whom the critique is articulated exists largely as a vehicle for those criticisms. But when writers take aim at themselves as much as at their societies, and when they begin to be engrossed by the potential for a disruptive self-consciousness on the part of both of the Saturnalian dialogue's antagonists, then the metamorphosis of the licensed fool into the Abject Hero becomes possible.

The desire to be free, at least in one's fantasies, from the tyranny of one's own governing convictions and the moral obligations they impose is no doubt part of an author's motivation in exposing his ideas to the Abject Hero's corrosive mockery. But there are other factors involved as well, including an urge to crack the armature built up by even the most secure and respectable of one's accomplishments, in order to break free from the expectations built up by previous successes. And because every success is always partial, always a compromise formation, the Abject Hero can crystallize one's repugnance at all the half-measures and surrenders that lie behind the most glittering of triumphs. More generally, there is the longing to keep open imaginative options that *any* decisive action or position, no matter how right, inevitably forecloses. To produce the kinds of bitter dialogues in which the Abject Hero can flourish, an intellectual-aesthetic excitement at pushing further the formal possibilities inherent in the genre unites with an imaginative need to risk everything in a Saturnalian clash that is like the gambler's desperate self-testing on the edge of ruin.

In order to fascinate, the Abject Hero must first persuade us that in spite of the obvious unpleasantness—or, more accurately, exactly because of that unpleasantness—conversation with him will yield the benefit of an otherwise unavailable insight into both human nature and the workings of society. Crucial to his success is the Abject Hero's exploitation of the knowledge that the dominant culture itself has endowed his marginal position with the compensatory prestige of an access to truths supposedly "denied to those blinkered by or imprisoned in the assumptions of their own society."[25] Paradoxically, to refuse the Abject Hero his say would risk condemnation by the eminently reputable conventions that branded him disreputable in the first place. For example, in the anecdote I just recounted, the unwilling listener might as easily be telling himself, "Well, yes, everything I'm hearing is just a garbled compendium of literary citations. But how can I be sure he isn't suddenly going to reveal something true that I've always been afraid to acknowledge? If I dismiss him without a thought, am I just exposing myself as one more smug coward? Even if he is just parroting Rameau and the Underground Man, how does my repugnance distinguish me from the *philosophe*'s complacency or the obtuseness of Dostoevsky's rationalist 'gentlemen'?" And so the dialogue continues, between the speakers and within each one as well, the voices doubled and then doubled again until it is closing time in the bar, or the bus finally arrives, taking each man in a different direction, one home to his burrow in the Underground, the other to his duplex in the company (or faculty) compound.

Two

O Totiens Servus: Horace, Juvenal, and the Classical Saturnalia

We stand in the tumult of a festival.
What festival? This loud, disordered mooch?
    (Wallace Stevens, "The Auroras of Autumn")

LIKE SO MUCH else in contemporary theory, our newfound faith in the liberating power of carnival laughter returns for much of its rhetoric to the cardinal example of Friedrich Nietzsche. In *Beyond Good and Evil*, for example, Nietzsche claims for his own age a unique preparedness

> for a carnival in the grand style, for the laughter and high spirits of the most spiritual revelry, for the transcendental heights of the highest nonsense and Aristophanean derision of the world. Perhaps this is where we shall discover the realm of our *invention*, that realm in which we, too, can still be original, say, as parodists of world history and God's buffoons—perhaps even if nothing else today has any future, our *laughter* may yet have a future.[1]

Yet even this affirmation, although regularly quoted as a kind of crystallization-in-advance of the whole modern longing for the cathartic energy of the Saturnalia, is more equivocal than commonly recognized.[2] A phrase like "that realm in which we, too, can still be original" betrays a profound anxiety about the possibility of finding any sphere in which to invent the new, and Nietzsche's solution is itself so dependent on that which it would replace—a parodist, no matter how brilliant, is always in a derivative relationship to the object of his parody—that it hardly seems to satisfy the demand for an "original" future.[3] To me, this passage reads more like a mockery (or even an Aristophanean derision) of our hope for a transcendental carnival than an announcement of its imminent likelihood. But if my interpretation seems overly pessimistic, consider how bitter Nietzsche's judgment is when he specifically interrogates the all too-human appeal of the Saturnalia:

> How can man have pleasure in nonsense? . . . The overthrowing of experience into its opposite, of purposefulness into purposelessness, of necessity into what is wished for, but in such a way that this process causes [us] no harm, but is

simply imagined once out of wanton exuberance, delights [mankind] because it liberates us momentarily from the compulsion of necessity, of what is appropriate to [quotidian human] purpose and experience in which we ordinarily see our inexorable masters. We play and laugh when the expected (which usually makes us afraid and tense) reveals itself without causing harm. It is the slave's pleasure at the Saturnalia.[4]

Throughout his writings, the word *slave* served Nietzsche as a synecdoche for a whole range of contemptible moral and intellectual qualities, and in these reflections from *Human, All Too Human* his scorn for the slave's joy at the temporary license of the carnival is unmistakable.

One reason for such scorn is the fact of the Saturnalia's brevity ("it liberates us *momentarily* from the compulsion of necessity"). For someone who believes as deeply as Nietzsche that "all desire longs for eternity, / longs for deep, deep eternity,"[5] a joy that is confined to a preordained timetable must seem trivial, and an officially sanctioned reversal of conventional hierarchies must appear more like a parody than a genuine instance of liberation.

The strict temporal limits of the Saturnalia and its character as an official state holiday do not trouble Bakhtin in the same way, and he describes the "essence of carnival" as "most clearly expressed and experienced in Roman Saturnalias."[6] Bakhtin recognizes, moreover, that "the tradition of the Saturnalias remained unbroken and alive in the medieval carnival, which expressed this universal renewal and was vividly felt as an escape from the usual official way of life,"[7] and sees its final triumphant expression in Rabelais's tales.

But while the continuity between the Roman Saturnalia and the festivals of medieval and Renaissance Europe has been recognized for a long time, there is certainly no agreement about which fictional works best embody "the quintessence of the Saturnalia."[8] Instead, what unites the diverse characterizations of the Saturnalia is the nostalgic appeal with which such rituals are invested by theoreticians as part of an argument about a more desirable society. In his study of "la fête," Roger Chartier challenges such nostalgia by showing how the contemporary carnival is always seen as a degradation of an earlier, more vital one, and how different theories about the meaning of festivals all tend to merge into the projection of an imaginary and idealized collective past.[9] Chartier further warns that the whole relationship between the narration or representation of a carnival, whether in literature, folk art, or paintings, and the festival as a collectively lived social experience is often far more problematic than theoreticians like Bakhtin acknowledge. Even in Rabelais, for example, it seems to me that for our delight in his inventiveness to be uninterrupted, he must ensure that we do not respond to all the killings, maimings, humiliations, and catastrophes as if they happened to real human beings. The excesses are so exuberantly and self-consciously verbal that no identificatory anxieties are likely to be triggered by what is recognized as a celebration of language's generative potency rather than an inventory of possible human actions. Only because Rabelais's stories are manifestly nonmimetic can critics like Bakhtin speak of "the redemptive energy of the [Rabelaisian] Saturnalia" and assimilate them to anthropological records of particular carnivals—many of which, as recent studies have shown, ended in a violence that proved devastating both to the actual victims and to the community as a whole.[10] But when I return to Rabelais from reading such accounts, his glee in depicting the various torments inflicted on the books' villains often leaves me considerably more nervous than Bakhtin's interpretation would suggest possible. Indeed, the energy released by Rabelais' laughter or by the literary depictions of medieval and Renaissance carnivals (e.g., Ben Jonson's *Bartholomew Fair*) has an element of deliberate cruelty, and the complexity of different narratives depends in no small measure on the author's skill in first arousing, and then assuaging, the nervousness such cruelty elicits.[11] René Girard's *Violence and the Sacred* offers a view of the Saturnalia diametrically opposed to the one endorsed by Bakhtin, and although I am far from sharing all of Girard's conclusions, his vision of the "mimetic violence" underlying the carnival's rites and his description of the revelers' Dionysus as a "god of homicidal fury" contains a salutary counterbalance to any populist and idealizing optimism.[12]

When one examines the use of historical, ethnographic, and literary data in the models of Saturnalian carnivals proposed by contemporary theoreticians, then in spite of any specific divergences three general themes emerge with notable consistency.

1. The first is the prevalence across numerous cultures, whether literate or not, of some ritual occasion during which, as for the Ashanti of central Ghana, "every man and woman, free man and slave, should have freedom to speak out just what was in their head, to tell their neighbors just what they thought of them . . . [and] also [of] the king or chief."[13] The festivals of classical Greece also included outbursts of extravagant obscenities, the public exchange of sexual and class roles signaled by "youths in girls' clothing and girls with beards, *phalloi*, and satyr costumes . . . [and] days when slaves were waited on by their masters, and treated as the superiors."[14]

2. The second is that the carnivalesque ceremony can be interpreted as a specific kind of language through which the tensions in a society are articulated and made visible.[15] The interpreter's risk, though, is to misunderstand the proportion of anarchic versus bound energy released by the carnival and to misread the festival's characteristically contradictory aims and correspondingly doubled (destructive/restorative) tropes.

3. The third theme does not directly address the nature of carnival itself, but rather the polemical function of its rites when they are invoked as models of a less hierarchic, more tolerant and spontaneous social organization. The most persuasive example I know of a culture actually based on "eternal recurrence" is that segment of the modern intelligentsia that continues to long for the *frisson* of a gratifyingly safe "textual" anarchic license. It is, moreover, a radical intelligentsia whose own writings, in spite of the blatant imperialism of such a quest, have eagerly ransacked the globe's most diverse societies for supposed instantiations of the unconstrained liberty about which it fantasizes.

It is largely because of their own longings that literary scholars find accounts of ceremonies like the Ashanti's *Apo* festival or the medieval Feast of Fools so attractive a guide for their interpretations of Western Saturnalian texts. Habitually in such interpretations, ethnographic data is introduced in a more or less random manner, without attention to the basic distinction between a textual representation of carnival and the actual festival rituals. The arbitrary appropriation of Saturnalian imagery, rather than any close attention to the history of the rite, has also shaped recurrent efforts to inaugurate a new carnival. That such attempts have usually been ideologically inspired, and intended, especially in the last two centuries, to serve direct political ends, will become increasingly evident in the course of this book. And since it is precisely the uses of, and longing for, a new Saturnalia that most concerns me, I want to focus on the Saturnalia primarily as represented in a fictional narrative or theoretical speculation and will scrutinize the historical and anthropological records only when they can directly illuminate the image of the carnival as a specifically literary and speculative topos.

In its classical incarnation in Roman culture, the Saturnalia designated a distinct religious festival held in honor of the mythical Golden Age of Saturn. During the time of the Saturnalia (December 17–19) a special license to speak their minds freely was accorded to everyone, irrespective of rank. This freedom is normally the only characteristic of the festival that classical poets found sufficiently intriguing to make central to their texts. Other, equally crucial, features of the Saturnalian rites, like the agrarian celebrations linked to the sowing of crops, the ritual exchange of presents, the public banquet that anyone could attend, etc., tend to be entirely absent from Saturnalian texts like the two satires Horace set during the festival period.[16] Indeed, in one of these, Satire 2.3, Horace views the Saturnalian tumult only as a distraction he must escape, and the poem opens with an account of his having fled Rome during the festival in order to try to find the quiet necessary to compose new verses. But irrespective of how the Saturnalian days were regarded, it was not the rites as such that writers sought to represent but certain specific features, selected because of their inherent literary potential. Foremost among these was, inevitably, the right of slaves to criticize their masters.

As a literary setting, the Saturnalia lends itself particularly well to satiric attacks both on specific individuals and on the larger customs of the age, because criticism can be introduced into the work with a minimum of prefatory explanation to justify its audacity. By placing these attacks in the mouth of someone without any social standing, like a slave, the satirist can permit himself a degree of acerbity in his observations that might be unseemly, or even dangerous, if uttered in his own voice. This literary use of the slave as ironist accords with Aristotle's advice in his *Rhetoric*: "There are some things which . . . you cannot say about your opponent without seeming abusive or ill-bred. Put such remarks, therefore, into the mouth of some third person."[17] The universal Saturnalian freedom to speak one's mind also affords the artist many technical as well as thematic opportunities; it allows him to experiment with mixed tones, expressions, and idioms that would violate the decorum appropriate to most other narrative situations.[18]

Finally, the questioning and rebellious stance permissible in a Saturnalian context also proves particularly fruitful for utopian speculations, with the description of a better society either explicitly narrated or at least unmistakably implied as the direct opposite of an unsatisfactory present. Thus, as Robert C. Elliott rightly argues, Satire, Saturnalia, and Utopia are linked in a clear continuum, but this continuum is determined as much by the formal possibilities inherent in the convention as by the universal longing that Elliott posits for a carnivalesque suspension of daily norms.[19] Such a distinction is worth emphasizing, because literary historians have been tempted to apply such powerful accounts of the festival's capacity to abolish time and history to the fictional presentations of a carnival as well.[20] In works like *Le Mythe de l'éternel retour*, for instance, Eliade describes the participants in a ritual as experiencing an unmediated contemporaneity with the timeless world of myth. But this abolition of their daily consciousness is precisely what characters like Horace's slave Davus cannot feel, since the threat of the next day's punishment intrudes even into their hours of Saturnalian liberty. But paradoxically, just because it actually is *not* liberating for the slave, the Saturnalia becomes all the more freeing for the master-artist, for the poet who can use the carnival setting to probe the most risky issues with a generically assured seemliness. The guaranteed boundaries permit him to ask real questions that he might be afraid to articulate in a context where the stakes were less mediated and revocable.

Horace never pretends that his poem returns him to the condition of timeless and universal equality of the Golden Age. He is acutely alert to the fact that the act of writing already draws attention to the separation between mythic experience and literary artifice. It is worth reminding ourselves that in a Saturnalian dialogue like Horace's Satire 2.7, we do not overhear a plausible rendition of a complaining slave briefly allowed to voice his grievances. Rather, we read the poet exercising his consummate metrical skill in the creation of Davus's speech, and it is the craftsman's cunning in satisfying the expectations of the satiric form and in expanding the genre's thematic range that gives his text its authority.

But even as a literary topos, the Saturnalia is considerably more ambiguous than descriptions like Bakhtin's or Elliott's suggest. If Saturn (Saturnus, "the sower," later identified with the Greek Cronus) introduced agriculture to Rome and founded the citadel on the Capitol, he also castrated his father and ate his children.[21] Saturn was thus linked both with a time of earthly paradise and with a threatening malignancy, a sense that still carried meaning in the Renaissance notion of a "saturnine" temperament, one embittered or melancholy as a result of Saturn's influence. Even in Latin poetry, the Age of Saturn was not uniformly associated with an epoch of human freedom from labor and class divisions. In the most famous of the *Eclogues*, for example, Virgil cries out with hope that a child might be born to inaugurate a new Saturnalian era of peace and stability after decades of civil war—"redeunt Saturnia regna"[22]—and in the *Aeneid* he characterizes the original Golden Age of Saturn as an era marked not by anarchic license but by the people's natural orderliness and just behavior, maintained through their own free choice rather than under compulsion of the law:

> neve ignorate Latinos
> Saturni gentem haud vinclo nec legibus aequam,
> sponte sua veterisque dei se more tenetem.

> [Know that our Latins
> Come of Saturn's race, that we are just—
> Not by constraint or laws, but by our choice.]

(7.202–4)[23]

No matter how the mythical Age of Saturn was conceived, however, there is no doubt that for poets of Horace's generation (65 B.C. to 8 B.C.), the idea of a carnivalesque suspension of social norms had very little appeal, since much of their lives had been spent witnessing or, as in Horace's case, briefly participating in, the chaos and bloodshed that marked the end of the Roman Republic. The literary excitement of imagining an apocalyptic breakdown of all social restraints is usually thrilling in direct proportion to its improbability, and Céline is among the very few writers I know who not only lived through a global cataclysm but actually found in that devastation something to applaud.

Horace, like all the writers of his day, reached a point where the near anarchy of daily life made the idea of a permanent Saturnalia deeply repugnant. As W. R. Johnson reminds us, Horace was only sixteen when Caesar and Pompey fought for supremacy in the Latin world, twenty-one when Caesar was murdered, and twenty-three when, as a student in Athens, he joined Brutus's army as a military tribune, only to flee "relicta non bene parmula [leaving my shield ingloriously behind]" in the rout at Philippi in November 42 B.C.[24] One historian estimates that "in the twenty years after Caesar crossed the Rubicon, some 200,000 Italians were often under arms."[25] Throughout this time Rome itself suffered through a series of bloody proscriptions, during one of which "Appian puts the number of those murdered as high as two thousand knights and three hundred senators."[26] Even after Horace's safe return to Rome, pardoned but bankrupt, he still had to experience the protracted struggle among Caesar's successors, and not until Augustus's victory at Actium in 31 B.C. did peace return to the Empire. As Niall Rudd observes, "when, after Actium, Octavian finally turned to the task of rebuilding the Roman state, the wonder is that there was anything left to rebuild."[27]

I cite these facts in order to emphasize that Horace's famous advocacy of moderation and balance was formulated in the aftermath of wholesale and almost continuous violence, during which much of the social order in which he believed perished. His advocacy of a reasoned, prosaic civility was purchased with far more strain and under far greater pressures than traditional readings recognize. Horace is both a darker and a more disturbing writer than his conventional image suggests, and W. R. Johnson's account of the poet's situation provides a valuable corrective to that image:

> Horace . . . was a poet at the edge of a chasm beyond which he could not see. What he saw was a ruin of the world he loved and the death of freedom. His vision was the more bitter because . . . he had almost learned to hope . . . that his culture would not collapse and his freedom would not die. . . . The desolation of outward freedom ultimately forced him to search out the inner freedom of the heart that each man has if he wills to find it. Political crisis and cultural crisis had provoked from Horace an astonishing number of complex, successful songs in which hope warred against despair and celebration of the human spirit warred against dark intuitions of abiding failure and futility.[28]

But even so acute a reader as Johnson is misleading when he speaks of "the inner freedom of the heart that each man has if he wills to find it," since it is precisely this liberty that Horace is also compelled to cast into doubt, or, perhaps more accurately, on whose possession Horace keeps overinsisting, as a barrier against the suspicion that in Augustan Rome private freedom, too, has become only a particularly alluring form of self-deception. François Furet describes a post-Revolutionary situation as replacing "the conflict of interest for power with a competition of discourses for the appropriation of legitimacy," and it is clear that Augustus saw the work of his favorite poets as a powerful weapon in the legitimization of his own regime.[29] R.O.A.M. Lyne puts the matter with characteristic brevity: "Augustus and the state were effectively synonymous. To be in his patronage, directly or indirectly, was to be in the patronage of government, and there was a pressure to publicize the government's policies and to burnish its image."[30] Although history has confirmed the brilliance of the Emperor's and Maecenas's choices for Imperial approval and patronage, the responsibility of the poets so honored to the Augustan "party line" was, if delicately imposed, nonetheless quite unmistakable.[31]

And so, if Horace learned the narrow limits of political integrity and justice from the public events of his era, his own spectacularly successful career showed just how uncertain a thing "inner liberty" was and how vulnerable all his claims to independence might prove when challenged. That Horace had to endure such challenges on numerous occasions is clear from the repeated insistence in the satires, odes, and epistles on his enemies' *invidia* (envy) to account for the hostility he seems to have encountered throughout his career.[32] But his self-defense, although phrased with disarming straightforwardness, only helps to keep the issue alive, and a tone of aggrieved uneasiness resonates very close to the surface of such seemingly untroubled narratives as the famous account of Horace's own childhood and early career in Book 1, Satire 6.[33] When his antagonist is one of the Roman patricians, shocked by the intimacy this freedman's son and ex-rebel enjoys with Augustus and Maecenas, Horace always deflects the charge of toadying to the great by pointing out his indifference to politics and his entire disinterestedness in the struggle for influence or position. One of the poet's favorite strategies is to reverse roles, and, as in Book 1, Satire 9, to show his loathing for those courting favors from the great, thus implicitly demonstrating how aloof he himself remains from such ignoble desires.[34] But Horace's switching of perspectives can also lead to some remarkably unsettling poems like Epode 4, a dramatic monologue in which an aristocrat rages against a freedman who dares to sit among the knights and even has the presumption to be named a "tribune of the soldiers." Considering that the speaker's description of the *parvenu* so closely matches Horace's own situation, the fact that the aristocrat's contempt is itself never undermined seems extraordinarily provocative, all the more so since we know how it galled Horace to endure just such taunts. As an imaginative act of "identifying with the aggressor," Epode 4 is unique in Horace's oeuvre; normally he finds more nuanced ways of confronting his situation. Typically, Horace marshals his most effective *apologia* and counter-accusations when challenged by an antagonist of patrician rank and presumption. In such a conflict, Horace elegantly inverts the customary roles and reveals that it is his nobly-born interlocutor, not he, who suffers from the plebeian vices of frustrated ambition and greed. But Horace's situation is entirely different when the accuser's voice is that of a household slave, speaking not with the arrogance of an aristocrat's *invidia* but with the license of a single day to vent a whole year's accumulated irritation. The speaker, of course, is merely a Davus—almost the generic name for impertinent slaves in Roman comedy—but the questions are those of Horace himself, distanced, no doubt, but nonetheless edged with genuine force.[35] In Satire 2.7, as in its most notable descendant, *Le Neveu de Rameau*, the satire's leveling is directed not only against society's stale conventions but, more importantly, against the carefully built up self-image of the author, whose life and consciousness constitute the real "tumult" of the festival's "loud disordered mooch."

> Dulcis inexpertis cultura potentis amici:
> expertus metuit.
>
> [Those who have never tried think it pleasant to
> court a friend in power; experience teaches one to
> fear it.]
>   (Horace, *Epistles*, 1.18)
>
> Love work, do not domineer over others, and
> never seek the intimacy of public officials.
>   (Rabbi Shemaiah, *Pirke Avot*)

Like most of the satires in Book 2, the seventh, "Iamdudum ausculto," is cast as a dialogue in which Horace is not an instructor but instead the more or less captive audience to someone else's unsolicited urge to give advice. Yet Horace is careful to frame the poem with a clear indication of the limits within which the conversation takes place. Davus is eager to talk to Horace but knows his position well enough to resist doing so until given permission by his master. Although the Saturnalia has already begun, it requires a formal confirmation of Davus's rights before the slave dares to use the traditional freedom of the holiday period:

> Iamdudum ausculto et cupiens tibi dicere servus
> pauca reformido. . . .
> . . . age, libertate Decembri,
> quando ita maiores voluerunt, utere; narra.
>
> ["I've been listening for some time, and wishing to speak to you, but as a slave
> I dare not. . . ."

"Come, use the license December allows, since our fathers willed it so. Have your say."]

(1–2, 4–5)

Similarly, at the satire's conclusion, Horace reasserts his authority by threatening his slave, first playfully with stones and arrows (116), and then, more plausibly, with banishing Davus from the privileged position of household servant to the harsher duties of a farm laborer:

Ocius hinc te
ni rapis, accedes opera agro nona Sabino.

[If you don't take yourself off in a jiffy, you'll make the ninth laborer on my Sabine farm.]

(117–18)

The central part of the poem is thus framed by the guarantee of a "normal" world order in which the relationship of master and slave will continue untroubled by its brief suspension. But the confidence that such a frame inspires, as well as the insignificance of his interlocutor, permit Horace to introduce questions whose resonance he might have been less willing to confront in a different context. In essence, the entire satire turns on the question of who is a slave, and the centrality of this theme is clearly signaled by the way the poem's opening hexameter ends on the word *servus*. There are two ways to define a slave: one legal and the other moral-philosophical, and Davus, following the convention of the genre, spends most of his lines demonstrating that his master is conspicuously lacking in true inner freedom. But more unusually—and far more riskily—Davus further hints, without ever quite stating, that Horace, like all dependents on Maecenas, the chief distributor of Augustan patronage, had far less effective legal and political autonomy than his habitual rhetoric was at such pains to assert.

Davus's bill of charges moves through several distinct stages, increasing in specificity as the slave gains in vehemence and audacity. At first (6–20), Davus limits himself to safe generalizations on the order of "man is a slave because of his inconsistency, unable to stay firmly committed to any course of action whether noble or vicious": "vixit inaequalis" (10). Here Davus, as though not yet daring to implicate his master directly, draws his examples from the behavior of others, like the senator Priscus, whose life had no unity of purpose or character, as opposed to the obsessive gambler Volanerius, who at least maintained a certain constancy, if only in his mania.[36] Niall Rudd points out that "the problem of consistency, which in morals involves the integration of the personality and in art the achievement of unity amid variety, held a special interest for Horace."[37] Such an interest,

it may be worth adding, must surely have been augmented, or at least nourished, by the example of Caesar Augustus, a man whose single-mindedness
and ambition resulted in such spectacular accomplishments. But in spite of
his admiration for men whose lives testified to the focused intensity of a
single aim, Horace, much like Diderot after him, appeals to us largely by
dramatizing his own mercurial emotions and motives. Like Diderot,
Horace learned how to exploit his fickleness as an essential characteristic of
his literary *persona*, and the astonishing variety of genres, tones, and rheto-
rics within which both men composed is a direct formal analogue to the
explicit thematization of their inconstant temperaments.[38]

After a brief transition (21–22), in which Horace virtually compels
Davus to explain the point of all these examples, the slave begins to take
direct aim at the poet himself: "ad te, inquam" (22). In rapid succession,
Horace stands accused of wavering in his proclaimed values, of being divided in his desires, of a readiness to change his mind under circumstances
that suggest rank opportunism, of hypocrisy in his self-description, and
finally, of being even a greater fool ("stultior") than is Davus himself (23–
45). The most interesting aspect of Davus's catalogue is introduced with
seeming casualness amidst the deluge of other charges: Horace is not only
a weak man but a dependent and a parasite, as subject to Maecenas's whims
as the poet's own *scurrae*, or hangers-on, are subject to his:

> si nusquam es forte vocatus
> ad cenam, laudas securum holus ac, velut usquam
> vinctus eas, ita te felicem dicis amasque,
> quod nusquam tibi sit potandum. iusserit ad se
> Maecenas serum sub lumina prima venire
> convivam: "nemon oleum feret ocius? ecquis
> audit?" cum magno blateras clamore fugisque.

[If it happens that you aren't asked out to supper, you praise your quiet dish of
herbs and, as though you were in chains when you do go anywhere, you call
yourself lucky, and hug yourself, because you don't have to go out to some party.
Let but Maecenas bid you at the very last minute, just at lamp-lighting time, to
attend him as a guest, "Won't somebody bring me oil this instant? Does nobody
hear me?" So you scream at the top of your lungs, and go rushing off.]

(29–35)

Although couched in the conventional satiric topos of the dinner party
and deliberately denied any prominence by being merely one of a torrent of
insults, Davus's observation is of primary significance in light of Horace's
customary insistence on his liberty. In Satires 1.6 and 1.9, for example, the
poet emphasizes that his relationship to the second most powerful man in
the empire was one of simple friend to friend, and that neither Maecenas's

wealth and position, nor the poet's poverty, influenced the nature of their ties. Yet here we see Maecenas inviting Horace as a kind of afterthought, apparently needing him only to fill an empty couch at his banquet, and Horace is shamelessly eager to oblige. Beneath the ostensible charge of fickleness and gluttony, the far more serious one of servility is unmistakable, and Horace's own anxiety about his ascendancy into the inner circle of Rome's rulers is at least partially acknowledged. If the "Epistle to Lollius," from which my epigraph about learning fear in the company of the powerful is drawn, shows one side of Horace's experience, he was also not above an occasional tone of boasting about his success. In Satire 2.1, for example, he declares:

> tamen me
> cum magnis vixisse invita fatebitur usque
> invidia.
>
> [Yet Envy, in spite of herself, will ever admit that I have lived with the great.]
> *(75–77)*

Much of Horace's ambivalence about his ascension can be crystallized by juxtaposing the lines from Epistle 1.18 and Satire 2.1. From such a juxtaposition, we can see that Amy Richlin's description of his customary stance as "defensive and vulnerable, dependent on politically powerful men whose acceptance he craves, with only his own provocative poetry to use as a weapon" is, if too one-dimensional, more accurate than earlier accounts that had stressed Horace's unshakable equanimity.[39] But in none of his satires is the issue pressed as far or with as much polemical energy as in Davus's image of the poet as Maecenas's all too eager dinner guest. As though to deflect attention from so painful a picture, the poem immediately continues with a further inventory of distinctly minor instances of Horace's weaknesses, particularly of his supposed sexual misadventures (46–67). Although the Stoic philosophers, whose precepts Davus parrots, condemn sexual servitude as another instance of man's enslavement to his baser instincts, Davus's moralizing is irritatingly beside the point. In Satire 1.2, Horace had already shown a remarkably prudential and untroubled view of regulating one's sexual conduct, arguing for the advantages, in terms of personal safety, reputation, and cost, of liaisons with a *meretrix*, or common prostitute, rather than with a well-born Roman matron (57–59), and now the poet easily shrugs off Davus with the simple declaration, "I am no adulterer" (72).[40]

Readers have often expressed surprise that the satire should devote so much energy to a theme that swerves ineptly past its intended target, leaving Horace scarcely nicked. Revealingly, the poem itself registers that something is amiss here. Davus feels compelled to give some account for

why Horace has deflected his accusation with so little strain. But the explanation he does offer, that it is only Horace's cowardice that prevents the
poet's surrender to sexual excess, is so feeble as to make the original puzzle
stand out all the more. A typical recent defense for the sequence is offered
by Rudd, who recognizes how clumsily the argument proceeds but hopes
to justify it on other grounds: "this point takes the argument to another,
more purely Stoic, level. For while the Cynics and Epicureans condemned
adultery because of its risks, the Stoics concentrated on the unhealthy state
of the offender's soul. Even if there were no risks, they said, the virtuous
man would abstain because of his inner discipline. This helps to prepare us
for the noble description of the truly free man."[41] But thematically as well
as poetically, so extended a digression is a remarkably unsatisfying prepara-
tion "for the noble description of the truly free man," and a more pertinent
strategy might be to ask, why was Horace eager to introduce the digression
in the first place, and what function is served by a lengthy accusation which
the poet could refute in a single phrase?

I think the operative principle here is a particularly cunning form of
"innocence by association." The earlier charge that Horace was only
Maecenas's *scurra* had raised too much anxiety to be openly acknowledged
or laughingly brushed aside, and the digression on adultery enables Horace
to deflect some of the threat of the previous image. Since Davus is manifestly wrong about Horace's sexual conduct, his earlier accusations are now
likewise less convincing, especially since the proportion between them
(roughly two to one) makes it clear that, for Davus, the sexual is by far the
more serious of the two issues. By charging his master with sexual misconduct, Davus is not only inaccurate but he effectively returns the whole
satire to the safe ground of traditional Roman comedy, in which the slave
is usually heavily involved in his owner's sexual intrigues. The image of
Horace as a typical *jeune premier* of classical stage comedies is obviously
intended to be amusing in its implausibility, but both its very convention-
ity and its peculiar placement within the satire raises rather than disarms
suspicion. There are times when the reliance on generic models seems as
much a strategic search for refuge as a coherent poetic decision.[42] An interpretation along the lines I am suggesting also helps to explain the famous
image that ends this section of the poem, since Davus now returns to the
theme of Horace's servitude under another master:

> tune mihi dominus, rerum imperiis hominumque
> tot tantisque minor, quem ter vindicta quaterque
> imposita haud umquam misera formidine privet?
> adde super dictis quod non levius valeat: nam
> sive vicarius est, qui servo paret, uti mos
> vester ait, seu conservus, tibi quid sum ego? nempe

tu, mihi qui imperitas, alii servis miser atque
duceris ut nervis alienis mobile lignum.

[Are you my master, you, a slave to the dominion of so many men and things—
you, whom the praetor's rod, though placed on your head three or four times
over, never frees from base terror? To what I have said, add something of no less
weight: whether one who obeys a slave is an underslave, as the custom of your
class names him, or a fellow-slave, what am I in respect to you? Why, you, who
lord it over me, are the wretched slave of another master, and you are moved like
a wooden puppet by wires that others pull.]

(75–82)

Writers like Diderot have found this peroration sufficiently powerful to
appropriate for their own purposes, but in the immediate context of
Davus's grievances the very vehemence of the image makes it appear
strangely excessive.[43] As a summary of Horace's supposed cowardice and
sexual indiscretion, the lines seem both too charged and insufficiently motivated. But as a return to the earlier description of Horace's embarrassing
eagerness to please Maecenas, the image acquires an immediate and vicious
sting. The aporias in Horace's satire teach a provocative reversal of our
current theoretical orthodoxies. The poem encourages a psychological interpretation of some of its moves (especially in the ways it almost forces
one to take note of its evasions and gaps by making them so blatant), but
once one follows its hints, the reading that ensues contests the primacy of
any sexual thematics. Horace, I am arguing, uses sexual motifs as a sublima-
tion of, and disguise for, political anxieties, not the other way around. The
contemporary reflex that understands the social and political as a thin superstructure, ultimately grounded on and determined by the sexual, plays
wonderfully into Horace's hands, sanctioning the very sublimations that
the poem is intended simultaneously to mobilize and to undermine.

The sweep of the satire's political reproach extends beyond Horace to
everyone in Augustus's Rome: senators, slaves, and poets alike all moved
"like wooden puppets by wires that another pulls," and although Horace's
intimacy with Rome's rulers might mitigate the rawness of their commands, it could scarcely conceal the strength with which the wires were
secured. When Davus calls his master "O totiens servus," a slave many
times over (70), the grounds of the charge are scarcely touched upon in the
description of the anxious adulterer. Essentially, Horace is accused of being
the court poet to an absolute master, one with the same power over the
poet and his cherished "Republic" as Horace exercises over Davus. But
because Horace insists on lying to himself about his real position, he only
adds the inner chains of self-deception to his outward political subjection.

For the Stoics, a refusal to recognize one's true situation is evidence of
folly and a guarantee that one will remain forever a slave, in the fullest sense

of that word. It is in contrast to this quite specific view of Horace's nature as enslaved by self-deception that Davus embarks on the portrait of the noble sage, free from outside control or untamed desires (83–88). The Stoic wise man lives self-containedly, "et in se ipso totus [complete within himself]" (86), in vivid opposition to men like Priscus, who lead lives of random inconstancy. Horace, according to Davus, utterly fails to live up to this standard, and in the penultimate section of the poem the slave continues to berate his master for a host of greater and lesser vices, including, once again, sexual misconduct, gluttony, and the curious new charge of affectation in judging works of art.[44] Davus, though, does make one last effective point. The real consequence of not being free is always to be in flight from oneself, and Horace tries in vain to "baffle Care" only to feel it pursuing him like an anxiety-stricken fugitive:

> adde, quod idem
> non horam tecum esse potes, non otia recte
> ponere, teque ipsum vitas fugitivus et erro,
> iam vino quaerens, iam somno fallere Curam;
> frustra: nam comes atra premit sequiturque fugacem.[45]

[And again, you cannot bear to be in your own company, you cannot employ your leisure aright, you shun yourself, a runaway and vagabond, seeking now with wine, and now with sleep, to baffle Care. In vain: that black consort dogs and follows your flight.]

(111–14)

By now, however, Davus's complaints have begun to be both repetitious, and in the main, ill-directed, and Horace interrupts the harangue with the threats that close the poem's Saturnalian frame and reestablish the post-festival power relationships in all their stark inequality. The license to speak freely has expired; neither master nor slave seem to have changed as a consequence of their encounter, and nothing suggests that next season's Saturnalia will differ in kind or effectiveness from this one. But the day has been rich in literary, if not in social, consequences: a pair of antagonists has been delineated, a dialogue begun, and a host of questions raised that will make us read the rest of Horace's satires, as well as the long list of their fictional descendants, both "more truly and more strange."

> It is the privilege of the rich
> To waste the time of the poor.
>   (Stevie Smith, "Childe Rolandine")

> If men are forbidden to speak their mind seriously
> . . . they will do it ironically. . . . 'Tis the persecut-

ing spirit has raised the bantering one. . . . The
greater the weight is, the bitterer will be the satire.
The higher the slavery, the more exquisite the
buffoonery.
(Lord Shaftesbury, "An Essay on the Freedom
of Wit and Humor")

Thus far, I have emphasized those elements in Davus's criticisms that seem
to cause Horace the greatest anxiety, or that strike most directly at the
reassuring image the poet has constructed with such effort in his other
satires. In Satire 2.7 Horace stands accused of precisely the same faults for
which he had mocked others in earlier poems, and the inversion of positions nicely enacts the fundamental aim of the Saturnalia itself. Horace is
judged deficient not only by the strict criteria of a stoic Sage but also according to his own proudly announced principles of personal integrity and
independence. But the pressing issue of determining who is a slave and
who is free is not untouched by Saturnalian irony either. Positions presented in such a satire, no matter how serious they might be in another
context, cannot fail to be affected—and infected—by the comic extrava-
gances of the depicted situation as a whole, as well as by the formal expectations inherent in the genre. In this poem, for example, a slave like Davus,
who himself confesses to gluttony, laziness, and excessive love of wine, is
hardly offered as a reliable guide to the characteristics of a free man in
either the legal or the moral/philosophical sense. Davus is a typical *sper-
mológos* (a "picker-up of learning's crumbs," hence a babbler),[46] and his
reliance on the philosophical authority of Crispinius's door-keeper is not
designed to give us much faith in the slave's discernment—all the more so
since Crispinius himself is one of the Stoic writers and moralists whom
Horace detests (cf., Satires 1.1.120, 1.3.139, 1.4.14). In fact, the poem,
much like Erasmus's *Praise of Folly*, relies on the common paradox of a
member of a discredited group describing someone else as having that
group's characteristics, a version, that is, of the Cretan Epimenides' claim
that all Cretans are liars. Since the manipulation of such logical conun-
drums was an essential part of Stoic training, its use in this satire helps to
subject Stoicism itself to a kind of Saturnalian upheaval by pitting one
doctrine ("only the wise man is free") against another ("a slave cannot
adequately know or describe what it means to be free").[47] Many of Davus's
accusations are also formulaic and thus unconvincing, and so, at the satire's
end, neither Horace nor his slave is left in a position of moral authority: the
roles are not so much reversed as they are set awhirl, until servitude and
self-deception seem, again like Erasmian folly, the common property of
everyone in the text.

For all its complexity, however, Horace's satire is not ambiguous in the
same way as some of its literary progeny, and although it powerfully influ-

enced both the structure and some of the specific images of *Le Neveu de Rameau*, in a deeper sense it is more like a richly suggestive precursor than a full marshaling of the resources of the topos. Neither Horace nor Davus approaches the wisdom of the truly free man, but the pertinence of that ideal is itself never questioned seriously. Beyond its rehearsal of the Stoic apothegms about freedom and self-knowledge, the subtlety of the poem is due largely to two distinct features. First, its technical mastery, especially Horace's ease in framing so fluid and volatile a dialogue within the hexameter's metrical exigencies, and the vividness of the exempla with which Davus and the poet embellish their dispute; second, the ways in which the text keeps touching on—only to withdraw again as though in contact with too nakedly exposed a nerve—the anxieties Horace felt about his role as Maecenas's dependent.[48] But neither the two characters nor the reader are ever troubled in their fundamental confidence about which values are to be defended and which condemned. The Saturnalian transformation of all values applies only to the worthiness of the men holding those beliefs, rather than to the beliefs as such, and it is not difficult when reading the poem to determine the degree of justice with which each speaker frames his utterances and the extent to which he is deluded about himself. Horace and Davus know, as the opening lines make clear, that they are participating in a time-honored ritual ("since our fathers willed it so"), but this knowledge only enables a dialogue to take place; it does not essentially inflect the argument or shift the stance of either interlocutor. The fact that this particular master and slave are only the latest in a long series of conventional Saturnalian pairings is not regarded as thematically or psychologically important in its own right. The very availability of the convention to be used in so untroubled a manner ensures both the dialogue's internal coherence and the re-emergence of a normative social order at the poem's close.

Horace may be amused to hear the recital of some of his more venal failings. In a darker vein, he may be deeply troubled by the thought of his willing complicity in a network of political and social subjection. But his role as a master, compelled by tradition to hear his slave's grievances, does not cause him any anxiety. The Saturnalian convention, to put the matter as starkly as possible, is itself not subject to Saturnalian derision, and not until that final twist of the paradigm is incorporated into its literary realization is the reader truly discomforted and the stage set for the emergence of an Abject Hero. Davus, with some justice, calls his master "you slave many times over." But what if participating in such a form is already a guarantee of enslavement, of servitude not to any particular vices or inadequacies but to the increasingly uncomfortable demands of the Saturnalian dialogue itself? If taking part in a Saturnalian dialogue is sufficient to merit the title "O totiens servus," then as soon as one has been trapped in the carnival tumult, there is little to do except struggle futilely against an already scripted part, waiting for the inevitable, and always partially irrefutable, deluge of accusations.

> Adulation bears the ugly taint of subservience,
> but malice gives the false impression of being
> independent.
>   (Tacitus, *The Histories*)

Roughly a century after Horace, Juvenal, a very different kind of satirist, would open his collection of poems with the outraged question

> Semper ego auditor tantum? numquamne reponam
> vexatus totiens rauci Theseide Cordi?

> [Must I *always* be stuck in the audience at these poetry-readings, never / Up on the platform myself, taking it out on Cordus / For the times he's bored me to death with ranting speeches / From that *Theseid* of his?][49]

Of all the writers we shall be considering, only Horace felt certain of being listened to in the appropriately attentive manner and by the era's most distinguished audience. And only Horace could know and give voice to the particular anxiety such attentiveness could evoke. In Horace, the desire of less successful aspirants for admission to the circle whose intimacy the poet enjoyed became a favorite target of his satiric mockery (e.g., the portrait of the social-climbing bore in 1.9). Later authors, though, were far more likely to echo Juvenal's injured pride and share his anger at being excluded from the rewards doled out by the great. Indeed, most of Western literature's subsequent railers and malcontents continue more or less explicitly framing their own versions of Juvenal's opening verses. In the course of their literary evolution, however, these succeeding figures reveal themselves as increasingly less certain of their genius, increasingly haunted by the fear that even if they were granted their hour on stage it would only result in abject self-embarrassment. It is as though, to the weight of their own anger and sense of exclusion, the identical feelings of all their predecessors has been added as an additional burden, a legacy that deprives even their "savage indignation" of any personal authenticity. Although Juvenal may claim that it is scorn, not poetic genius, that prompts his verse ("Si natura negat, facit indignatio versum"),[50] the satires exhibit no doubt about either the legitimacy of his indignation or, more importantly, about his ability to give that indignation proper expression. The Abject Hero, on the other hand, may feel a Juvenalian outrage at his society, particularly at his exclusion from its privileges, but, like Horace's Davus, he will never be able to shake off a servile longing for approval from the targets of his wrath.

Still worse, he will be lacerated by the galling suspicion that in truth he deserves no better than his subservient status.

In one of his most striking phrases, Freud described "the narcissism of minor differences," the need we have to distinguish ourselves from others, no matter how paltry the demarcations are in objective terms.[51] It is here that the Abject Hero is most vulnerable, his narcissism most easily wounded: since the accents of his anger are themselves only quotations, his claim to even the most "minor differences" is necessarily suspect. Out of this wounded narcissism arises a compensatory urge: the fantasy of seizing the platform, not just to draw everyone's eyes to himself and exhibit his humiliations as evidence of a victimized sensitivity, but to insult and injure the audience that has "compelled" him to become a licensed mountebank. The initial theatrical image is gradually transformed from Juvenal's vexation at being relegated to the audience and denied his rightful place on stage to Céline's hallucinatory vision of everyone trapped together in the same violent arena, without either stage or stands remaining as a place of refuge. The most intriguing aspect of this transformation is that it found its literary structure not in Juvenal's monologic indignation but in Horace's subtly modulated dialogues, in the metamorphic possibilities of a Saturnalian confrontation between servitude and mastery, wisdom and folly. The crucial difference between Juvenal and Horace seems to me best crystallized in Elias Canetti's distinction between a psychologically complex authorial voice and the self-regarding anger of a pure satirist: "Another reason for the strength of these characters [in Büchner's *Wozzeck*] is no doubt that they are given the full value of the word 'I,' which a pure satirist grants to no one except himself."[52] Horace grants this "I" to his minor characters; Juvenal, the great railer, only to himself, and although his satires are swarming with an enormous variety of figures, his is the only realized voice we ever hear with any clarity.

If Juvenal insists it is anger that prompts his verse, there is a counterclaim that seems at least as plausible; namely, his verse itself entirely creates the anger in the first place, an *indignatio* that exists only for its rhetorical possibilities as a poetry-engendering stance. Moralistic critics have often censured Juvenal's "cowardice" for his refusal to take aim at living figures, a decision he openly acknowledges at the end of the First Satire: "For myself, I shall try my hand on the famous dead, whose ashes / Rest beside the Latin and the Flammian Ways [experiar quid concedatur in illos / quorum Flaminia tegitur cinis atque Latina]."[53] But beyond what seems a perfectly sane refusal to jeopardize his life—armchair audacity can be exercised with rather more impunity by tenured scholars than by one of Domitian's or Trajan's subjects—the implicit premise that Juvenal's verse might depend in some way on the identity of its targets fundamentally mistakes the nature of his poetry. Juvenal has no reformist or pedagogic impulse: the satires only exist in order to rail and by virtue of the breathtaking technical brilliance of their raillery. For Juvenal, the kind of "wisdom" Horace both accepts and mildly satirizes (largely a form of humane Stoicism) is essentially irrelevant. The world has gone so totally astray that the wisdom of the all-observing Juvenalian eye can breed only anger, disgust, or despair, and beneath these emotions a distinctly audible delight at its own wit in fashioning a matchingly corrosive idiom. Moreover, in the Juvenalian canon one vice immediately turns into another and still another, thereby generating both the poet's vision and the poem's structure: a kind of epic catalog of horrific negative exempla (cf., Satire 8.183–84), linked by a kind of demented *metamorphosis vitiarum* in which degeneracy and folly reign supreme. In such a universe, the concept of a meliorative wisdom seems the height of delirium because, were it to exist, it would be so utterly impotent.

Since the Juvenalian voice can do nothing but rail, the suggestion that virtue may actually exist is registered as only another provocation, as something the poem can not incorporate except by denouncing. In Satire 6, for example, the lengthy description of the horrors of female sexuality is interrupted by a crucial supposition. What if there really still existed, Juvenal asks, a woman who embodies all the perfections, who is the exact opposite of the monsters he has expended such vitriol denouncing?

> sit formosa decens dives fecunda, vetustos
> porticibus disponat avos, intactior omni
> crinibus effusis bellum dirimente Sabina.

> [with beauty and charm, fertile, wealthy, her hall / A museum of old ancestral portraits, grant her Virginity more stunning than all those dishevelled Sabine / Maidens who stopped the fighting.][54]

Surprisingly, Juvenal does not deny the possibility that so rare a Roman maiden can still exist amidst the corruption of the age. Instead he takes the more shocking tack of insisting that this picture of perfection is actually the most appalling prospect of all:

> quis feret uxorem cui constant omnia? malo,
> malo Venusinam quam te, Cornelia, mater
> Gracchorum.

> [Who could stomach such wifely perfection? I'd far sooner / Marry a penniless tart than take on that virtuous / Paragon Cornelia, Mother of Statesmen.][55]

Beyond the obvious, and probably self-mocking, misogyny characteristic of the whole satire, what is more revealing about this passage is that Juvenal's verse cannot tolerate any sort of "paragon." What cannot be attacked also can not be narrated within the restricted emotional compass of his lines. Juvenal continuously decries his era's lack of genuine nobility or virtue, but his poetry is deeply complicit with the corruption it indicts since it is incapable of accommodating even a fragmentary remnant of an ideal without renouncing its character as monologic raillery. Like all raillery, Juvenal's satire is tremendously excited by what it attacks. The imaginative energy of each satire is roused into the greatest verbal activity by the most ferocious examples of degradation, and the poem's savage indignation is entirely dependent on fantasizing an in principle unending puppet-show of human viciousness, each instance compelling the poet to new—and more thrilling—verbal pyrotechnics. But because Juvenal is neither a reformer nor particularly interested in problems of representation, his satires are united purely by a narrative voice, rather than by any consistent psychological self-portraiture (e.g., the often contradictory description of his tastes, etc.) or moral/logical thematic unfolding. Juvenal writes about the pleasures of writing, specifically about the pleasures of writing about being furious, and he does so by blatantly undermining both narrative plausibility and authorial psychology.

Of course, I am not interested in claiming that Juvenal was a "postmodernist" before there ever was a modernism, but only that satire of pure raillery tends to be more static both in its structure and in its tones and to have less formal capacity for radical transformation in different contexts than does the apparently less flamboyant genre of the dialogic Saturnalian confrontation. Juvenal provides the most powerful instance classical literature has left us of the strength of a single, outraged voice inventing image upon image of fresh vexations to justify and stimulate itself, and there are clear echoes of this voice still audible in the subsequent texts of rage and *ressentiment*. But the most effective of these, as we shall see, will have learned to reinvent and expand the resources of the Horatian dialogic satire as well—in large part, I suspect, because only a dialogic form has a chance of entrapping its reader into its conflict. We can admire, be shocked by, or grow weary of, a superbly solo performance like Juvenal's; but it is hard to see how such a form can either implicate its reader or seek to thrust that reader into the role of one of its interlocutors, since the existence of any other consciousness is, at least at the formal level, not pertinent to the poem at all. Nor does a form like Juvenal's enable a writer to question his own beliefs and practices, since the rhetorical pressure of the work makes it impossible to posit *any* values with the initial plausibility required to generate much tension out of their subsequent undermining.[56]

One powerful solution that later writers worked out was to appropriate the sweep and vehemence of the Juvenalian raillery, but as only one of the voices of a complex dialogic *agon*. The most fruitful form for that *agon* was the Saturnalian dialogue whose initial terms Horace set down in Satire 2.7. The Horatian model taught writers to dialogize—and thereby open to contradictory and critical voices—the limited focus of Juvenalian indignation.

But the ferocious energy tapped by a Juvenalian anger raised the stakes of succeeding Saturnalian confrontations, exposing the text's characters, ideas, and readers to risks Horace would never have allowed.

From Horace's once-a-year banter with Davus and Juvenal's outcry at his exclusion from the platform and the patron's purse to the Underground Man's *ressentiment* or the Célinian narrator's fury may seem like an untraceably far-reaching evolution. But the decisive mediating link of this development, Diderot's dialogue between a bankrupt parasite and a typical Enlightenment *philosophe* makes clear the logic by which just such a transformation and adaption occurred. Accordingly, it is to *Le Neveu de Rameau* that our attention should be directed next, for the first real encounter with the Abject Hero as both instigator and victim of the Saturnalia's increasingly bitter turbulence.

Part II

THE ABJECT HERO EMERGES

Estragon: We've lost our rights?
Vladimir: We got rid of them.
  (Samuel Beckett, *Waiting for Godot*)

Three _____

Oui, Monsieur le Philosophe: Diderot's
Le Neveu de Rameau

> May he not be knave, fool, and genius altogether?
>   (Herman Melville, *The Confidence Man*)

IN PLAUTUS's comedy *Persa*, the parasite Saturio reassures his daughter that far from having nothing to give her as a dowry he actually possesses "a whole hamper full of books." Saturio promises that if she cooperates with his schemes he will give her "a good six hundred witticisms" from his collection as her marriage portion, and, to make her dowry truly rare, will select only the choicest of them: "all Attic ones without a single Sicilian jest among them."[1] What is so striking about this scene is less the high value placed on books—a commonplace of literature before the seventeenth century—but the information that anthologies of humor were in general circulation, that they were ranked according to the prestige of the jests they contained, and that such compendia represented a significant legacy. As a parasite living off his wit and needing to please his patron every day to be certain of a dinner, Saturio can turn to his library for professional advice on how to be entertaining. He has at hand a treasury of well-tested jokes that he can study, adapt to his changing circumstances and draw upon whenever his own inspiration flags.

This scene from classical Roman comedy is particularly revealing because the situation is entirely different in later European drama. Although scholarship has documented the existence of numerous sixteenth century "jest-books" written to pass on the most successful witticisms and tricks of such famous court fools as Killian, buffoon to the King of Hungary, these are never consulted by any of the "licensed fools" who populate the plays of the period.[2] In the world of the Renaissance stage, each fool is an original, with no prior history or formal training; none of them avails himself of the considerable literature left by his predecessors in the art or shows much awareness of the rich heritage available to him for study and imitation. But *Le Neveu de Rameau* relies on a thorough familiarity with the tradition from which it derives, not only on the part of its readers, but on the part of its two characters as well. An intimacy with the Latin and French satiric tradition is shared equally among *Moi*, *Lui*, and the author who provides the opening epigraph, and the dialogue's speakers are able to marshal the resources of a common culture *against one another's positions*. *Le Neveu de Rameau* depends on this shared knowledge as part of its fundamental enabling condition and employs it as the single most important factor in creating the dialogue's atmosphere of dazzling—but also deeply unsettling—emotional and intellectual playfulness.

When Diderot risked pitting the central tenets of his daily activity as a *philosophe* and leader of the Enlightenment against Rameau's laughter, the Saturnalian provenance of that derision was far more than an ancestral echo.[3] *Le Neveu de Rameau* confines its tumult to the interior of a famous Parisian coffee house,[4] but from the outset, the one unmistakable guide Diderot provides to the nature of his work is its character as a Saturnalian dialogue. That such a guide should be at once indispensable to an understanding of the text, and yet helpless to resolve the multiplicity of antithetical thematic interpretations it has evoked, is due to the inherent power of the topos and Diderot's masterly unfolding of its potential.

Le Neveu de Rameau opens with a direct citation from line 14 of Horace's Satire 2.7, to remind us of Priscus, the unstable senator, "born when every single Vertumnus [the god who presided over the changing of the year and assumed any shape he pleased] was out of sorts [Vertumnis, quotquot sunt, natus iniquis]."[5] I say remind *us*, because these lines are spoken neither by *Moi* nor by *Lui* and so do not actually enter into the dialogue proper; rather, they serve as a frame alerting the reader to the work's genre. Since Ernst Robert Curtius first called attention to the importance of the Horatian epigraph for *Le Neveu de Rameau*, critics have found themselves in the curious position of recognizing a clear generic affiliation while in fundamental disagreement about how its literary genealogy should govern the interpretation of Diderot's satire.[6]

The character of Jean-François Rameau shares numerous traits with Horace's Priscus, a character whose fickleness of temperament was matched only by the constant reversals in his fortunes.[7] Indeed, *Le Neveu de Rameau* is full of echoes, not only of Horace's Saturnalian dialogue, but of numerous other Horatian and Juvenalian satires as well.[8] Although scholarship continues to find ever more instances of Diderot's debt to Horace and to the entire tradition of Roman satire, there is a remarkable lack of consensus about the thematic consequences of those debts.[9] In part, no doubt, this absence of critical accord is a tribute to the productive uncertainties Diderot's text generates. But it is also due to the particular nature of the Saturnalian dialogue as a genre. For all their canonic force, it is impossible to appeal to Diderot's classical models for help in resolving any of the specific issues under contention in *Le Neveu de Rameau*, if only because his exemplary source-texts are themselves inherently resistant to closure. That the contest between *Moi* and *Lui* takes up in a different age and dispensation the *agon* inaugurated by Horace and Davus is indisputable, but this knowledge cannot settle any interpretive controversies, since

Horace's satire, as well as the principal intervening examples of the genre, are invoked by Diderot exactly because of their open-ended disputatiousness. The introduction of a quotation uttered by neither *Moi* nor *Lui* must be seen as issuing from the dialogue's author and addressed directly to the reader; both Diderot and that reader are thereby brought into the text as participants. The Horatian epigraph implicates rather than shelters Diderot, who may be distinct in traits and opinions from *Moi* but who is nonetheless, via the framing citation, himself enframed within the work. Finally, since *Moi* and *Lui* borrow vital aspects of their arguments and self-definitions from the same classical sources as determined Diderot's choice of an initial epigraph, a hectic circulation of topoi occurs that keeps the entire satire spinning and that deprives anyone—author, character, or reader—from enjoying an unchallengeable last word. When so much of a book's dialogue is a matter of direct quotation and close echoes of prior texts, the whole question of autonomous individual authorship and control is rendered suspect, a victim, and perhaps the most distinguished one of all, of the Saturnalia's leveling energy.

The twin themes of control and mastery versus impotence and anarchy are central to *Le Neveu de Rameau*, as they are to the whole tradition of the Saturnalian dialogue. From his first self-description, *Moi* insists on his willed surrender to stray thoughts, indulged at the close of a busy day ("sur les cinq heures du soir") as a form of harmlessly agreeable diversion. But to bandy words with so disreputable a character as Jean-François Rameau is clearly more than the *philosophe* can tolerate very often, since he emphasizes that such encounters are kept strictly to an annual event: "I stop and talk to them once a year."[10] *Moi* immediately justifies the expense of time and spirit by subsuming it into his regular reflections. Talking to men like Rameau is really a form of educational amusement:

> because their character stands out from the rest and breaks that tedious uniformity that our education, our social conventions, and our habitual good manners have brought about. If a man like that makes his appearance in some circle, he is like a grain of yeast that ferments and restores to each of us a part of his innate individuality. He shakes and stirs things up, tells us what to praise or censure, brings out the truth, reveals who is decent and unmasks the scoundrels. It is then that a man with genuine discernment keeps his ears open and sifts out the real state of affairs.[11]

It is worth paying close attention to this first account, as much for what it reveals about *Moi* as for its description of the Nephew.

Initially, it is hard to quarrel with *Moi*'s account, and his qualified justification for chatting with "such eccentrics"[12] has been echoed by virtually every commentator on the dialogue. Indeed, *Moi* recapitulates the classical defense of the "licensed fool" as an agent of social unmasking who exposes the falsehood and conventionality of his more fully socialized interlocutors.

More elegantly, and consonant with *Moi*'s position as a professional man of learning, the role he assigns the Nephew corresponds closely to the pedagogic function Stoic logic attributed to paradoxes.[13] In Stoic theory, just as in *Moi*'s summary, the paradox has no intrinsic value except as a means to an end: its propositional force is exhausted as soon as the one central truth has been extracted from the surrounding conventionally false doctrines. As a kind of living incarnation of the Stoic paradox, Rameau offers only a preliminary stage in the neophyte's quest for genuine wisdom; it is a challenge the sage no longer needs, although he occasionally may indulge in the exercise as a kind of intellectual *divertissement*. Crucial, too, is that the sage always retains the final word; it is his judgment that determines the relevance and utility of the paradox, and it is in his wisdom alone that the largely negative force of the paradox finds its positive resolution.

Even in this passage of seeming commendation, then, *Moi* asserts his superiority to the Nephew. Rameau may "bring out the truth," but he does so blindly, and it requires a philosopher to recognize it as such. The observer *Moi* confidently calls "a man with genuine discernment" is never unsettled by the paradoxical arguments, and since, presumably, he is always identical to himself and true to the truth he serves, he wears no mask for the paradoxialist to strip off.[14] It is to hear about the failings of *others* that *Moi* is willing to banter words with Rameau, certain that his own certainties can never be challenged seriously in the dialogue.

Five o'clock is a nicely appropriate hour for such encounters, since it is an in-between time: neither day, when thoughts should be on serious public matters, nor night, with its more inward claims, and yet partaking of both. It is also the time of entertainment, as the closing references to a new opera make clear, and one of *Moi*'s strategies is to treat his dialogue with Rameau as a kind of spectacle in which he may participate without serious implications for his important functions. It is particularly fitting, moreover, that the conversation takes place in the Café de la Régence. As Stallybrass and White remind us, in the eighteenth century the institution of the coffeehouse quickly emerged as a privileged setting for the new bourgeois humanism: it was kept more orderly and calm than the "sordid" alehouse, and it served a drink that was supposed to encourage clarity and concentration instead of the fuzzy dissipation induced by alcohol. "Its great claim to superiority over the alehouse was that it replaced 'idle' and festive consumption with *productive* leisure."[15] Ironically, then, the Nephew's wild antics and the chaos he spreads in the course of his dialogue re-carnivalizes a setting designed expressly to shelter its inhabitants from the carnival-like atmosphere of other public meeting places. Rameau brings the marketplace and tavern into the coffeehouse, just as he brings idleness and parasitism into philosophical discourse, thereby inverting the specific values characteristic of the *Encyclopédistes'* locus and language.

But if an encounter with Rameau is potentially so amusing, and, in a limited sense, even instructive a part of twilight relaxation, why does *Moi* set a strict annual limit on its occurrence? Formally, of course, the phrase signals an explicit parallel to the classical Saturnalia, recapitulating the genre affiliation announced by the opening Horatian epigraph. Additionally, the temporal restriction testifies to *Moi*'s sense of having graduated beyond the need for an ephebe's lessons in manipulating paradoxes. More subtly, though, by his insistence *Moi* shows that he too recognizes his conversation with Rameau as a Saturnalian dialogue. He is as aware of the encounter's provenance as the author who provided the initial framing tag. The difference is that *Moi*'s confidence permits him to envisage a safe carnival in which he will observe the false values of men he already scorns held up to ridicule and in which he will be able to "praise or censure" the sallies of the licensed clown. But *Lui* is no less aware of the conventions, both spoken and implicit, governing their exchange, and he will match the *philosophe*'s relaxed expectations with a bitter will to make the most of his chance and turn the moment into a wild Saturnalian upheaval, in which nothing evokes more mockery than the sage's pretensions to judge and to know.

> His choice was between playacting and no action
> at all. There are situations in which people are
> *condemned* to playact.
>   (Milan Kundera, *The Unbearable Lightness of
>   Being*)

In the *Persa* it is clear not only that wit can leave a written legacy of its triumphs but that the professionals of such wit must have reflected on their roles sufficiently to encourage the establishment of a proper historical record. The clowns and parasites of Roman comedy are entirely creatures of literary convention, but those conventions include at least a limited kind of self-knowledge and a separate, domestic existence apart from the exercise of their trade. But in medieval and Renaissance drama, for all of the self-reflexive wit and understanding of a clown like Feste or Lear's Fool, there is no "Mrs. Fool" to whom the jester returns at the end of the day's work,[16] or a "Fool Junior" to whom his father could will the catalog of his best sallies.

Diderot's single most significant transformation of the figures of the licensed clown and his interlocutor is to endow both of these figures with a densely particularized historical, biographical, and professional identity, as well as with a radically new awareness of their genealogies. If Bakhtin laments the decline of the carnival's original universality into the privatized "chamber" world of post-Renaissance writers,[17] it is just as plausible to understand the genre's evolution positively, as an unfolding of an ever-increasing historical specificity and individualization.

Le Neveu de Rameau is such a decisive turning point in the history of the Saturnalian dialogue because its "licensed fool" is endowed with a complex personal history, an emotional inscape that is not entirely subsumed by his formal role as ironist and mocker. Jean-François Rameau is clearly a direct descendant of Horace's Davus; he is also the inheritor of the Renaissance tradition of the "wise fool." Unlike either of these two figures, though, Rameau is not merely a parasite and unmasker but also a father, grieving widower, and failed artist, whose familial relationships—he is, after all, known primarily as the crazy nephew of France's greatest living composer—and debilitating penury are crucial both to his temperament and to the specific charges he levels against *Moi*'s complacent confidence.[18] An equally significant consequence of this particularization is that the Nephew reflects on his role as a "licensed fool" and makes of that condition his central grievance against himself, the *philosophes*, and the society in which occupations like his are simultaneously sought after, scorned, and rewarded. For Rameau, the banter of the "licensed fool" is a grotesque kind of career decision, and much of his self-laceration consists precisely in trying to understand and justify what he sees sometimes as an involuntary degradation of his voluntary stance and other times as a voluntary self-abasement to which he is driven by ineluctable human need.[19] Folly may be common to everyone in the world of Shakespeare's *Twelfth Night*, and servitude may be the lot of all of Augustus's subjects, but Rameau is the first literary character to unite both the fool and the slave with the painful self-consciousness of a man convinced both that he is doing exactly what most fits his skills and that he has been debased by a world in which survival is possible only by letting one's own ignobility flourish. Finally, and perhaps most surprisingly, the Nephew is widely, if eccentrically, well-read, and it is his reading that gives him the knowledge of what he and *Moi* are doing in their complex reenactment of a contest inaugurated centuries ago and in another tongue.

> They chanced to think. Suppose the future fails.
> If platitude and inspiration are alike
> As evils, and if reason, fatuous fire,
> Is only another egoist wearing a mask
>   (Wallace Stevens, "A Duck for Dinner")

In his mocking description of the intellectual and moral bankruptcy of the *anti-philosophe* clique represented by characters like Bertin, Palissot, and Fréron, Rameau is only voicing, although with unusual acerbity, the "licensed fool's" customary scorn at the pretensions of the corrupt. That Diderot used the dialogue to settle old scores is undeniable, and there is a particular elegance in allowing the condemnation of his enemies to be articulated by one of their intimate associates, a participant in the very cabal that had exposed Diderot to ridicule on the public stage in works like Palissot's *Les Philosophes*. But Rameau does not confine his sarcasm to any single sect, and the gratification *Moi* derives from hearing his foes' baseness so thoroughly exposed is soured by an acute discomfort at seeing his own ideals treated with equal disdain.

Throughout the dialogue, Rameau denies the ethical and philosophical universality upon which the *Encyclopédistes* had based their claims as public benefactors, and he subverts their self-flattering division of all Parisian intellectual life into camps of committed allies and unyielding antagonists. (It is amusing to note *Moi*'s eagerness to associate himself with men like "Voltaire, d'Alembert and Diderot [!]")[20] *Moi* clearly relishes the late–eighteenth-century cult of *les grands hommes*, the age's veneration of men who were neither warriors nor aristocrats but leaders in science and the arts, whose labors would dissipate ignorance and bring benefits to the whole nation.[21] No doubt *Moi* hopes that at least some of the prestige acquired by these distinguished names will devolve unto him as well, through a kind of "trickle-down" effect of cultural prestige. For *Moi*, an awareness of the venality of the enemy must lead to an acknowledgment of his own party's virtue, but Rameau makes evident the absurdity of such categorizations by occupying what, in *Moi*'s eyes, ought to be the untenable position of finding both sides ridiculous. Of course, in so doing, Rameau is still acting in keeping with the traditional role of the "licensed fool" like Feste, whose wit spared neither Olivia nor Malvolio, or the momentarily enfranchised slave, Davus, whose reproaches are directed at everyone from his masters to his fellow laborers. Indeed, it is only *Moi*'s vanity that permits him to enter what he explicitly recognizes as a Saturnalian dialogue while still imagining himself invulnerable to criticism, and Rameau's irony is a powerful way of reminding his interlocutor of the ground rules of their meeting. But what is recognizably unique about Jean-François Rameau is that he has pondered the canonic sources of his designated function and is quite prepared to provide *Moi* with a thoughtful bibliographic and existential account of his education in parasitism and mockery:

> That, said he, is because bad company is as instructive as debauchery: one is indemnified for the loss of innocence by the loss of prejudice. In a society of bad men, vice reveals itself without a mask, and one learns to see people as they really are.[22]

In his *apologia*, the Nephew makes the identical claims for the pedagogic value of associating with the corrupt that *Moi* had originally offered for talking with such types as Rameau himself. In the Bertin-Hus household, Rameau has taken on the role of the *philosophe* willingly attending the de-

praved for the instruction their company can provide, and the ease with
which the Nephew can appropriate *Moi*'s rhetoric for his own behavior
helps to destabilize the solidity of the philosopher-parasite distinction.[23]
Indeed, throughout their encounter, both men engage in a continual effort
to claim the word *philosophe* for their own purposes, and near the end of the
dialogue, in one of his most characteristically acute (because also emotionally touching) jibes, Rameau describes his dead wife as "a kind of *philosophe*," who understood the need to prostitute herself to a wealthy admirer.[24] The description of Mme. Rameau ("Mrs. Fool" as would-be tart)
indirectly satirizes Diderot's own relationship to patrons like Catherine the
Great, and it explicitly parodies *Moi*'s initial, complacent description of his
more venturesome ideas as "my sluts."[25]

But Rameau's challenge strikes more deeply, since the main sources he
draws on for guidance in his activities are the same canonic masters who
had also enthralled and directed the studies of the *philosophes*:

> LUI. . . . And then I've done some reading.
>
> MOI. - What have you read?
>
> LUI. - I keep rereading Theophrastus, La Bruyère and Molière. . . . What I find
> there is a compendium of what to do but never to articulate. When I read
> *L'Avare*, I tell myself: "Be as stingy as you like, but don't talk like a miser."
> When I read *Tartuffe*, I say: "Be a hypocrite if you want, but don't talk like
> one. Keep any useful vices, but don't acquire the tone and mannerisms that
> would make you ridiculous." But to avoid these lapses one must know what
> they are, and the classical authors have given us excellent portraits. . . . I recall
> whatever others have said, whatever I have read, and I add to all this my
> original contribution.[26]

Irrespective of the justice of Rameau's interpretation of the great satirists,[27] there is no doubt that his account closely follows the normative
description of artistic development mapped by Horace in the *Ars Poetica*
and adopted by Diderot himself in countless passages throughout his writings on aesthetics. The three stages, first studying the Old Masters, then
imitating them as faithfully as possible, and finally adding one's own particular discoveries and personal refinements, constitute the traditional journey
from ephebe to original creator, but Rameau diligently follows the path of
the Masters only in order to become a more accomplished scoundrel. Such
a trajectory thrusts directly at one of the *Encyclopédistes*' central beliefs: the
value of a classical education in forming a nobler kind of citizen, freed from
religious dogmatism and clerical superstition. The unique efficacy of the
classics for this project lay in their capacity to unite, according to one of
Moi's typical Horatian borrowings, "entertainment and learning"[28] in a
universally transmissible manner.[29]

Diderot consistently upheld the centrality of classical authors because
they presented examples of how to live a life of virtue through reason alone,

without the need for Christian revelation or priestly mediations. More-over, classical philosophy seemed to the *philosophes* to have sought for truth in public dialogues and open debate rather than in a monastic withdrawal from communal affairs. Thus, when Rameau turns for advice in villainy to the very models *Moi* venerates as instructors in a life of civic virtue, he trivializes the grounding certainties of the *philosophe* as public educator. That he should do so, and in a "philosophical dialogue," a form which traditionally leads to the logical confirmation of the indissoluble link be-tween truth and virtue, only makes his mockery all the more effective. In-deed, the whole structure of the satire ironizes Diderot's self-identification with Socrates, since, as Carol Blum points out, it is exactly the Socratic role of the "quirky gadfly, needling a pompous or rigid opponent" that Rameau appropriates.[30] Disconcertingly enough, Rameau most resembles Socrates when the issue is one of moral corruption, since he describes himself as quite ready to die for his educational theories—or at least to face with equanimity the prospect of being murdered for his money by a son who has absorbed only too well the lesson of his father's pedagogic pantomime with the *louis d'or*.

Just as *Le Neveu de Rameau* enacts a carnivalesque disruption of the con-ventional philosophical dialogue, refusing that genre's teleological closure in the enunciation of a unique, globally authoritative truth,[31] so *Lui*'s lu-cidity in his corruption negates the central premise of Socratic/Platonic ethics. In theory as well as in his practice, Rameau severs the link between intellectual knowledge, aesthetic discrimination, and moral integrity that Diderot identified as the core of classical ethics and that he invoked when he insisted that the *Encyclopédie* would improve public virtue by spreading learning.[32] What Rameau finds so ludicrous is exactly the confident self-aggrandizement of the professional intellectual:

> You think that everyone could be made happy in the same way. What an absurd idea! . . . You ennoble your idioscyncracies by calling them virtue, or philoso-phy. But is this particular virtue and philosophy really suitable for everyone?[33]

But Rameau's targets include more than the universalist arrogance of the *Encyclopédistes*, uncanny though it is to watch Diderot frame so dismissive a jibe at theories he himself helped formulate and whose propagation took up so many years of his life. What the Nephew derisively rejects is any global truth divorced from the particularized, specific needs of individuals seeking to survive comfortably in determinate historical circumstances:

> Moreover, bear in mind that in a matter as variable as behavior there is no such thing as the absolutely, essentially, universally true or false. . . . Supposing virtue had been the road to fortune, either I should have been virtuous or I should have simulated virtue as well as the next man. But people wanted me to be ridiculous, and so I have made myself that way.[34]

Rameau's outburst crystallizes in advance the critique against Enlightenment pretensions that would be taken up throughout the nineteenth and twentieth centuries.[35] Central to Nietzsche's thinking, for example, is the affirmation that only the truly heroic and free spirit can conceive of its own value system as simply one perspective among many, a perspective appropriate only to itself. Such a spirit is content in its singularity and feels no need to generalize its point of view into a moral/transcendent category with equal claim on everyone. But Nietzsche also believes that those not free in this way suffer from a *ressentiment* that finds its chief outlet in the compulsion to impose their values on the whole world. What is remarkable is that Diderot not only had anticipated Nietzsche's argument, but had already deconstructed the Nietzschean hierarchy by showing that the abject, base *Neveu*, who is full of *ressentiment*, is precisely the consciousness most free from any moralisms, free, that is, from both the religious moralism of the Church and the philosophical-scientific moralism of the *philosophes*. *Le Neveu de Rameau* is so unsettling because it exposes the will-to-power not only of the *Encyclopédistes*, but of all aspirants to the status of universal educators. Diderot's critique, unlike Nietzsche's, is formulated as a voice *from below*, a cry issuing from the groveler's viewpoint, rather than from the more typically heroic perspective of the *Übermensch*. While Nietzsche emphasizes the nobility of the irreverent mocker, Diderot shows that that same mockery functions even more disconcertingly when it is articulated from the opposite camp, by an Abject, rather than an aristocratic, Hero.

In the face of so radical a re-evaluation of all values, Bakhtin's regret at the decline of the post-Renaissance carnival into the privatized realm of the individual consciousness seems oversimplified. In *Le Neveu de Rameau* this "decline" is the first step toward an all-encompassing Saturnalia from which a return to normalcy the next day becomes increasingly more difficult to effect. Jean-François Rameau knows his Rabelais as well as his Horace and Molière, but his profit on it is to have learned how to mock and curse both himself and his patrons more savagely. In *Le Neveu de Rameau*, the Saturnalia itself is carnivalized, and the carnivalesque de-idealized, until neither hierarchy nor rebellion are given any priority, and neither sage nor fool allowed to triumph for more than a moment before being compelled once again to yield the initiative.

Born Originals, how comes it to pass that we
die Copies?
   (Edward Young, "Conjectures on Original
   Compositions")

Because Rameau has pored over the appropriate classical models, he knows quite well the ambiguous authority traditionally alloted to a "wise fool" and does not hesitate to invoke it in his quarrel with *Moi*. In chapter 1 we already heard Rameau's boast that great rulers have always welcomed "an official fool," without ever requiring the services of "an official sage."[36] He is equally ready, however, to shift the grounds of his critique and mock the *philosophe*'s striving for secular wisdom and morality by opposing to it a self-serving version of the Judeo-Christian theme of the folly of human knowledge. In a deliberate echo of the medieval "Feast of Fools," Rameau misappropriates Ecclesiastes as readily as he does the motifs of classical comedies: "Listen! I say, Long live philosophy and wisdom—the wisdom of Solomon: to drink good wines, stuff oneself on exquisite food, tumble gorgeous women, sleep in soft beds. Apart from that, all is vanity."[37] Included in Rameau's catalog of "vanities," moreover, are just those qualities the *Encyclopédistes* most often held up as the cardinal virtues of an enlightened age: patriotism, friendship, the faithful discharging of social obligations, and the education of one's children. To all of these, Rameau's answer is "Vanity!" and he justifies his scorn with some of his sharpest—and most Juvenalian—outbursts:

> There is no longer any such thing as one's homeland. All I see from pole to pole is tyrants and slaves. . . . Does one really have friends? And even if one had them, should we make them ungrateful? . . . Gratitude is a burden, and all burdens are meant to be shaken off. . . . No matter what you do, it is impossible to disgrace yourself if you are rich.[38]

Repeatedly, *Moi* is compelled to admit that "there's some sense in almost everything you have been saying,"[39] only to be met with the irritation of a man who realizes full well that there are numerous domains wherein his knowledge exceeds that of the *philosophe*:

> That's typical of people like you. If *we* say something intelligent, it's like madmen or people possessed—purely by accident. It's only men of your kind who know what they're saying. Yes, Mister Philosopher, I know what I'm saying, and I understand it as well as you understand your own thoughts.[40]

Yet Rameau derives remarkably little benefit from his self-awareness. The knowledge of his position as generically privileged ironist is undoubtedly useful for refuting *Moi*'s pretensions, but it has yielded the Nephew neither material comfort nor self-esteem. Rameau is simultaneously wretched and arrogant in a way that differs incrementally from the traditional sad clown or hungry slave, and his wretchedness and lucidity about his own talents are intimately linked to one another. In one of the crucial passages of *The Phenomenology of Mind*, Hegel used, without ever citing directly, *Le Neveu de Rameau* as the principal example of an unhappy consciousness, seeing in Rameau's plight "The Spirit in Self-Estrangement," for whom

Everything that has continuity and universality, everything that bears the name of law, good, and right, is torn to pieces . . . all identity and concord break up, for what holds sway is the purest discord and disunion, what was absolutely essential is absolutely unessential, what has a pure being on its own account has its being outside itself.[41]

Rameau's rage is the inverted mirror of eighteenth century optimism and propriety, which, in its confidence of spreading benefits to all, had overlooked what Hegel goes on to call the "secret rebellion of the other self," "this pure disintegration" in which only "sheer internal discordance" can still be heard.[42] But for Hegel, the Nephew's "absolute frankness" and cynical candor, as well as his moments of ecstatic, musical rapture, finally effect a dialectic reconciliation between negative and affirmative impulses and save him from utter abjection.[43]

But I think it is truer to the dialogue to see how Rameau's depth of feeling and inspiration only render his abjection all the more painful. Instead of mitigating his sense of abject debasement, his ecstasy only confirms it; indeed, the experience of such rapture is a constituent element of, not a transcendence over, the depth of abjection. Later Marxist interpretations of *Le Neveu de Rameau* do not duplicate Hegel's tortuous formal analysis of the Nephew's consciousness but instead take over the Hegelian concept of a productive negativity for its ideological utility. Henri Lefebvre, for example, argues that *philosophes* like *Moi*, who speak on behalf of a prosperous bourgeoisie, hope to silence their critics by the proclamation of a purely abstract conception of human equality, and that the dialogue forces them to confront what Lefebvre calls Rameau's "inner revolt, the complete emancipation of the poor wretch through his very abjection and laceration."[44] *Le Neveu de Rameau* undoubtedly contains a number of striking aphorisms that seem to privilege class conflict.[45] But paradoxically, so politically interested a reading is much too positive and optimistic. It misses exactly what is most tragic about Rameau: his total internalization of the most corrupt values and paltry aspirations of the society he mocks.

Starvation might be sufficient excuse to drive a failed composer to the life of a licensed jester and parasite, and Rameau, echoing Juvenal, often resorts to just this kind of self-justification, as in his famous outcry: "The voice of conscience and of honor is pretty weak when one's guts are screaming."[46] But if hunger were Rameau's sole spur, then it follows that if this spur were ever removed, the degrading and degraded existence he knowingly leads would be fundamentally altered and a different kind of life become possible. Rameau, according to this logic, might be too cowardly or lazy for an open revolt, but his lucidity in degradation should imply a rejection of the whole value system whose victim he is. Yet Rameau is not only unwilling to rebel on an empty stomach, he makes clear that even if he were well fed he could still not imagine any alternative to society's grotesque comedy of servitude.[47] Indeed, Rameau is so "perfect" an incarnation of the Abject Hero because his very consciousness exists "at the confluence of contestation and conformity" and all of his words and actions "both speak for and against the very order that he constructs as excluding him."[48]

In what is perhaps his most demoralizing admission, Rameau declares that if he were suddenly wealthy, his new life would mirror in every detail the daily routine he has observed *chez Bertin*. He would use his money to purchase precisely the same goods and command the same services as his former masters already enjoy, and his imitation of their routine would even extend to hiring his own set of parasites to flatter and amuse him, although his entire experience has taught him just how thoroughly such creatures despise their patrons. Even some of Diderot's most alert readers have made what seems to me a crucial mistake by speaking of Rameau's "unsocialized desire," not realizing that to do so is merely to second *Moi*'s judgment of the Nephew.[49] In fact, Rameau's desire is socialized in the extreme, constituted as it is entirely by the lowest common denominator of his age's goals. This trait of the Nephew is exactly what enables the dialogue to function as a satire of eighteenth-century Parisian life, since both speakers agree that Rameau's cynicism only gives voice to the desires that most of society feels but dares not articulate. Rameau depends so entirely on the opinions of others that his fantasies about being rich are remarkably similar to his fantasies about being a genius: in both cases, what really matters is the knowledge that now people would say gratifying things about him. In spite of his conventionality, it actually makes more sense to speak of the *philosophe*, not the Nephew, as having "unsocialized desires." At least at the level of theory *Moi* argues for the need to sacrifice material comfort to the demands of ideals that do not depend on popular support for their validity. But there is no rebellion, or even a possibility of rebellion, in Rameau—not because of his cowardice or poverty, but because he can envisage no acceptable alternative to the values he finds so contemptible.

The claims of public duty and social virtue represented by *Moi* hold no appeal for *Lui*, either on their own terms or as a counterweight to those of his corrupt circle, since he denies both their internal coherence and their pertinence to his aim of achieving a pleasant life. Hence his scorn for the education *Moi* plans for his daughter, an education which *Lui* regards as better suited for a life in Sparta than in contemporary Paris and therefore certain to make the child wretched in her adult life.

In this debate, it again becomes apparent how mimesis—its ethics, aesthetics, and pedagogic function—provides the dialogue's harmonizing strand, the overarching issue that unites both speakers precisely by foregrounding all their differences.[50] Both men agree on the paramount significance of mimesis, but they differ radically on the question of whom and what to imitate (*Moi*'s Socrates versus *Lui*'s sycophantic courtier, Bouret); on the appropriate lesson to be derived from the chosen models (*Moi*'s moralistic reading of Molière versus *Lui*'s); and on the kind of imitation that parental education ought to encourage (*Moi*'s plans for his daughter versus *Lui*'s for his son).[51] On all of these issues, the *philosophe* can mount no effective refutation of his antagonist's position. The *Encyclopédiste*'s universal norms ought to provide him with a stable ground from which to judge Rameau. Instead, *Moi* admits himself confused by, and even suffering from, the contradictions between his simultaneous aesthetic admiration and moral repugnance for Rameau's performances (e.g., during the Nephew's account of his seduction of a young girl). Similarly, since he cannot resort to the threat of an afterlife with appropriate rewards and punishments, *Moi*'s argument that unvirtuous but materially successful people must be inwardly unhappy is altogether feeble. Finally, his praise of Diogenes living naked in a tub and eating wild berries is so sanctimonious in the face of *Lui*'s immediate want of adequate food, clothes, and a bed that he has to switch from articulating general and reasonable principles to defending extreme responses appropriate only for a fanatic.

Both men accept happiness in this world as their chief aim. But for Rameau, this happiness depends purely on the position one occupies on the ladder of patron and client, possessor and dispossessed. The criteria by which the *philosophes* would determine personal satisfaction are as willfully self-deceiving in Rameau's eyes as were those of Alceste to all the other characters in Molière's *Le Misanthrope*. According to Juvenal, "rara in tenui facundia panno [eloquence doesn't often wear rags],"[52] but Rameau does both; he is remarkably eloquent in his rags, and the very fact of being so ill clothed and housed forms the principal theme of his eloquence. But his concerns about poverty and class injustice, though fierce, are entirely personal and immediate. Rameau is clearly not a revolutionary. He is not even a spokesman for a possible change, whether fundamental or cosmetic, in the social structure, and a reading that slights the extent of his willing participation in the shabbiness he anatomizes with such accurate glee risks missing the true bitterness of the dialogue.

Considering the paramount importance of material comfort to Rameau and the absence of any counter-ideal to which he might be drawn, *Moi* is quite right to ask why the Nephew ever sacrificed his position as Bertin's jester in the first place: "Nevertheless, you must have sinned at least once against the rules of your art and accidentally have voiced one of those bitter truths that causes offense."[53] Why, to return not just to the beginning of this chapter but to the opening of the book as a whole, does the encounter between *Moi* and a starving, newly patronless Jean-François Rameau even take place? What provoked the adequately fed and housed licensed fool to become a rebel after all, or, more accurately, what kind of rebel can be so abject a participant in his own degradation?

> A yes-man will strain his guts to produce . . . but
> strain a gut as they may they cannot strain it past its
> true natural elasticity.
> (Norman Mailer, *Why Are We in Vietnam?*)

In an explicit quarrel with Hegel's reading of *Le Neveu de Rameau*, Lionel Trilling offers what remains one of the most succinctly accurate remarks about the Nephew's plight: "But despite his native abilities and the cruel self-discipline to which he has subjected himself, he must endure the peculiar bitterness of modern man, the knowledge that he is not a genius."[54] Above even wealth, Rameau desires proof that he is not an "espèce," a "typical mediocrity," which he calls the most degrading appellation of all, and more than penury he fears the knowledge that he will never be other than ordinary.[55]

It does not matter to Rameau in what domain his skills might flourish and his originality become manifest; music, parasitism, and crime are all equally plausible candidates. The paramount goal is to excel, both in his own eyes and in the world's, irrespective of the project finally chosen, but at each step Rameau is too lucid not to realize that his abilities, although considerable, fall far short of the standard of a true innovator. His close reading of the classics, and his even closer observations of such contemporary prodigies of servility and cunning as Bouret or the Renegade of Avignon bring him face to face with his position as merely one more in a chain of licensed fools and parasites, and it is this self-knowledge that renders his daily existence so painful. Since for Rameau "the best order in the world is the one in which I am to exist,"[56] *Le Neveu de Rameau* is a chronicle of his attempt to find the rightful and validating order for his existence—in a Saturnalia, in the texts of the past, in immediate performance, or in the commission of an especially shabby deed. It is as though Rameau were an artist endowed with unmistakable gifts of technique and execution and yet haunted in all of his performances by the sense of never quite managing to create the work that would confirm his equality with the exemplary masters of his craft. In music, moreover, it is his loathsome uncle, whose name he must bear, who is universally acknowledged as the age's standard of excellence.

Nowhere are Rameau's keen powers more in evidence than in his analysis of the achievement of his rivals. He recounts the story of two such men, Bouret (pp. 51–52) and the Renegade of Avignon (pp. 72–75). Each exemplary tale is intended as a "scene of instruction," bringing into prominence the theme of mimesis and the problem of the gulf between moral and aesthetic excellence. Rameau introduces his narration of Bouret's mask through a subtle hint that raises curiosity, mentioning how the story has already won acclaim throughout Europe. Instead of following a chronological sequence, Rameau presents his version by considering the problems Bouret faced. What he creates is a structure of obstacles to overcome (signaled by the triple repetion of "Bear in mind that . . . "),[57] so that when the solution of the mask is presented, it is startling in its elegance and economy. Even *Moi* is fascinated by the resolution, his moral outrage temporarily overcome by the power of the Nephew's artistic representation and Bouret's problem-solving intelligence. But this shaping power regularly deserts Rameau, and much of his discourse abandons the craftsman's control that made this story so seductive.

His account of the Renegade of Avignon, for example, is undermined, not only by the vileness of the actions described, but also by the way in which he tells it. The Nephew keeps interrupting his tale, and in his overinvolvement he continually interjects distracting comments on the action and the characters' behavior. Oddly enough, Rameau himself praises the Renegade's artfulness in controlling his discourse—"Too much intensity would have risked jeopardizing the whole scheme"[58]—but he is incapable of exercising similar restraint. His sadistic zeal in repeating the appalling story distances both *Moi* and the reader and makes Rameau aesthetically, as well as morally, repugnant.

Rameau narrates these anecdotes in part for the shock value of their immoralism, a deliberate and successful gambit designed to *épater les philosophes*, but also, and more importantly, to make clear the criteria by which he judges his own performance.[59] I intend the sense of *performance* here literally, since the profession of licensed fool and parasite is preeminently a matter of acting, and Rameau's failure is above all a question of a simultaneous insufficiency both in himself and in his audience. If, as he admits, he could never attain the heights of inventiveness scaled by Bouret, he was certainly adept enough to amuse the circle around Bertin and Mlle. Hus. Yet here too he suffered dismissal, although it was in part deliberately provoked, and in the vicissitudes of his most recent fiasco we can see the characteristics of Rameau as Abject Hero displayed with a singular narrative economy.

The insult that led to Rameau's dismissal is no more biting than the banter that had secured his position with Bertin in the first place. Rameau is not punished for the *inaequalitas* and impertinence that marks his nature, but, on the contrary, for being so *consistent* with his chosen role, for acting entirely "in character." His fidelity to the demands of the role results in disaster, because Bertin, like Malvolio, lacks the aristocratic knowledge that there is "no slander in an allowed fool, though he do nothing but rail," and his anger violates the generic contract governing the relationship between master and licensed jester. As Wilda Anderson remarks, the structural link between patron and fool is so intimate that a failure in the one function assures a failure in the other.[60] Rameau's situation also satirically duplicates that of Diderot himself, whose pride was bruised by the public's indifference to his play, *Le Père de famille*. Diderot probably began work on *Le Neveu de Rameau* around the same time that he suffered this semi-humiliation, and a host of coincidences, ranging from Palissot's vicious but popular satiric piece, *Les Philosophes*, to Jean-Jacques Rousseau's spectacular success with *La Nouvelle Héloïse*, united to make Diderot especially anxious about his worth as a writer. Under such circumstances, the wit with which he dramatized—and mocked—his own fears by setting up an ironic analogy between his situation in the world of letters and that of Rameau in Bertin's household is astonishing for its emotional largess. (There is also a nice irony in the fact that Diderot, who so often polemicized against the formal requirements of the three "unities" in French drama, should obey them with such fidelity in *Le Neveu de Rameau*.)

But the responsibility for Rameau's expulsion can not be attributed exclusively to Bertin. Rameau's contribution to his disgrace is profound, and it touches the core of his unstable self-conception. He declares, "I am willing to be abject but not under duress."[61] This single outburst crystallizes the Nephew's predicament and that of the subsequent Abject Heroes in modern literature. To insist on one's right to choose when to be abject and when to claim one's share in "mankind's natural dignity"[62] is to inhabit a logical and emotional oxymoron whose internal contradictions in no way minimize its compelling emotional force. Rameau's appeal to the "natural dignity of man" is particularly dubious because the phrase itself is so central an element in the rhetoric of his antagonist and owes its force to the very perspective Rameau normally despises and mocks when he hears it articulated by *Moi*. Yet Rameau, lacking an adequate rhetoric of his own for these kinds of arguments, is compelled to draw on the language of his opponent to explain the laceration he endures as a self-conscious licensed fool in a world of contemptible patrons whose contemptible creature he must strive to remain.

Unlike the ideal actor Diderot praised in *Le Paradoxe sur le comédien*, an artist who never identifies with the character he plays but figures it perfectly for his audience by remaining coolly detached himself, Rameau failed as Bertin's licensed fool by losing emotional control.[63] The irony of the ensuing dialogue is that in *Moi* Rameau has finally found the ideal audience for his role, but one that will engage him only for a once-a-year limited run. Unlike Bertin, *Moi* does fulfill all of the conventional demands of the licensed fool's Saturnalian antagonist, and the confrontation is so rich in resonance because each of the speakers is willing to stay "in character" for the duration of their encounter. In terms of the dialogue's structure, *Moi* replaces Bertin, but he does so with a literary foreknowledge the financier lacked. Matched against *Moi*, Rameau has a final chance to establish his claim to a kind of genius after all. He can choose to be abject while insisting on his "natural dignity," and even use the claims of that dignity to fuel his impulse toward utter abjection. What ensues, though, is another failure, and perhaps, because the chance of a certain kind of success lay so close, the most painful debacle of all.

> We are always on stage, even if, at the end, we are
> stabbed to death in earnest.
>   (Georg Büchner, *Dantons Tod*)

If Jean-François Rameau has failed as a musician, there is another art, that of the actor and mime, in which his skills are undisputed. Throughout *Le Neveu de Rameau* he astonishes both *Moi* and the reader with a series of five main and countless smaller pantomimes ("L'Oncle Rameau," "La supplication à la Hus," "La pantomime du violon et du piano," "Les airs d'opéra," "La danse des gueux") that reveal immense powers of observation and artistic reproduction. Most of the critical attention has always been focused on the "pantomime des suppliants," and considering its thematic importance this emphasis is no doubt justified. But from a strictly artistic point of view, Rameau's miming of a violin player may well be an even greater triumph. It is the attention paid to the smallest details (something Diderot had praised so much in the *Éloge de Richardson*) that distinguishes Rameau's performance, for not only does he make *Moi* hear the notes played on a non-existent violin and piano, he is even capable of suggesting a specific piece of music. More striking still is that his mimetic accuracy includes "correcting errors" in a musical performance that is, after all, imaginary.

At least since the Renaissance, the roles of buffoon, parasite, and mime have been closely linked, and Rameau's talents in all of these spheres are intended to remind us of his ancestry in the court fool and carnival trickster. But his brilliance as a mime is particularly significant because it comes so close to overwhelming *Moi*'s critical distance. Rameau *embodies* the art Diderot was so concerned to legitimize, an art whose affective power Diderot consistently championed both in his own plays and in his critical writings.[64] In pantomime Diderot found a vitalizing, gestural corrective to the declamatory style of classical French drama, a way of returning the primacy of the human body to the problem of dramatic representation.[65] Pantomime makes the body into a medium of artistic representation, and since *Lui*, quoting Juvenal, always insists that genius and inspiration have their origins in the belly, it is fitting that he should excel at so physical an art.

Pantomime is to classical French acting what the Saturnalian dialogue is to a conventional philosophical treatise, and for Diderot pantomime and dialogue are twin manifestations of a single intellectual/artistic impulse. The dialogue form appealed to Diderot for many reasons, among the most powerful of which was the effect it creates of a constantly labile, almost inchoate configuration of themes and points of view. The closer a literary dialogue comes to creating what one could call "the dialogue effect"—the textual simulacrum of a conversation in which issues are raised, then dropped, only to be picked up again later, or simply abandoned—the more convincingly it achieves the aesthetic instantiation of a form at once evanescent and structured. The "pantomime effect" is the closest in any art to the sensation of overhearing an actual dialogue, because in pantomime there is not even a distinct text to be composed, worked on, and published; unlike the reader of a literary dialogue, who can still turn back a few pages and trace the development of an argument, the observer of a pantomime has only the single moment of pure artistic creation before his eyes. In short, pantomime and dialogue are parallel forms, and much of the formal play in *Le Neveu de Rameau* arises from Diderot's exploration of their shared properties.

The joining of dialogue and pantomime is particularly intimate, both in terms of the text's characters (i.e., Rameau's need for an audience to admire his skills and the *philosophe*'s commitment to public debate as the proper testing ground for his theories) and in terms of the text's generic affiliation. Rameau's gift for pantomime makes him, at least temporarily, not so much a modern Davus as the very incarnation of the Saturnalia's destructive fluidity. What Bakhtin called the "ever changing, playful, undefined forms" demanded by the Saturnalian experience is exactly the impression *Le Neveu de Rameau*'s dialogic structure manages to achieve.[66] The text as a whole embodies the oppositional energy of the Saturnalia at so fundamental a level that we continue to respond to its mocking energy even when the particulars of its satiric attacks on contemporary Parisian society no longer compel our identificatory sympathies.

In his confrontation with *Moi*, Rameau performs a series of pantomimes with which he seeks to captivate his interlocutor, to keep the beholder's eyes fixed on his own inventiveness. As the dialogue continues, the significance of the concept and act of *pantomime* continues to expand, until in the "pantomime des gueux" it becomes a metaphor for social interaction (i.e., human life) itself. All the descriptions of the Nephew's performances suggest an element of pain and hysteria. Rameau's final musical pantomime, the fragments from a dozen or more operas, is a true "satire" in the etymological sense of *satura* as a mishmash, a random heaping-up.[67] He is no longer concerned in this frenzy with translating musical sound into bodily gesture, but with creating a new kind of corporeal-imaginative totality, a plenitude of all things as present at once, a desire utterly replete and satisfied (and hence a delusional absurdity). As Elisabeth de Fontenay remarks, Rameau's "ruinous effort to restore the simultaneity of instruments . . . based upon music's supposed capacity to express everything . . . is both obsessive and ludicrous. . . . [His] ecstasy's failure is presented as a farce and the extreme of pleasure is turned into a mockery."[68] Almost at the dialogue's end, though, Rameau creates his most haunting pantomime image, a picture of basic human need figured by a finger pointing desperately into an empty mouth.[69] Gesture and need are here fundamentally linked, hence Rameau's definition of "position" as the result of bitter necessity: "The worst of it is the contorted position in which need confines us. The needy man doesn't walk like the rest, he skips, twists, cringes, crawls—he spends his whole life picking and performing 'positions.'"[70] Needy men are forced to enact positions as though obeying a musical score. The mouth is the locus of music, speech, and hunger, as the body is the instrument with which the mendicant assumes the required contortions demanded by his patrons.

Yet for all Rameau's brilliance, his performances lack the power to sustain their hold on *Moi*, and for exactly the same reason that Rameau was unable to retain his position as resident buffoon with Bertin. He is incapable of restraint; he fails to preserve enough distance from his own performance to keep in reserve the strength needed for his next tableau. The issue here is one of an economics of energy, not of inspiration, since according to Diderot, the sublime actor is distinguished by his ability to repeat the same performance daily with no discernible loss of intensity. A precise calculation of expenditure is required in order to guarantee the continuing availability of the actor's affective power, and this rationing of energy is what Rameau so conspicuously lacks. He is capable of reaching the highest levels of any performer and initially succeeds in overwhelming *Moi* with the authority of his skills. But Rameau cannot hold on to his advantage. Just when the sheer brilliance of the pantomimes seems to have his adversary overwhelmed, Rameau, in what is almost a physiological analogue to the *temporary* nature of the Saturnalia's reversal of power, collapses and allows *Moi* not only to reassert the contrary opinion but, even more devastatingly, to revert to his initial patronizing attitude toward the exhausted Nephew: "He didn't notice anything; he continued, gripped by a kind of mental aberration, by an enthusiasm so close to madness that one couldn't be sure if he'd ever recover, and I wondered if he shouldn't be thrown into a cab and taken directly to the Psychiatric Hospital."[71] Even in his most successful pantomimes, Rameau increasingly approaches the enactment of a state of pure folly. The Nephew's performance is at once inspired and pathetic, and typically, in the pantomime of the opera airs, it is because Rameau so genuinely loves music that he loses the cynicism that had given his earlier exhibitions their controlled edge.[72] As Starobinski notes, in the 1770s and 1780s "music was considered a propitious medium for folly to manifest itself in to an extreme degree."[73] The folly of Rameau's musical panto-mimes ends up ruining him once again, debilitating his energy and drain-ing his inventive impudence. At the dialogue's end, Rameau is no longer even authoring his own mimes; he is merely acting out *Moi*'s philosophical reflections. It is *Moi* who conceives of and articulates the various characters and their positions in the pantomime of need. *Lui* performs the scenes splendidly, but he has surrendered the *agon*'s inventive energy as well as its conceptual daring to his antagonist.[74]

But *Moi*'s triumph is essentially hollow, in part because it is won over a temporarily exhausted and incoherent antagonist, and in part because it does not result from any of the principles he is dedicated to championing. On the contrary, by in essence jumping in "to write" Rameau's last major tableau, the "pantomime des gueux," *Moi* actually collapses the distance between them. The pleasure he takes in his authorship, his scripting of a world in which everyone—monarchs, priests, lovers, etc.—is condemned to dance the beggar's pantomime, except, as he self-praisingly notes, for "the philosopher who has nothing and asks for nothing"[75] betrays the nar-cissism of his reflections and undercuts the moral stance on which his self-representation depends. Diderot is never dialectical—the antitheses the speakers set in motion are impossible to resolve and there is no synthesis that could subsume the dialogue's combat into its higher unity—and hence it would be simplistic to suggest that *Lui* triumphs at the end precisely by allowing *Moi* to appear the conqueror. But by the same logic, Rameau's defeat is far from equivalent to his opponent's victory. Through his very collapse, the Nephew does manage both to remain himself and to deny the *philosophe* an intellectually respectable triumph. The same mercurial, Ver-tumnus-like instability that ruins *Lui* also succeeds in emptying each fiasco of any serious meaning. Rameau exists, as both *Moi* and he admit, as a series of moments, each only loosely bound to its predecessor, and his im-perviousness to either logical persuasion or empirical demonstration makes Rameau an unmanageable opponent in terms of the conventions of a philo-sophical dialogue. (Consider, for example, how important a part of Soc-rates' aim it is to elicit his interlocutors' agreement about their misconcep-tions.) What Rameau wrests from his abasement is, not victory, but the knowledge that his humiliation condemns himself and his opponent equally. He knows that in the Saturnalia into which he has drawn *Moi* there can be no ultimate reckoning because the whole scale of immutable judg-

ments and incontrovertible evidence required for any verdict is exactly
what is denied from the outset. To invoke these categories, as *Moi*, by both
temperament and conviction, must do, can never settle the dispute, but
only, as both *Moi* and *Lui* understand, begin it all anew. Jean-François
Rameau lacks the "estimable unity of character" to be a successful villain, or
ultimately even an eminent parasite or mime, but if he is not a genius, he
is sufficiently lucid in the confused intensity of his passions and the accuracy of his observations to make abjection into a new kind of quest, and
almost, at the end, by his sheer persistence and unyieldingness, into a desperate form of heroism.

> Clov: What is there to keep me here?
> Hamm: The dialogue.
>   (Samuel Beckett, *Endgame*)

What both fuels and vitiates Rameau's gamble that his very abjection may
give rise to at least a simulacrum of genius is the burden of the tradition
that he, part deliberately, part helplessly, assumes. Rameau understands
that he is only a licensed fool, a creature who is free to speak his mind solely
because no one need ever take him seriously: "a freedom that I use without
consequences, since I myself am without consequence."[76] But his reading
has also taught Rameau that this seemingly ignominious role contains the
always possible metamorphosis in which the jester is suddenly revealed as
the unexpected truth-teller, and he knows that according to generic expectations his wildest outbursts may contain a deeper wisdom than the educated knowledge of more successful men. He is haunted by the awareness
that, at least according to literary tradition, he may, *intermittently*, be a
genius after all. Abjection itself, so the classical dramas and jest-books he
consults have taught him, may be a path to insight, and the self-lacerating
vanity and cringing defiance of the abject often retain a stronger grip on the
imagination of their interlocutors and audiences than untroubled virtue or
nobility of character.

   The possibility that he has genius is partially sustained by *Moi*'s reluctant
admiration and attentiveness, both of which are more tense and anxious
than the amused patronage of the master and his "licensed fool" in traditional comedy. Rameau's problem, though, is that as a fool he can never
know, either in advance, or even after the fact, when one of his sallies
articulates some deep truth and when it is sheer splenetic raillery. When
Moi seeks to patronize Rameau's moments of lucidity, the Nephew's scorn
is instantaneous, and he insists on his consciousness-in-folly, certain that
often his perceptions are more accurate and socially pertinent than those of
the *philosophes*:

I'm sure that you are laughing at me. But, Mr. Philosopher, you have no idea who it is you are up against: you don't even suspect that at this very moment I represent the beliefs of the most important elements both in the city and at court. . . . But I am too generous with you. You are an ignorant layman who doesn't deserve to be instructed in the miracles that go on all around you.[77]

But when not directly challenged, Rameau admits that he is unable to distinguish between his moments of folly and wisdom, that there are simply no criteria by which to separate the proportion of genuine insight from the hollow banter in his discourse. Anticipating both the Freudian and the Surrealist argument for the revelatory power of free association, Rameau joins an intuitive faith in the haphazard to the requisite nimbleness and spontaneity of the professional clown (p. 56).

Just because Rameau speaks with a knowledge of what a "wise fool" should be, his inability either to control the mixture of wisdom and folly in his words or to master the social rituals required for worldly success as a licensed fool becomes a source of constant frustration and self-abnegation, combined with a kind of desperate pride in the chance—always formally present—that the next moment's words will strike home with the authority of a genuine insight. Rameau's Nephew is simultaneously a "wise fool," a cynical parasite, and a madman, and because it is impossible to tell who is speaking at any given moment, his entire discourse—the arguments that, in another mouth, we might recognize as plausible, as well as those that seem obviously ludicrous—is infected with a fundamental instability. His "truth," throughout the dialogue, is as compromised by madness as his madness is tempered by the possibility of concealing a deeper truth. In this confusion, induced by an exacerbating self-reflexiveness and literary sophistication, lies the core of the Nephew's anguish and the impetus for the development of an Abject Hero out of the traditional licensed fool.

Rameau's speech lacks all of the customary contextual cues locating an articulation according to its degree of truth, folly, or humor. Even the most carefully nuanced attempts to arrest the uncertainties of Le Neveu de Rameau fail because the reader has no independent standards by which to gauge the dialogue's speakers. Identification with either Moi or Lui alone is clearly unsatisfactory, since each so effectively undermines the authority of the other, but for the reader to venture any judgment about the issues they are contesting is merely to occupy one of the positions already articulated by the speakers themselves. Diderot's satire so consistently acknowledges and self-consciously exploits the literariness of the satiric tradition that it is able to turn that acknowledgment against any inherently stabilizing tendency in the reliance on generic expectations. Bakhtin, we recall, considers the existence of "footlights," the distinction between actors and spectators, sufficient to destroy carnival. Yet I have argued that some framing device is already implicit in the institution of the carnival, and doubly so in its literary representation. Diderot's way of negotiating this problem is not to deny the preexistence of the unavoidable "footlights" but rather to hollow out their stability until they occupy the peculiar position of being neither fully within nor entirely external to the turbulence of his dialogue. He admits the privileged position of the reader but only in order to subvert entirely the reader's traditional self-confidence in his right/capacity to be the work's spectator-judge. The reader is drawn into the carnivalesque uncertainty because the entire literary tradition he has inherited has schooled him to assume the role of arbiter, and in the endlessly renewed and perpetually frustrated effort to fulfill the demands of his own expectations, he is compelled to recapitulate the same dilemma confronting both of the dialogue's fictional characters. No one in *Le Neveu de Rameau* can escape the pressures of the generic expectations inherited from the Saturnalian tradition, but neither can anyone perform what is expected of him without the demoralizing awareness of his own failure. Thus, paradoxically, it is when the laughter turns bitter, and when, instead of an affirmative celebration, there is a dialogue of frustrated latecomers, imitating models whose naive confidence they can never get quite right, that the Saturnalian paradigm of an all-inclusive carnival comes closest to its realization.

Instead of providing a normative framework, the reader's own literary background and personal interests only help entrap him in the text's debate. The opening Horatian epigraph, which seemed to promise a touchstone by which to understand the dialogue, is, at the end, revealed as only the first snare by whose means *Le Neveu de Rameau* incorporates—and thus renders problematic—all external guideposts. In his torment Rameau knows that he has added something decisively new to the tradition of the wise fool.

> A hundred fools like me! Look, Mr. Philosopher, they're not so easy to find. Ordinary fools, yes. But people are more demanding when it comes to folly than either talent or virtue. I'm a rare example of my kind, yes, very rare.[78]

What Rameau has added is the burden of understanding his role more deeply than did any of his predecessors and experiencing at every moment the helplessness of that understanding. Rameau's Nephew is, I believe, modern literature's first fully realized Abject Hero, the first self-conscious "wise fool" sufficiently versed in the traditional satires to understand the requirements of his role, precariously enough situated in his milieu to feel he has no other social position open to him, and embittered to the extent that he becomes unable, as well as intermittently unwilling, to fulfill these requirements.[79]

It is Jean-François Rameau's painful privilege to have united licensed folly, crippling penury, a haunted knowledge of literary belatedness, and the rudiments of an almost Dostoevskian *ressentiment* as constituent elements of a new sensibility. His closing line, "He laughs best who laughs last,"[80] terminates without in any way resolving Diderot's dialogue, and it opens an equivocal laughter that has continued to trouble literature until today.

Part III ⸻⸻⸻⸻⸻⸻⸻

THE POETICS OF *RESSENTIMENT*

Vileness sometimes demands as much self-
renunciation as a feat of heroism.
   (from a letter of Leonid Andreev)

Four

Lacerations: The Novels of Fyodor Dostoevsky

Everyone, as it were, wishes to revenge himself
upon someone for his [own] nullity.
  (Fyodor Dostoevsky, *Diary of a Writer*)

FEW EPISODES in Diderot's life have provoked as much curiosity as his brief stay in St. Petersburg at the court of Catherine the Great (October 1773–March 1774). Among the very wildest of the speculations concerning this visit is the following, supposedly much repeated folk-legend version of the encounter between the archetypal representative of an atheistic Parisian Enlightenment and the Russian Orthodox ecclesiastical hierarchy:

> Did you ever hear, most Holy Father, how Diderot went to see the Metropolitan Platon, in the time of the Empress Catherine. He went in and said straight out, "There is no God." To which the great Bishop lifted up his finger and answered, "The fool has said in his heart there is no God." And he fell down at his feet on the spot. "I believe," he cried, "and will be christened."[1]

Of course the narrator of this edifying tale is himself a fictional character, one of literature's most disagreeably tormented and tormenting buffoons, and neither he nor his listeners believe a syllable of the anecdote. Indeed, when Fyodor Pavlovich Karamazov recounts his miniature "Legend of the Grand Philosophe" to the appalled circle gathered in Father Zosima's cell, it is not even clear whom he is actually mocking. Among the likely targets are: (1) Father Zosima, the holy elder, as the embodiment of a religion in which miracle stories, no less improbable than this patently spurious one, figure prominently; the story of Diderot and the Metropolitan Platon thus uncannily prefigures Ivan's "Legend of the Grand Inquisitor," and it does so through a kind of proleptic parody in which the themes that so disturb the son are treated as occasions for grossly offensive humor by the father. (2) Pyotr Alexandrovich Miüsov, the smugly cynical Westernizer who resents seeing his own shallow anti-clericalism satirized in Fyodor Karamazov's buffoonish version of it. Here Karamazov's jests are aimed not at the faithful, but at the mockers of faith; Fyodor thus also anticipates the paradoxical reversals of sense and intention that characterize the typical rhetorical strategy of one of his other sons, Smerdyakov, and again, he does so by way of parody. And most interestingly, (3) Fyodor Karamazov himself, who is trying to *disprove*, by the deliberate ineptitude of his performance, that he is merely an abject buffoon.[2] Fyodor Karamazov, in this last interpretation, is so anxiously conscious of his compulsion to be witty and entertaining—and so deeply outraged at himself for this compulsion—that he willfully sabotages the urge by parodying it, thereby attempting, in a single movement, the impossible task of incarnating and demolishing a role that is hateful to him but that he is incapable of shaking off. In the peculiar economy of his narrative gesture, Fyodor Karamazov produces an outburst of deliberately offensive rubbish, not solely to offend, but also, and more importantly, to short-circuit what he knows to be his parasite's contemptible urge to please. Thus, when he declares, "One must be agreeable, mustn't one? . . . I play the fool, Pyotr Alexandrovich, to make myself agreeable" (pp. 33–34), he is being maliciously disingenuous. Fyodor Karamazov is certainly playing the fool, but with the typologically incompatible aim of making himself as disagreeable and unamusing as possible. Instead of the toady's low murmur of trivially agreeable background chatter, Fyodor Karamazov seizes center stage and proceeds to insult everyone gathered around him in order to demonstrate his indifference to their favor. But as he knows all too well, he thereby only confirms his abject lack of real independence.

If the insulting anecdote reveals what I have called a peculiar economy, it is still a relatively straightforward one when compared to the full resources of abjection. Although the major abject figures in literature, from Jean-François Rameau to Louis-Ferdinand Céline, regularly turn to insult as a means of breaking out of their entrapment in buffoon's motley, abjection is sufficiently cunning to turn the hoped-for avenue of escape into another snare enmeshing the imprisoned psyche all the more firmly.

As a young man, Fyodor Karamazov played buffoon and parasite out of economic want—"he ran to dine at other men's tables and fastened on them as a toady" (p. 2)—but by the time of the meeting at the monastery, he was rich enough to count as one of the wealthiest men in the district.[3] Karamazov's self-abasement is thus largely divorced from any question of material advantage. In him, abjection has become a spiritual and psychological characteristic existing on its own terms, and in its materially undetermined disinterestedness it is like a grotesque inversion of the Kantian aesthetic sublime. Karamazov acts "sometimes without any motive for doing so, and even to his own direct disadvantage" (p. 6); his contortions and rages are no longer, as in Horace or Diderot, linked to a servile economic or social position, and this very absence of explicable motivation is the source of their ability to shock and surprise. Karamazov's abjection may have been triggered initially by the experience of dependence on others, but it has long outlasted its original aim; it has now assumed a fully independent status, and in the process, a far more virulent and self-destructive intensity.

Jean-François Rameau, we remember, could envisage no plausible alternative to the social order of his day: in his view, one was either a wealthy patron or a wretched supplicant, and if ever Rameau-the-parasite were to acquire an adequate income, he would simply take up the habits, activities, and tastes of his former masters. A wealthy Rameau's Nephew would then be a more intelligent Bertin, but he would retain, we can reasonably assume, no trace of the abjection that marked his life as the financier's toady. Fyodor Karamazov, on the other hand, has succeeded in acquiring the wealth that always eluded Rameau, yet he has done so without managing to shed his abjection. It is true that "the former buffoon showed an insolent propensity for making buffoons of others" (p. 16), and his mockery reduces men like Miüsov to helpless rage, but what is so fascinating in this description is that Karamazov's "insolent propensity" does not in the least exempt its possessor from being treated like a buffoon by everyone around him, and most especially not by himself. In Dostoevsky's novels there are certain temperaments in whom the urge to abjection is itself fundamental, a kind of compulsion, impossible to eradicate or even to restrain. Like an addiction, it drives one to increasingly more lurid and flamboyant expressions, each such episode leaving a new residue of self-contempt, which both confirms and exacerbates the conviction of one's permanent arrest in the role of lacerated buffoon.

Compared to its literary ancestors, the Dostoevskian version of the lacerated buffoon embodies what amounts to a kind of absolute, autonomous, and sublime abjection, one that is all the more galling for its paradoxical "purity." With considerable justice, Rameau, at least, could tell both *Moi* and himself that the Parisian social order of his day made abjection an especially effective survival tool, and thereby distance himself from his degrading actions by the plea of *force majeure*. Dostoevsky's Abject Heroes can offer no such eudaemonic rationalization to give a semblance of worldly calculation to their self-debasement, and no prudential tallying of advantages can hope to offset the ignominy of their role. It is his awareness of how painful such a role must be that makes Father Zosima tell Fyodor Karamazov, "and above all, do not be so ashamed of yourself, for that is at the root of it all" (p. 35). To be ashamed of oneself is more often the consequence of a boundless and wounded vanity than of any finely tuned moral scruples, and knowing this himself, Fyodor Karamazov echoes and elaborates on the elder's advice: "Indeed, I always feel when I meet people that I am lower than all, and that they all take me for a buffoon. So I say, 'Let me really play the buffoon. I am not afraid of your opinion, for you are every one of you worse than I am.' That is why I am a buffoon. It is from shame, great elder, from shame" (p. 36).

But Fyodor Karamazov's account shows how entwined inner impulses and external judgments, the sense of being ashamed and the aggressive pleasure of exhibitionism, really are. The Dostoevskian buffoon humiliates himself to forestall the humiliations he knows lie in wait for him, and then revenges himself by bringing to light the buffoonery of his humiliators—a buffoonery that he hopes to mark as even more pettily sordid than his own because it is unwitting rather than "freely" chosen. But the hopelessness of such a tactic is evident when one considers how hollow the claim to a "free choice" really is. The endless reverberations between inner and outer scorn cannot be frozen in a single formula, since the original prediction about the reactions of the Other operates as a self-fulfilling prophecy and serves less as a plausible etiology of abjection than as another symptom of the disease it would diagnose. One of the central dilemmas of abjection is this impossibility of distinguishing between inner and outer pressures, between self-loathing and social humiliation, cunning mockery and a pathetic need for attention. Irrespective of its origin, Dostoevskian abjection functions as a weapon of global aggression, whose sting is all the more venomous for continually traversing the complex passage between internal and external targets. It is as though the initial, desperately seized-upon gambit of caricaturing one's own feelings not only justifies but also focuses the malice cascading outward from one's psyche in a kind of noxious deluge from whose contamination no one escapes unbesmirched.

The psychologization of the Saturnalian carnival is readily apparent in the image of such a leveling deluge. Indeed, Dostoevsky's novels are a potent index of how bitter such a carnival has become and how deeply wounded all of its participants must be to perform their customary parts. The Saturnalian dialogue is central to Dostoevsky's art, but instead of the usual optimistic interpretation of the carnivalesque, Dostoevsky insists on its kinship to the Gadarene swine's headlong rush to disaster. There is considerably more laughter in Dostoevsky's novels than we tend to remember, and there are times when he seems, after Flaubert, the supreme comic novelist of the nineteenth century. But his humor has a distinctly hysterical edge, and the most riveting moments of his characters' laughter are often accompanied by murderous impulses towards self and others. It is these impulses, the longing of the tormented for the absolution of utter chaos, that Dostoevsky depicts as underlying the Saturnalian ecstasy. Jean-François Rameau would have recognized the urge and would have been careful to keep his deepest longings in check, just like Fyodor Karamazov, who "in the last resort . . . could always restrain himself, and had indeed marveled at himself sometimes on that score."

He had no clear idea what he would do, but he knew that he could not control himself, and that a touch might drive him to the utmost limits of obscenity, but only to obscenity, to nothing criminal, nothing for which he could be legally punished. (p. 77)

Saturnalia may indeed abolish the "footlights . . . between actors and spectators,"⁴ but by making everyone an actor, the festival's histrionic element is dangerously heightened. And the problem with the histrion's role is that usually no one is willing, or indeed able, to separate the elements of charlatanism and sincerity in the performer's character. *Le Neveu de Rameau*'s constant reversals depend on this ambiguity and, more specifically, on the fact that *Moi, Lui*, and the reader are all equally unable to judge the Nephew's degree of folly and insight, charlatanism and inspiration. Fyodor Karamazov and Jean-François Rameau both demonstrate the gestural febrility and inventive verve of virtuosi, especially in their wickedly precise characterization of everyone's—including their own—ignominious traits. But because Karamazov does so in a less materially determined context, his confusion is all the greater and the reader's consequent uncertainty proportionally heightened.

Fyodor Karamazov knows that he is usually acting a part, that even his "righteous anger" no longer exists except as a series of poses in a third-rate spectacle:

> With old liars who have been acting all their lives there are moments when they enter so completely into their part that they tremble or shed tears of emotion in earnest, although at that very moment, or a second later, they are able to whisper to themselves, "You know you are lying, you shameless old sinner! You're acting now, in spite of your 'holy' wrath and your 'holy' moment of wrath." (p. 64)

It is often unclear if he has any emotions left at all that are not in large measure dramatic performances. Dostoevsky had already written what is virtually the comic apotheosis of this dilemma fifteen years before *The Brothers Karamazov*, in the Underground Man's description of "the moans of an educated man of the nineteenth century who is suffering from a toothache":

> particularly on the second or third day of the attack, when he has already begun to moan not as he moaned on the first day . . . simply because he has a toothache, . . . but as a man affected by progress and European civilization. . . . His moans become nasty, disgustingly spiteful, and go on for whole days and nights. And, after all, he himself knows that he does not benefit at all from his moans . . . he knows that even the audience for whom he is exerting himself . . . do not believe him for a second . . . they understand that he could moan differently, more simply, without trills and flourishes, and that he is only indulging himself like that out of spite, out of malice.⁵

The Underground Man's whole confession, as is often remarked in Dostoevsky criticism, is very much like the toothache he has himself described. In both, genuine pain and the self-contemplating expression of it are present in roughly equal measure; real suffering and melodramatic self-indulgence can perfectly well coexist, seeming to cancel one another at one moment, and to intensify each other's effect at the next.[6] What Father Zosima offers histrions like Fyodor Karamazov or Mme. Khokhlakov is an acknowledgment that their suffering is sincere, that their constant self-dramatization has not eradicated a kernel of genuine anguish beneath the posturing.[7] Such faith in one's own pain, that it really *is* one's own and not merely another theatrical costume, is what abjection makes impossible, and this denial of any authenticity constitutes a central strand in the net of abjection's worst torments.

Abjection entails an obsessive and involuntary theatricality, expressed in a kind of manic logorrhea that is haunted by the fear that every genuinely inward feeling has been leached out in the very act of representation.[8] This fear is one of the many ties uniting figures like Rameau and Fyodor Karamazov and helps explain their frequent moments of fatigue and depression. But abjection is also the one category able to make clear the common nature of such otherwise diverse character types as, for example, Fyodor Karamazov and Katerina Ivanovna. Traditionally, Dostoevsky criticism has found it useful to distinguish the buffoons from the lacerated souls in the novels. Robert Belknap has articulated this disjunction with the greatest precision:

> Gratitude implies benefits received, and just as buffoonery was a twisted response to poverty and blows received, so the *nadryv* [lacerated soul] is a twisted response to wealth and benefits received, or at least offered. . . . The *nadryv* is the exact opposite of buffoonery, involving pride, riches, dignity, and a pressing fear of being base, while the buffoon embodies humiliation, poverty, shame, and pursuit of baseness. The buffoon makes himself laughable in order to make others so. The *nadryv* causes a person to hurt himself in order to hurt others, or, perversely, to hurt others in order to hurt himself.[9]

I think there is a good deal of justice in Belknap's analysis, but he seems to me to ignore one of the central features of Dostoevsky's characters: that is, their nervous motility, their disconcerting tendency to switch in an instant from buffoon to lacerated soul and back again, or, still more alarmingly, to exhibit both personae at the same time. When the Underground Man, for example, paces the floor for hours in the restaurant, hoping to attract the attention of Zverkov and his cronies by ignoring them, is he a buffoon or a soul writhing with the pangs of an ineradicable laceration? Or, consider the case of *The Brothers Karamazov*'s Captain Snegiriov, the "wisp of tow," who is both a buffoon and a lacerated soul, a duality perfectly revealed in the instability of his language, tone and demeanor:

> There was extraordinary imprudence in his expression, and yet, strange to say, at the same time there was fear. He looked like a man who had long been kept in subjection and had submitted to it, and now had suddenly turned and was trying to assert himself. Or, better still, like a man who wants dreadfully to hit you but is horribly afraid you will hit him. In his words and in the intonation of his shrill voice there was a sort of crazy humor, at times spiteful and at times cringing, and continually shifting from one tone to another. (p. 181)

The same duality is even more striking in Fyodor Karamazov, which is precisely what Father Zosima recognizes when he acknowledges the lacerations goading the buffoon to his exhibitionism. The whole dialogue between Father Zosima and Karamazov shows how abjection incorporates both buffoonery and self-laceration, and how each of these is only the unstable and easily reversible way abjection manifests itself in a specific moment of tension.

"He laughs best who laughs last," is how Jean-François Rameau took leave of *Moi*. It is undoubtedly a long journey from the Paris of the *Encyclopédie* to St. Petersburg, "a most fantastic city with the most fantastic history of any city on the globe."[10] But, as we know, Diderot himself made just such a voyage, and as we shall see throughout this chapter, the Abject Hero did so as well. Only, in his case it was to take up permanent residence in his new environment and to flourish there as never before.

> "Underground, underground, *poet of the underground*," our feuilletonists have been repeating over and over again, as if this were something derogatory to me. Silly fools, it is my glory, for that's where the truth lies.
> (Fyodor Dostoevsky, *The Notebooks for The Idiot*)

Because the most complex Dostoevskian Abject Heroes often lack Rameau's grounding in the precarious struggle for sheer survival, their anguish can be more varied and internalized, and their critique of society less obsessively focused on the problem of its inequitable distribution of riches. For the novelist, such an evolution of the type is particularly beneficial, since it permits the Abject Hero to figure in a potentially limitless range of contexts and situations. Each of these elicits new possibilities and responses in the character, as each context, in its turn, is narratable in a radically new way by being viewed through the simultaneously clarifying and distorting gaze of an Abject Hero. Only by having been successfully adapted to the formal demands and opportunities of the novel did the Abject Hero continue to develop as a figure of such disturbing imaginative force. Just as Diderot was able to exploit the resources of the Abject Hero with exemplary literary self-consciousness, so it was Dostoevsky who worked out the next stage in the unfolding of the topos with an unmatched rigor and inclusiveness. But any formulation that talks like this of a character in isolation is, in some measure, misleading, since what is at issue is less a single character than a paradigmatic situation, a bitter Saturnalia whose central celebrant and victim, the Abject Hero, only comes into being in and through his confrontation with his equally crucial antagonist(s). Accordingly, significant evolution in the nature of the Abject Hero necessitates a corresponding change in his interlocutor(s) as well, and a reliable gauge of Dostoevsky's (and later Céline's) craft in creating a new novelistic version of the Abject Hero is the precision with which he was able to adjust all of the roles in the carnivalesque *agon*.

Dostoevsky's familiarity with Diderot extended considerably beyond the ludicrous anecdote narrated by Fyodor Karamazov. Bakhtin, for example, cites the "fundamental significance for understanding Dostoevsky's generic traditions [of] the menippea of Diderot."[11] More specifically, he links *Le Neveu de Rameau* directly to Dostoevsky's important short tale "Bobok," through "the motif of extremely frank confessions without a single grain of remorse."[12] The Nephew is certainly a prototype of Peter Klinevich, the impudently cynical truth-teller in "Bobok," whose cry to his neighbors in the cemetery, "Ladies and Gentlemen! I suggest we should get rid of all sense of shame!" sets off a macabre Carnival of the Lately Dead.[13]

But *Le Neveu de Rameau*'s importance to Dostoevsky goes beyond thematic echoes. Although specialists agree that he knew Diderot's work well, the genealogy I am tracing is independent of such direct transmissions. Instead, what matters is the "genre memory," the ways in which Diderot and Dostoevsky each appropriated a classical topos and then uncovered, through the act of "making it new" for their own eras and idioms, fresh formal and thematic possibilities in its structure. Even though I am often unconvinced by Bakhtin's larger claims for the menippea, he is surely correct to stress the greater significance of "generic traditions" and "generic contact" over individual models in shaping an author's sense of the resources available to be drawn upon, contested, or transformed.[14]

Undoubtedly characters like Fyodor Karamazov and the Underground Man have a multitude of literary ancestors, among the most obvious and regularly cited of whom are Gogol's downtrodden clerks and the numerous variations on the "superfluous man" in nineteenth-century Russian fiction. But it seems to me that the differences between Dostoevskian abjection and

its supposed ancestry in these models are more telling than such a genealogy recognizes. For all of the "superfluous man's" ineffectualness, he is an
important bearer of culture. The irrelevance of his ideals to contemporary
life and his passivity are held up for criticism, but the worthiness of those
(often distinctly Westernizing) ideals is itself rarely contested. Moreover,
although both Turgenev's Chulkaturin and Dostoevsky's Underground
Man feel themselves cut off from society, from love, and, in the deepest
sense, from their own psyches, the "superfluous man" is not concerned
with blame or vengeance. George Steiner rightly speaks of the "grace and
compassion" of *The Diary of a Superfluous Man*,[15] but these qualities characterize not just Turgenev's attitude toward Chulkaturin but the protagonist's own toward himself and his world. "I die. . . . Live on, ye who
live!"[16] are the superfluous man's final words. Turgenev's American transla-
tor rightly emphasizes that "Chulkaturin is not petty; he holds no grudge
against those among whom he could not find a place."[17] But pettiness and
an unforgiving, self-tormenting grudge is exactly what is most urgent in
the Underground Man, in Fyodor Karamazov, and in all the desperate
buffoons and abject souls writhing through Dostoevsky's fiction.

It is the violence of their "grudge against those among whom [they]
could not find a place" that indicates the family resemblance between characters like Jean-François Rameau and the Underground Man, and it is their
bitter commentary on the society in which they have been unable to secure
a place commensurate with their intelligence and vanity that makes them
such powerful satiric voices.[18] Yet the fact that they are speaking from a
position of rejection and humiliation distorts their sharpest insights and
distances both the reader and their fictional antagonists at the instant their
embittered eloquence should be most convincing. All of these characters
regularly confuse tantrums and traumas, and because each of them is so
thoroughly alienated from his own nature, from the values of the other
voices in the text, and from the values of the work's implied reader, abjection is a particularly potent distancing device: its satiric edge and promise
of psychological revelations draw us into the narrative, but its spiteful aggressiveness and self-alienation prohibit any full identification with the
characters, thereby forcing the reader to work through the text's arguments
without being able to rely on an authoritative guide within the tale itself.

The Underground Man comments on the frustration of dealing with a
"friend [who] is a compound personality, and therefore it is difficult to
blame him as an individual" (p. 20). Since suffering from such a "compound personality" is precisely the nature of abjection, no doubt the Underground Man is talking about himself again; but his point about the
difficulty of judging such a creature is nonetheless accurate, and where
blame is so difficult to assign, praise is equally problematic. In this sense, all
Abject Heroes are doomed to, and glory in, a radical instability of charac-

ter. They are each, like Rameau's Nephew and the Nephew's Latin ancestors, "born when every single Vertumnus was out of sorts," and in their
very inconsistency they embody a challenge to the notion of a permanent
identity and globally valid standard of behavior on which most ethical and
psychological norms depend. Their challenge is, in uneven measure, both
repellent and attractive—all the more so since our culture already includes,
with qualified approval, the theme of a rebellious denial of conventional
presuppositions—but it rarely elicits either full agreement or utter rejection. Instead, there is a kind of "abjection effect" worked on the reader,
whereby his engagement with, and distance from, the character is rendered
as unstable and volatile as the Abject Hero's problematic relationship to his
own persona.

Although the Dostoevskian underground men are genuine descendants
of Jean-François Rameau, the fact that the psychic economy of their
"grudge" has evolved beyond the Nephew's Juvenalian hunger for a meal
and a secure position entails a whole series of other important changes as
well. The Abject Heroes of Dostoevsky's novels are usually not crying out
with the pain of hunger, like their Parisian ancestor,[19] but their sense of
social marginality is, if anything, still more acute and their derisive laughter
at the complacencies of their opponents even more contemptuous. The
society of nineteenth-century Czarist Russia, with its glimpse of an element
of new social mobility, generated its own form of "class rage," especially
among the educated, which was fueled less by a fear of destitution than by
frustration at the extraordinary disparity in the various positions attained
by members of the same youthful circle. Dostoevsky's understanding of the
dangers of this kind of rage, whose worst effects would not be felt until this
century, was prescient in its clarity, and it is fascinating how many of his
most tormented Abject Heroes are unemployed, or merely embittered,
university intellectuals.

If Dostoevsky boasted in his journals that "I have been the only one to
bring out the tragedy of the underground, which consists of suffering, self-
laceration, an awareness of a better ⟨life⟩ coupled with the impossibility
of attaining it, and, most important of all, a strong conviction on the part
of these unfortunate people that everybody else is like them and that it is,
therefore, not worthwhile to improve oneself,"[20] it was because he felt that
within certain limits the underground was "where the truth lies."[21] But the
"truth" of the underground was always only partial and relative, potent as
a corrective to the meliorist fantasies of his opponents, but disastrously
flawed as a value in its own right. Dostoevsky knew, perhaps more fiercely
than any similarly polemical thinker before him, that the expression of a
truth is inseparable from the temperament of the character who articulates
and/or embodies it. It is the nature of this deeply divided and ambiguous

truth, the tension between the "truths of the underground" and the tormented underground men who express them, that we must learn to perceive with particular vigilance.

> the wound of a doubt, the pain of a laceration,
> soon becomes confined to the one who is ill, in
> whom others are right to lose interest.
>   (Pier Paolo Pasolini, *The Divine Mimesis*)

> We are all, to the last man, Fyodor Pavloviches.
>   (Fyodor Dostoevsky, *The Notebooks for*
>   *The Brothers Karamazov*)

I often think that what we most value in our first encounters with Dostoevsky is neither the complex dialogism of his novels nor the celebrated intensity with which his characters incarnate and voice their psychological-moral convictions, but rather the ways in which the books seem to grant each reader something like the recognition Father Zosima extends to Fyodor Karamazov's self-dramatizing lacerations. We shall see how this all-too-human desire for acceptance, even for a kind of absolution, often blinds us to the most corrosive effects of Dostoevskian irony, but it is initially helpful to emphasize how generous and vivifying such a recognition must be. Its generosity is all the more striking because (1) much of our practical and communal existence necessarily minimizes the worth of something as isolating, socially unproductive, and tortuously histrionic as the misery of an abject consciousness; and (2) we ourselves, at least intermittently, are only too aware of the petty and melodramatic stratagems through which we not only express but, far worse, actually feel our feelings. Although his theme is depression rather than abjection, Michael Ignatieff brilliantly summarizes the essential link between the depths of our personal agony and our conviction that it is precisely in those depths that we can locate an otherwise inaccessible truth:

> Of all the painful features of a depression, the worst may be its truth. As long as some portion of our mind believes that our reactions and emotions are exaggerated, we can shield ourselves from the full force of melancholia. But if we convince ourselves that depression lays bare the reality of our existence, we experience our own despair as the scourge of truth. . . . Our despair seems to cast the sinister light of truth on all our former experience. In this phase, depression appears as the bearer of bad but indisputable tidings.[22]

Because we sense that our unhappiness has brought us in touch with a core of meaning more authentic than the assumptions on which quotidian existence bases its habitual justifications, we are at once indebted to anyone who agrees with our estimation of its meaning and outraged at anyone who would question its revelatory authority. As Ignatieff notes, "Nothing is more likely to arouse rage than the tinny eudaemonism of the variety 'Look on the bright side,' 'Don't let things get out of proportion.' The insult here is an insult to the truth of lived experience."[23]

With this observation, we are plunged directly into the world of *Notes from Underground*, where the "tinny eudaemonism" of self-improvement and social responsibility—themes as dear to the Russian Westernizers of Dostoevsky's era as to Diderot's *Encyclopédistes*—and the vengeful misery of abjection exchange insults and incomprehension with a verbal dexterity unequalled since the days of the Café de la Régence. Again and again, the Underground Man defends his isolation, depression, and nastiness against the rational criticism of his fantasized interlocutors, the "gentlemen readers" whose rhetoric and judgments he has internalized enough to mimic with brutal accuracy, and whose attention represents the minimum necessity for his sense of existence. His defense adopts many stratagems, but it always reverts back to some version of the equations Dostoevsky himself repeats throughout his writings: consciousness = lacerations, and underground = truth. Miserable and degraded though he knows himself to be, or, more accurately, *through* the experience of his own misery and degradation, the Underground Man derives the energy for his scornful rejection of the rationalist view that human existence is a calculable striving after maximum advantage for the self. He has little beyond spite and self-destructive perversity to hold up against the utilitarian anthropology of his "gentlemen" antagonists, but by exhibiting his own abjection as the extreme counter-example to their assumptions, he offers, if only in the form of a nasty "Non serviam," a gratingly dissenting chord in the paean of self-satisfied historical meliorism: "man everywhere and always . . . has preferred to act as he wished and not in the least as his reason and advantage dictated. Why, one may choose what is contrary to one's own interests, and sometimes one *positively ought* (that is my idea)" (p. 23).

It is the resistance to any systematic, calculable account of human behavior that Dostoevsky cherishes as the "truth" of the underground. It is also this resistance that has made the Underground Man so prolific an ancestor, spawning an enormously heterogeneous herd of twentieth-century descendants, from Roquentin in *La Nausée* to Randle McMurphy in *One Flew Over the Cuckoo's Nest*. But with few exceptions, the Underground Man's literary progeny tend to lack the quality of abject shabbiness and spiteful self-injury that makes his revolt so problematic. For his inept buffoonery, they usually substitute heroic defiance, and in contrast to his tawdry longing to be admired and made welcome by the socially prominent, they prefer the accents of a scornful solitude. They have, in other words, made a conventionally Romantic monster, although one dressed in the rags of modernist alienation, out of the far less glamorous figure of the Abject Hero.

The distinction between the types is never starker or more revealing than in the case of works like *Notes from Underground*. The Dostoevskian Abject Hero is certainly driven by contempt for the "progressive" ideas of his Chernyshevsky-inspired opponents. But his "reactionary" rage never becomes a conservatism on the rostrum—still less on the barricades—but remains a series of poses in front of the mirror of his own self-regard. Spite like his can be a potent catalyst and purgative, but it has grievous limitations as either a political program or a personal ethics. The lesson of Dostoevsky's writing, from *The Insulted and the Injured* on, is that once in power, victims can become the worst tormentors of all, finding in their former victimization the emotional need and ideological justification to oppress others.

Earlier, I spoke of Dostoevsky's generosity in acknowledging the truth value of our self-dramatizing woes. The artistically decisive aspect of Dostoevsky's writing, however, is that while embodying that generosity in the fundamental structure of his novels, he remained just as alert to the banality and shabbiness, the murderous rages and jealousies, that the self-same suffering both feeds upon and leads to. Dostoevsky is as powerful an *anti-*existential writer as we have, anticipating with contempt most of the standard moves of subsequent existentialist writers. Unlike novelists like Camus, for example, Dostoevsky refuses the notion that lucidity about one's condition suffices to make one a tragic figure.[24] Characters like Raskolnikov or the band of revolutionaries in *The Possessed* fill their brains with all the conventionally "progressive" clichés of their era and pose in an endless variety of hand-me-down attitudes redolent of "world historical significance." Dostoevsky shows no indulgence toward the self-aggrandizing psychological scenarios that his underground men rely on to flesh out their compensatory fantasies. He makes painfully evident that their solitude is chosen out of wounded vanity—out of their fear of rejection or, just as torturing, the fear of being welcomed, but at less than their own self-estimation—and not out of inner self-sufficiency. But by the same token, Dostoevsky utterly despises the cheery optimism and complacency of the underground men's opponents, whether these appear as the internalized readers of the *Notes from Underground* or as the famous defense attorney Fetyukovich in *The Brothers Karamazov*. Simultaneously to reject the rationalist dismissal of marginal figures like the Underground Man, to see in the underground malice a lucidity about the paltry values and ideological *idées reçues* of the era, and yet to refuse to heroicize a spiteful resistance to conventional society requires an altogether rare sense of balance, and although Dostoevsky is not always able to sustain that balance, at his best he negotiates the challenge with unique authority.

George Steiner remarks that, "We tend to picture the soul in tiers and have formed habits of language suggesting that the forces of protest and unreason mount 'from below.'"[25] It is difficult to resist the lure of this image long enough to remember that while writing his "Notes," Dostoevsky's Underground Man lives in an upstairs flat (although a "wretched, horrid one") on the outskirts of town, and that he still maintains a servant, a disagreeable "old country-woman" who has replaced the terrible Apollon of part 2 (p. 5).[26] The Russian word (*podpol'e*) suggests only the space immediately beneath the floorboards of an ordinary room, and in spite of its by now inescapable cultural echoes, Dostoevsky's underground is equally remote from both the Freudian unconscious and the proletarian novel's image of the milieu of the oppressed working classes (e.g., Maxim Gorky's *The Lower Depths* or Gissing's *The Nether World*).[27] The locus from which the Underground Man vents his nastiness is not a zone of primal energy or raw desire; still less is it the unacknowledged foundation upon which the rest of social existence is constructed; and least of all is it a site free from the compromises, deferred desires, and substitute gratifications of life at street level. Rather than thinking of ordinary existence as a fragile superstructure everywhere vulnerable to the upsurge of forces from its repressed underground base, it would be more accurate to see the underground as the secondary phenomenon, a tenuous and partial resistance to the pressures of the normative. It is the normal that structures the underground and not vice versa.

The Underground Man's obsessiveness, his spite and longing for power, tend to keep even his fantasies imprisoned within the rhetoric and imagery of the social world. As readers have noticed regularly, far from being an embodiment of the id's libidinal energies, "the Underground Man is so entirely a figure of consciousness that even his dreams are only an aspect of that consciousness."[28] Hence his desperate garrulity, his effort to seduce the attention of his questioners by any means—buffoonery, insolence, intellectual arguments, lurid sexual confessions, etc.—since without such attention his own sense of existence becomes too attenuated to sustain. The Underground Man may stay silent for a long interval, but it is only to store up energy for an inevitable explosion into hysterical and unstoppable speech. The "truth" of the underground is at best the truth of a compromised and impure refusal, a revolt already shaped by, and thoroughly saturated with, the values it seeks to deny.

Perhaps the best way to summarize the preceding argument is to see how the underground is really Dostoevsky's special term for the locus from which the Abject Hero emerges and in whose name he speaks. Abjection is so important in works like *Notes from Underground* or *The Brothers Kar-amazov* because it is by far the most effective means to register a pro-foundly satiric critique of social conventions and beliefs while simultane-ously emphasizing the shabbiness of the critic.

When Father Zosima told Fyodor Karamazov to act more naturally and not to be so ashamed of himself, the advice was both generous and (di-vinely?) foolish. Karamazov himself provides the first of what will be a series of ironic rejoinders to the idea that a return to some kind of pre-lacerated stage can cure a self-torturing buffoon. To the elder's invitation, Karamazov responds with comic justice, "Do you know, blessed father, you'd better not invite me to be my natural self. Don't risk it. . . . I will not go so far as that myself" (p. 35). The knowledge that the "natural self" is already entirely infected with abjection, that abjection is a constituent part of one's psyche, not a derivative and hence eradicable symptom, is one of the bitter truths of the human psyche of which Ivan is certain (p. 218) but that Father Zosima's faith cannot allow nor his generous understanding heal. If it could do so, we would witness a divine suspension of the "natu-ral," and, like Raskolnikov's Siberian redemption, such a manifestation of supernatural grace would belong in a miracle story rather than a novel. In most of Dostoevsky's books there is little risk of such a transcendent inter-vention, and the usual relationship between the Abject Hero and his fellow human is one of mutual contempt and suspicion. Usually, there is no one like Father Zosima to give sympathetic credence to the authenticity of the histrion's suffering. On the contrary, the gentlemen interlocutors derive considerable pleasure from telling the Underground Man a truth he knows only too well himself: "You may perhaps really have suffered, but you have no respect whatsoever for your own suffering" (p. 34), and they make clear that they too share this general lack of respect. But then how could he respect his own suffering, when he is aware, down to the slightest twitch, of how much tawdry artifice and malicious fantasy there is in his misery? While abjection's lacerations do bring insight, if only into the basest mo-tives of human behavior and the most self-indulgent of human illusions, they neither ennoble the sufferer nor give him access to any compassion. Only a saint like Zosima could respect an abject unhappiness that always thrusts itself forward as a performance.

The very theatricality that condemns abjection to display itself as an ag-gressive *public* spectacle is what makes it so entirely and essentially carni-valesque. But it is a carnival of rage in which every position and each pro-nouncement seems, even to its speakers, fissured by artifice. Of all the forms of theatricality that can torment, none is as painful as the sense of only speaking pre-scripted lines, of being, in one's very outrage and pain, just a histrion and bumbling latecomer. The more abjection is released from strict economic subservience and the despair of hunger, the freer it is to add the sting of *ressentiment* to its repertoire, a sting implicit in the topos from the outset but that only became capable of erupting with full virulence in the changed conditions of the Dostoevskian novel.

> Ah yes indeed, isn't education a wonderful thing!
> (Gustave Flaubert, *Bouvard et Pécuchet*)

When Nietzsche praised *Notes from Underground* for containing "the most valuable psychological material known to me"[29] and called its author "the only psychologist . . . from whom I had anything to learn,"[30] he was undoubtedly responding to the mordant accuracy with which Dostoevsky traced the lineaments of ungratified *ressentiment* in the psyches of so many of his major characters. For Nietzsche, understanding the psychological and historical power of *ressentiment* is one of the central tasks of contemporary thought, and in Dostoevsky he rightly saw both an anticipation and a crystallization of many of his own dominant preoccupations. The links between *ressentiment*, temporality, and the vicissitudes of the Dostoevskian Abject Hero, although never thematized in traditional philosophical or literary scrutiny, seem to me decisive, less for the understanding they can yield into Nietzsche's account of human motives than for the precision with which they locate the nervous pulse of novels like *Notes from Underground*, *The Brothers Karamazov*, and their most problematic modern descendants.

Reminiscence-as-suffering is the most succinct formulation I can imagine to suggest the complex range of meanings in Nietzsche's radical refashioning of the concept. Nietzsche defines *ressentiment* as the chief characteristic of "natures that are denied the true reaction, that of deeds, and compensate themselves with an imaginary revenge."[31] It is marked by an inability to forget, to rise above, or to avenge an injury. Each slight, each abject compromise or moment of cowardice is lived through again and again, and since the sense of injured vanity can never be assuaged, existence itself is experienced as an endless recurrence of humiliations, fresh only in their infinite variety but dreadfully familiar in their affect and structure. A maddening sense of impotence is united to a daemonically obsessive total recall, until the sufferer's entire consciousness is like an open sore which evokes only disgust in both the victim and those around him.[32] In fiction, it is hard to think of any work that has chronicled the inscape of *ressentiment* with greater narrative flair than *Notes from Underground*. Let us, for the moment, simply listen to an early passage in which the Underground Man offers, in the process of his ironic self-description, what is virtually an itemization of *ressentiment*'s major preoccupations:

There, in its nasty, stinking underground home, our insulted, crushed and ridiculed mouse promptly becomes absorbed in cold, malignant and, above all, everlasting spite. For forty years together it will remember its injury down to the
smallest, most shameful detail and every time will add, of itself, details still more
shameful, spitefully teasing and irritating itself with its own imagination. It will
be ashamed of its own fancies, but yet it will recall everything, it will go over it
again and again, it will invent lies against itself pretending that those things too
might have happened, and will forgive nothing. Maybe it will begin to revenge
itself, too, but, as it were, piecemeal, in trivial ways, from behind the stove,
incognito, without believing either in its own right to vengeance, or in the success of its revenge, knowing beforehand that from all its efforts at revenge it will
suffer a hundred times more than he on whom it revenges itself, while he, probably, will not even feel it. On its deathbed it will recall it all over again, with
interest accumulated over all the years. (pp. 10–11)

The crushing sense of one's own insignificance, evoked in the image of
a mouse, was prefigured earlier in the assertion that "I could not even
[manage to] become an insect" (p. 6)—a quest that Kafka's Gregor Samsa
carried to a successful conclusion—but what is crucial about this passage is
the thoroughness with which *ressentiment*'s grievances are itemized. The
spite is cold because it is denied any sudden and passionate purgation
through action; it is venomous because it poisons both the sufferer and
whatever he encounters; and it is everlasting because without forgetfulness, no release can be conceived. More important, though, is the admission that not only does the memory of an injury continue its torment forever but the passage of time adds fresh details and new provocations to the
reminiscences. *Ressentiment* does not merely recollect slights; it *creates* them
from its own imaginings, establishing a psychological economy of abjection in which time breeds a quarterly dividend of new shame to swell the
capital already deposited in the sufferer's emotional account. The whole
question of an original outrage is deliberately undermined, since the Underground Man freely confesses the fictional status of his sufferings and
admits his authorship of the very humiliations and reminiscences that vic-
timize him. What "might have happened," the degrading images of his
"own imagination," and the taunts actually encountered in society are all
spun into a single narrative, whose self-reflexivity heightens, rather than
mitigates, the intensity of the hysteria. In Nietzsche's lapidary account, the
cry of *ressentiment*, "I suffer: it must be somebody's fault,"[33] reveals both
the factitiousness of any external agent in creating the sufferer's misery and
the need to blame someone and everyone for his lacerations. Or, in the
Underground Man's parallel formulation: "though you can't come up with
an enemy, you do have pain."[34] *Ressentiment* is like an author in search of
characters to populate the seedy dramas of its own spite, and like an author

it creates scenarios to justify what is only—but also never less than—the narratives it will then remember and ceaselessly amplify. The narrative of memory and the memory of narrative are indistinguishable in their effects, and it makes no difference that *ressentiment* is as ready to blame itself as another, since the self is already experienced as radically multiple, constantly divided from itself in the exteriority of time experienced as pure repetition.

But if my description thus far sounds as much like a Freudian case history as a Dostoevskian or even a Nietzschean crisis of consciousness, it is only in order to highlight what I take to be a central difference between the two models: the subject matter and motivation of the memories themselves. Freud liked to say that his discovery of the unconscious had inflicted the third great injury on human narcissism, decentering the claims of a sovereign *cogito* much as Copernicus and Darwin had compelled a fundamental reevaluation of our place in the physical universe and our origin as a species. But perhaps Freud himself was too cheerfully self-congratulatory in his description, since his patients at least suffered their own impulses, enjoyed, that is, the admittedly thin consolation of taking their traumas as unique burdens, irreducible marks, if nothing else, of their existence as distinct beings. How readily even misery can be converted into a sign of individual distinction is amply demonstrated by the Underground Man, who, in some of his moods, makes precisely such a claim, locating in his very unhappiness the evidence of a singular identity. But the Underground Man, unlike the Freudian analysand, also knows well how dubious such a claim really is and how vulnerable even one's anguish can prove to the charge of plagiarism.

His sense of being only an ambulatory incarnation of literary clichés governs all of the Underground Man's other, more luridly visible grievances, and a crisis of citation constitutes the central injury of his reminiscences. The Underground Man is only the most extreme example of a problem that, beginning with Diderot's *Le Neveu de Rameau*, starts to dominate, with increasing ferocity, both the consciousness of major nineteenth century fictional characters and the narrative structures of the texts in which they appear. One could summarize this predicament by emphasizing that we may not always find the Underground Man's speeches easy to read, but it is usually very easy to know just what he has been reading. There is a careful and increasingly detailed body of scholarship that has traced the literary echoes in works like *Notes from Underground*, but this research has been aimed primarily at documenting the novel's polemical relationship to its contemporary context, that is, to showing Dostoevsky's fiercely partisan role in a moral-ideological debate in which works like Chernyshevsky's *What Is to Be Done?* and Henry Thomas Buckle's *The History of Civilization in England*, or the sentimental romanticism of the Schillerian 1840s, represent the main antagonists. But invaluable as such scholarship remains, its concentration on *Dostoevsky's* savage wit in exposing the intellectual and moral bankruptcy of socialist reformism or sentimental idealism has come at the price of slighting the problematic nature of the Underground Man's own relationship to these positions. It is undoubtedly true, to return to the cherished formulae of Bakhtinian criticism, that *Notes from Underground* is among the most profoundly dialogical works ever imagined, that its every utterance is, from the outset, already engaged in a torrent of other statements, its every word "is not only a word with a sideward glance; it is also . . . a word with a loophole,"[35] but it seems prudent to remind ourselves that this dialogism is not only a positive aspect of Dostoevsky's narrative practice but the very root of the Underground Man's whole dilemma. The "polyphony" of *Notes from Underground* functions primarily to create a character who undermines his own independence as a character. The paradox of the Underground Man's consciousness—the simultaneity of his powerful will and slavish dependence on others—is directly linked to the demoralizing contradiction that this fierce proponent of "free will" often acts and talks exactly "like an automaton" (e.g., at the Zverkov dinner), and that his whole behavior has already been determined by the models whose unhappy mimic he is.

The dialogic status of their words, ideas, and sentiments is experienced as pure entrapment, triggering only rage and *ressentiment* in the characters who must endure an endless chatter of already uttered utterances. In crisis after crisis, the Underground Man cries out for "a real regular quarrel—a more decent, a more *literary* one" (p. 43), and in the bitter narrations of his fantasies, what confirms the paltriness of his abjection is the knowledge that even his most "personal" longings are only commonplace quotations from Rousseau, Byron, Pushkin, Lermontov, etc., etc.: "I was actually on the point of tears, though I knew perfectly well at that very moment that all this was out of Pushkin's 'The Shot' and Lermontov's *Masquerade*" (p. 74). Everything about the Underground Man's psychic economy testifies to his indebtedness to others, both at the material and the imaginative levels.[36] Indeed, the link between his various borrowings makes problematic his insistence on an absolute gulf separating the laws of consciousness from those of physical need. For example, he must borrow money to dress up to challenge the Army Officer, attend Zverkov's dinner, visit the brothel, etc., but just as important is the fact that he borrows the whole idea of borrowing money from Gogol—and does so knowing full well the exact models he is imitating. Fiscally, as well as logically, it is impossible to constitute an independent self out of nothing but debts, and yet such debts are all that the Underground Man can rightfully claim as his own. But his emphasis on the principle of randomness and arbitrary free choice makes his IOUs worthless since he rejects the predictability upon which debts depend. Because he experiences subjection to the laws of temporality and sequence as the source of his most galling narcissistic injury, he refuses to acknowledge any moral or psychological continuity linking his present to the future. Hence the Underground Man cannot make a promise that has any meaning, either to himself or to his creditors, and even his debts are empty of content.[37]

It is a truism of literary history that the nineteenth-century novel substitutes "the hero's evolution through time" for the earlier structuring of narratives as physical journeys.[38] What has been less often remarked are the ways in which temporality and succession become increasingly marked by anxiety, and how time becomes less a novelistic resource than the occasion for a crisis of originality in which the book and all its characters can only repeat configurations and echo speeches already scripted by earlier narratives. As we have seen in *Le Neveu de Rameau*, and as Dostoevsky's novels demonstrate in still more feverish ways, one of the Abject Hero's principal attempts to escape this dilemma is to try and persuade others of his viciousness and to assume, if only for its conventional literary promise of originality, the mantle and accents of the monster. But unlike the genuine monsters of Gothic fiction or the great criminals of Balzac and Sue, the Abject Hero is far too lucid to believe his own pose—hence, of course, both his demoralizingly accurate moments of insight into human motivation and his almost unbearable incapacity to fashion a persona for himself that is both believable and possessed of a minimum of human dignity. It is the foreknowledge of the inevitable failure of his attempt and the experience of insults and misunderstanding from men lacking even the knife-edge of his own self-consciousness that drives figures like Fyodor Karamazov to playing the buffoon. In a case like his, a longing to cause everyone around him to share at least a portion of his embarrassment and shame, along with a compulsion to exhibit his very humiliation as a public spectacle, becomes the one "genuinely imitative" form of daemonic fury available to the abject consciousness.

It is not only the Bloomian "strong poet" who must endure "the anxiety of influence": even the characters of modern fiction are compelled to realize their *post festum* existence. Their development is permanently scarred by the rage against their belatedness. For them, self-consciousness is largely a question of recognizing the massive citations out of which their self is assembled. The Underground Man is not only "fictitious" (in the words of the "Editor's" curious footnote at the novel's outset) because he appears in a fictional text. He is fictitious because he is entirely composed of fictions, a being whose ideas, desires, and aspirations are only citations "gotten out of books" (p. 40). But so too, as he keeps insisting, are those of all the Underground Man's antagonists/interlocutors, including the "Editor," the "gentlemen readers" he ceaselessly addresses and whose attention he so fears losing, and his historical-ideological opponents like Buckle and Chernyshevsky, whose theories are only plausible to someone with a conception of human nature formed entirely by the naive abstractions of philosophical tracts. (In *The Genealogy of Morals*, his principal treatise on *ressentiment*, Nietzsche also rages against Buckle's intellectual vulgarity.) Like other anti-Utopian texts, *Notes from Underground* repeatedly affirms its own fictionality, its status as a book, in order to expose the falseness of conventional Utopian works like *What Is to Be Done?*, which disguise their imaginary nature and present themselves as "realistic" transcriptions of actual events.[39] But in *Notes from Underground*, the stress on fictionality is not merely one more polemical gesture. Instead, it is an expression of the dilemma that is common to all of the novel's characters. Both the Underground Man's own fantasies and those of his opponents are entirely derivative, so the only choice that remains to them is what kinds of narratives to quote and imitate: "Leave us alone without books and we will be lost and in confusion at once—we will not know what to join, what to cling to, what to love and what to hate, what to respect and what to despise" (p. 115).

Throughout his writings, Dostoevsky insists on the "unreality of St. Petersburg," on the capital's willed and artificial character, reflected even in the architecture of its massive public buildings.[40] And as critics have often noticed, the citizens of this "unreal city" have become equally fantastic, detached from reality and inhabiting isolated and isolating delusions in the hours not dedicated to serving the enormous, all-powerful, and largely anonymous Imperial bureaucracy.[41] Those Dostoevsky characters who are most like the crushed clerks of Gogol's tales surrender with neither resistance nor rage to their entrapment in daydreams and fantasies. But the more complex figures understand all too clearly how cut off they are from an authentic existence, how "we have reached the point of looking at actual 'real life' as an effort, almost as hard work. . . . without books we will be lost and in a confusion at once" (p. 115). Yet their self-awareness only helps to exacerbate their dilemma. The Underground Man rages against the Crystal Palace because he is afraid that it is "an edifice at which one would neither be able to stick one's tongue nor thumb one's nose on the sly" (p. 31), and he feels at home in the artificiality of St. Petersburg because it is an environment pre-eminently suited to *ressentiment* and abjection, that is, to sticking out one's tongue and thumbing one's nose—but, of course, only *on the sly*.[42] His pride in an acute self-consciousness is not posited in opposition to a psychological unconscious, but to the absence of conscious self-awareness in his fellow citizens.[43] But when such self-awareness is largely an acute ear for the citationality of one's own desires and the derivativeness of one's most "inspired" words, then the frustration with the abjection of one's existence becomes intolerable.

It is against fiction itself, against the fictional status of his own consciousness that the Underground Man's *ressentiment* explodes, and it is the peculiar logic joining fiction, dialogism, and temporality as mutually linked sources of *ressentiment* that determines the structure of texts like *Notes from Underground* and constitutes one of the central imaginative crises of nineteenth-century thought. Freudian neuroses may be specific and personal, but *ressentiment* is a herd phenomenon: the state of mind, temperament, and imagination of a being who suffers most from the realization that even his worst grievances lack any trace of particularity. And here the genealogical technique of examining a concept's etymology is especially fruitful, since if Nietzsche took over and extended the word *ressentiment* from the seventeenth-century French moralists he so admired, the dictionary reveals how at one time the word carried no pejorative connotations. Philologically, the *re* in *ressentiment* originally functioned purely as an intensifier rather than as a mark of repetition, and Littré, for example, offers several citations in which the word means no more than "sentiment de reconnaissance" (a feeling of gratitude).[44] It is only through a long temporal process that *ressentiment* became linked to time itself as the "feeling-again" of something vile, something whose vileness is precisely a function of its repetitive nature. It is this meaning to which Nietzsche gave a new depth and resonance, and his analysis decisively linked *ressentiment* to the lived experience of temporality.

Of all the emotions issuing out of the frustration of *ressentiment*, none is more striking than the desire for revenge. Revenge and *ressentiment* are twin movements of the same malign emotional orchestration, and their deepest rage is aimed at time itself: "'It was': that is the mark of the will's teeth-gnashing and most lonely affliction. Powerless against that which has been done, the will is an angry spectator of all things past. . . . This, yes, this alone is *revenge* itself: the will's antipathy toward time and time's 'It was.'"[45] This is how, in *Also sprach Zarathustra*, Nietzsche defined the fundamental nature of revenge as a constant and nagging rage at the human experience of temporality. All the slights and humiliations that formed the scenarios of *ressentiment* now turn out to be only manifestations of a still deeper sense of injury, a layer of impotent fury that finds the very fact of being delivered over to succession and history intolerable.

If we now return to Dostoevsky's introductory footnote, we read that the Underground Man is "one of the characters of the recent past" (p. 3). Undoubtedly, one sense of this phrase is the character's location as a man of the 1840s, a self-indulgent and nasty worshiper at the shrine of "all that is beautiful and sublime," unhappily surviving into the politically volatile atmosphere of the 1860s. But in a more radical interpretation, the Underground Man was always a personality of the past. As a creature of *ressen-timent*, haunted by memory and fashioned by citations, he can have no present except for his impotent misery at the process of time itself. The attempt to plot one's life according to the tropes of a prior author is to surrender any genuine relationship to temporality, and it ensures that only in borrowed dreams of fulfillment—dreams of whose fantastic nature one is only too aware—is there a compensatory satisfaction from the rancor and spite occasioned by real life. "The tradition of all the dead generations weighs like a nightmare on the brain of the living,"[46] wrote Marx in *The Eighteenth Brumaire of Louis Bonaparte*, and in coining what is surely one of the most romantically Gothic and anti-materialist images of his entire oeuvre, he crystallizes a sense of time-as-oppression that can be heard again and again throughout the century, even, and perhaps especially, in thinkers like Dostoevsky and Nietzsche, who might seem furthest removed from his views.

What makes the Underground Man's misery so acute, as he himself confesses with something akin to a perverse pride, is his awareness of how degraded his condition really is. But the reason this self-consciousness only intensifies his pain, or better, actually creates it, is that it is *not* an awareness of unconscious impulses (in the Freudian sense), but a too vivid recollection of the texts whose belated and trivial successor he is. *Notes from Underground* is a pastiche of countless prior texts, in part because that is all the Underground Man himself really consists of, except for his additional burden of finding this existence-as-pastiche intolerable. The hysteric of *ressentiment* also suffers reminiscences, but his particular tragedy, a specifically modern and abject one, is that these reminiscences are always recognized as borrowed from others. And if his suffering is one of reminiscence/quotation, so too is the only vengeance open to him. Because he is such a storehouse of clichés, he has the ability to wield those same tropes against someone with less self-awareness, against, that is, a creature whose mind is equally formed by literary commonplaces but who is not as self-conscious about this dependence on narrative models. Here, of course, I am thinking of the Underground Man's relationship to the prostitute Liza, an episode that seems to me among the most carelessly interpreted of any in Dostoevsky's oeuvre.

It is impossible not to notice how the stories the Underground Man tells Liza are a cento of literary commonplaces about the unhappy fate awaiting the "fallen woman," and at first his narrative aggression is so obvious that Liza herself is moved to mock him for speaking "'exactly like a book'" (p. 86). But gradually he begins to find the right models and succeeds in moving both of them to tears, "the lump in my throat" (p. 91) showing at once how vulnerable he is to his own sentimentality and how he shares the typical salesman's need to become his own first customer before being able to persuade anyone else to consider buying his obviously shabby goods. But Liza's reactions, down to tearfully showing him a letter written "to her from a medical student or someone of that sort—a very high-flown and flowery, but extremely respectful, declaration of love" (p. 93), are themselves straight out of typical nineteenth-century romances, and the Underground Man's emotional triumph over her in the brothel has less to do with her purity of soul than with a need to see her situation in exactly the terms laid down by such tales. All of this is clearly signaled by Dostoevsky himself in his ironic citation of Nekrasov's appalling verses at the outset of part 2—verses that are themselves only a pastiche of other poets, including Victor Hugo.[47]

The redeemed prostitute motif is the one trope common to both the types of fiction satirized in *Notes from Underground*, the sentimental novels of the 1840s and the socialist fiction of the 1860s, and in the Underground Man's relationship with Liza, Dostoevsky unerringly seized on the one literary cliché that could expose the common ground of moral-emotional bankruptcy in two otherwise distinct types of narrative. But the curious thing, surely, is how Dostoevsky—and, I am afraid, the vast majority of his readers as well—seems to be quite willing to embrace just this very cliché in his desperation to find some kind of positive beacon in the shabby and sleet-battered grimness of the novel's atmosphere. In *Resurrection*, Tolstoy offers a direct critique of precisely this cliché. There, the prostitute Maslova initially spurns Prince Nekhludov's marriage proposal because she realizes, in a way that both Dostoevsky's readers and his romanticized "fallen women" all too rarely do, what her suitor's motives are: "You want to save yourself through me. . . . You had your pleasure from me and now you want to get your salvation through me."[48] Indeed, the whole topos of the redeemed and redeeming prostitute was soon to be recognized as no longer suitable for anything but ironic treatment, and in tales like Chekhov's "An Attack of Nerves," there is a wonderfully comic itemization of the standard programs that sensitive young men draw on to rescue a "fallen woman":

> All these not very numerous attempts . . . can be divided into three groups. Some, after buying the woman out of the brothel, took a room for her, bought her a sewing-machine, and she became a seamstress. And whether he wanted to or not, after having bought her out he made her his mistress. . . . Others, after buying her out, took a lodging apart for her, bought the inevitable sewing-machine, and tried teaching her to read, preaching at her and giving her books. . . . Finally, those who were the most ardent and self-sacrificing took a bold, resolute step: they married the woman.[49]

When Liza visits the Underground Man in his tawdry flat and reacts to his tears and abject hysteria by rushing to him with a gesture of acceptance

and love, I have no doubt that Dostoevsky, the Christian apologist, intended this moment to seem like an instance of genuine self-sacrifice and
inspired comprehension, the revelation of a depth of heart unavailable to
either the Westernizing rationalists or the tormented dwellers of the underground. And it has been regularly accepted as such by subsequent readers,
even by commentators otherwise as canny in their judgments as Joseph
Frank, Tzvetan Todorov, Robert Louis Jackson, and Michael Holquist.[50]
But isn't Liza's gesture itself really another quotation, an essentially bookish cliché, even if a "noble" one, repeated by a regatta of similar women in
Balzac, Georges Sand, Victor Hugo, and, yes, in Nekrasov's poetry and in
Chernyshevsky's novel itself? Isn't her gesture just as pre-scripted as the
Underground Man's own, and the whole episode less the one chance for
redemption that he fails to seize than another proof of the terrible power of
the Library to create even our most passionately inspired moments?

I know that my interpretation of this scene will evoke disbelief or outrage from many readers. But in fact I am saying only that the Dostoevsky
who wrote *Notes from Underground* is more complex than the Dostoevsky
of the *Correspondence*, the *Diary of a Writer*, and the polemical journalism.
As a novelist, Dostoevsky was able to challenge the very ideas he valued
most and that this ability is what most obviously characterizes his particular
authority as a writer. Phrased in this manner, my observation is not only
uncontroversial but deliberately echoes a favorite commonplace of Dostoevsky criticism. What fascinates me, however, is how rapidly the difficulties accumulate when one tries to move from such a generalized critical
banality to a specific instance, how committed we are to siding with Dostoevsky *against* his fiction as soon as the pressures of the split become too
acute. Not only is Liza's very compassion, like her medical student's letter,
a citation from her predecessors in the trade, but the ensuing events reveal
how limited an emotional repertoire such citations offer. The Underground Man, we remember, reacts to her outpouring of sympathy with
what he—and most readers—agree in considering his vilest "atrocity." He
turns her "rapturous embrace" (p. 110) into a sexual provocation, then
dismisses her as quickly as possible with the added insult of thrusting a
five-ruble note into her unwilling hand. But why are we so ready to see this
"atrocity" as his *final* entrapment in the hell of the underground? After all,
in what way is his behavior here worse than the vituperations with which
he greeted Liza upon her arrival at his flat, or his earlier quest in the brothel
for the right narrative, the most efficacious "cute little pictures," to provoke
her tears?[51] Or conversely, why is this last gesture less a cry of pain than any
of the earlier ones? Why, if Liza's intuitive wisdom and depth of soul enabled her to see through and forgive his suffering before, can she not do the
same now? The answer, I think, is that in the narratives on which her consciousness is based, such scenes only happen once—that in the world of

sentimental novels the instant the "fallen woman" has compassion on the cruel man and recognizes that he, too, like her, is one of the "insulted and injured," he is released from his anguish, and the two are mutually purified by their shared ordeal. When the Underground Man does not act according to her sentimental scenarios, but instead reverts back to the revenge-centered paradigms of *ressentiment*, Liza is wounded beyond endurance, beyond, that is, her repertoire's capacity to find a consolingly redemptive narrative model. The Underground Man knows that the "atrocity was so phony, so cerebral, so deliberately contrived, so *bookish*,"[52] but because he draws from a different, more savagely wounded and wounding text than any Liza has encountered before, she can have no response but flight, her powers of interpretation exhausted.

Notes from Underground continuously satirizes the sentimental use of the prostitute figure in the tales of the 1840s, in Nekrasov's verses, and in Chernyshevsky's novel. Even though Dostoevsky finally intended Liza to function as such a figure of redemptive suffering and love, the logic of his own narrative undercuts this solution at every turn. Abjection can never be healed by copying anyone, not even the sacred example of Mary Magdalene. This is true because every act of imitation—no matter how worthy, or even divine, the model—simply confirms the initial predicament, and even the most uplifting narratives are transformed, through the very fact of being copied, into merely fresh aspects of, rather than solutions to, the crisis of reminiscences. (How clearly Dostoevsky understood this bitter truth is evident from the end of *The Idiot*, whose Christ-like hero, Prince Myshkin, finishes his life back in a Swiss sanatorium, completely incapacitated by his mental and physical collapse.) As long as one desires an original, authentic consciousness and voice, as long as the fact of living a belated and already scripted existence is seen as the ultimate wound, making any claim to personal dignity derisory, abjection must remain consciousness's dominant emotion, and *ressentiment* will structure the narratives one lives, the narratives one tells, and ultimately, the narratives in which one figures as one more increasingly wretched character.

> No festival without cruelty: this is the lesson of the
> most ancient and longest part of human history.
>   (Friedrich Nietzsche, *Zur Genealogie der Moral*)

In chapter 1, I said that the logic of abjection receives its ultimate articulation in Dostoevsky's most compelling figure of evil: Ivan Karamazov's Devil. The satanic is figured here "exactly like a poor relation who had come down from his room to keep his host company at tea" (p. 603). Instead of the conventional, and conventionally grandiloquent, fallen titan, full of grim defiance and stormy, Romantic rages, this Devil resembles only a Russian gentleman . . . no longer young . . . with rather long, still thick, dark hair, slightly streaked with gray, and a small pointed beard. He was wearing a brownish reefer jacket, rather shabby, evidently made by a good tailor though, and of a fashion at least three years old, that had been discarded by smart and well-to-do people for the last two years. . . . His linen was not too clean and his wide scarf was very threadbare. . . . In brief, there was every appearance of gentility on straitened means. (p. 602)

The crucial exchanges between Ivan and the Devil derive much of their power from showing how the core of a deeply Christian metaphysics (the soul-destroying nature of evil) exists independently of its conventional narrative and iconographic props (the fire-and-brimstone, horns-and-tail imagery). But perhaps still more uncanny is the way Satan so freely admits that he only exists by virtue of, and in order to engage in, just such conversations, in order, that is, to be given a palpable reality by what Bakhtinians have celebrated as "the dialogic principle": "Here when I stay with you from time to time my life gains a kind of reality and that's what I like most of all" (p. 605). Actually, what the Devil wants most of all is to be able to fascinate his conversational partner with "such artistic visions, such complex and real actuality, such events, even a whole world of events, woven into such a plot, with such unexpected details from the most exalted matters to the last button on a cuff, as I swear Leo Tolstoy could not create" (p. 606). But alas, the tone of helpless longing makes it clear that Dostoevsky's Devil is no match for Tolstoy. Being unable to create aesthetically convincing narratives of his own, Satan will need to cite those of his betters, though it is not only, nor even primarily, Scripture that he quotes to his own ends, and certainly not the novels of Leo Tolstoy, but rather the words of such congenial fictional frauds as Ivan Aleksandrovich Khlestakov, Gogol's fake Inspector General (p. 608). This is an incarnation of evil who, in Gary Saul Morson's phrase, "is content to be, if not a real, then at least an imitation imposter."[53] Ivan repeatedly accuses the Great Accuser of plagiarizing from his own adolescent anecdotes, but in a universe in which everything is pure citation, such a charge is essentially tautological and carries little sting.[54] In *The Brothers Karamazov*, the monstrous exists as pure mimic and as pure monstrosity at the same time, and in that simultaneity Dostoevsky has crystallized the most disturbingly modern theology of the daemonic that I know.

But it is not necessary to be haunted by specifically theological questions in order to be as unnerved as Ivan is by the dialogue his Devil initiates. This Satan is nothing if not shrewd, and he fully realizes how provocative his appearances as a poor toady must seem to anyone highly literate, whose expectations have been determined entirely by conventional literary images: "You are really angry with me for not having appeared to you in a red glow, with thunder and lightning, with scorched wings. . . . You are wounded, in the first place, in your aesthetic feelings, and, secondly, in your pride. How could such a vulgar devil visit such a great man as you!" (p. 614). The diagnosis is maliciously accurate. Since classical antiquity, the stature of a great man was confirmed in part by the quality of both his antagonists and his attendants, and to Ivan the ordinariness of "his" Devil is like a visible confirmation of his deepest fear of being only derivative and second-rate, even in his "rebellion" against God. Watching his ideas appropriated and put into action by Smerdyakov has forced Ivan to acknowledge their essential vulgarity, and the Devil's shabby appearance only underlines the shabbiness Ivan feels already marks his whole existence. He must now cope with the thought that instead of a heroic rebel, he is merely another philosophically confused and emotionally overwrought ex-student whose speculations have resulted in terrible consequences to everyone around him—but even then only once they were mediated through the deeds of his paltry double. Ivan confronts the banality of his satanic nature in a dialogue with a banal Satan, much as, although on a far less intense and metaphysically charged scale, Horace confronted his own servile tendencies in a dialogue with a petty slave like Davus.

We know from his correspondence that Dostoevsky was greatly worried about the persuasive intensity of Ivan's accusations against God in the chapters "Rebellion" and "The Grand Inquisitor." He assured men like K. P. Pobedonostsev, the powerful, ultra-orthodox tutor to the future czar Alexander III and Chief Procurator of the Holy Synod, that the account of Father Zosima's life, "The Russian Monk," would provide the required counterweight, although he confesses that "I am trembling over it [the life of Zosima], wondering whether it will be an *adequate* answer . . ."[55] But Dostoevsky provided a quite different—and psychologically far more effective—answer to Ivan's blasphemies in the description of his dialogue with the Devil. Instead of merely presenting, as the letter to Pobedonostsev had promised, "a world view that stands in direct opposition to the one previously presented [by Ivan],"[56] Dostoevsky shows us the lies and vanity at the heart of Ivan's accusations themselves.

For all his pride in his analytic powers, and in spite of all the charges of non-existence that he hurls at the Devil, it is indicative of Ivan's will to deceive himself that he never consciously articulates the uncanny and unmistakable resemblance between Satan and Fyodor Karamazov. Guilt at his complicity in his father's murder may be part of the reason for Ivan's failure to make the connection, but it may also be that he has internalized his father so entirely as the embodiment of everything loathsome in the world and in himself that he is no longer able to distinguish Fyodor's specific features from his own nightmarish self-image.[57] The whole dialogue with so maddeningly ordinary a Devil exposes the self-deception behind what Geoffrey Kabat perceptively describes as "Ivan's attempt to deny his relation to his father and to assert his total independence, his project of self-origination."[58] The text gives us numerous hints about how closely the figure of the Devil resembles Fyodor Karamazov. Not only are they explicitly linked through a common rhetoric of buffoonery and parasitical dependence on others ("prizhival'shchiki"), but their tastes in French literature, polemics against religious hypocrites, and sense of being victimized by unjustified slanders underline their temperamental and functional similarities.[59]

We have already seen how the initial encounter in Father Zosima's cell rehearses, but in the mode of ironic diminution, most of the novel's major themes, and it is hardly surprising that in the presence of the holy elder some of Fyodor's second-rate satanism (or, equally accurate, some of the Devil's flunky Fyodor Pavlovichism) rushes out. Fyodor calls himself "an inveterate buffoon," only to raise the stakes of his self-description slightly before dashing it all the more disparagingly to the ground: "I daresay it's a devil within me. But only a little one. A more serious one would have chosen another lodging" (p. 36). Here again, the debauched father knows more and speaks more justly than his intellectually trained son, and what he knows more clearly is just how petty he, and by extension, Ivan, really are. Each time Fyodor is tempted to claim a kind of higher daemonism for himself, a sense of proportion quite remarkable in a character universally described by critics in terms of excess and untrammeled energy intervenes and chastens the presumption: "Of a truth, I am a lie, and the father of lies. Though I believe I am not the father of lies. . . . Say, the son of lies, and that will be enough" (p. 37).

Smerdyakov, whose function it is to notice and bring to light everything Ivan refuses to acknowledge, has no difficulty seeing the resemblance between father and son: "You are like Fyodor Pavlovich, sir, you are more like him, sir, more like him than any of his children; you've the same soul as he had" (p. 599). If Ivan's Devil shares numerous features with Fyodor Pavlovich, he also at times resembles Smerdyakov, especially his ingratiating tone and irritatingly mock-servile speech rhythms (note especially the repeated use of "sir" in both their conversations). It is worth recalling here that at the end of *Twelfth Night*, Malvolio rushes off stage vowing, "I'll be revenged on the whole pack of you,"[60] and that in a sense Smerdyakov, the overreaching valet, educated beyond his station, represents a grotesque culmination of the entire Malvolio tradition. The vengeance the Elizabethan *arriviste* failed to exercise is exactly what Smerdyakov, who does succeed in destroying the entire Karamazov household, effects. As though to clinch the correspondences I have been tracing, Ivan's final interview with Smerdyakov immediately precedes his encounter with the Devil, and when he tells his half-brother, "Do you know, I am afraid that you are a dream, a phantom sitting before me" (p. 591), it is as though he were unconsciously practicing the lines he would shortly be trying on his most dangerous and mocking antagonist. The Devil departs from Ivan's room just before Alyosha brings news of Smerdyakov's suicide, news, that is, of Satan's "real" working in the world to seal Ivan's doom, and in the chaos that ensues, the four figures—Fyodor Pavlovich Karamazov, Ivan Fyodorovich Karamazov, Pavel Fyodorovich "Smerdyakov" [Karamazov], and the Devil [as-a-Karamazov]—begin to coalesce in the reader's mind almost like part objects of a single grotesquely torturing, because tormented, figure. It is a figure that in retrospect has functioned throughout the entire plot of the novel like a magnet, gathering fragments from the four individual characters into a single, larger image that I am tempted to call, were such an oxymoron not too provocative, the apotheosis of the Abject Hero.

> Novels are the Socratic dialogues of our epoch.
> (Friedrich Schlegel, "Kritische Fragmente")

For all its aphoristic authority, Schlegel's famous dictum is as misleading as it is suggestive. The novel's famously capacious and flexible structure certainly provided a hospitable setting in which the philosophical dialogue could flourish. Such a setting was all the more welcome since the Kantian redirecting of philosophy left little opportunity within it for dialogism as either a technique of inquiry or an epistemological category. The philosophical dialogue began to figure in the novel less like a master trope than like a refugee, exiled from its original home as a consequence of philosophy's altered conception of its methods and goals. And like a good refugee, the philosophical dialogue took on the local accents and customs of its hosts, becoming one more strand in the novel's variegated texture.

The best way to picture this development is to incorporate both sides of the Bakhtinian perspective, emphasizing that what writers like Dostoevsky achieve is not the dialogization of the novel, but rather the novelization of the dialogue. And in such a trajectory, the Saturnalian dialogue, whose fictionality is not merely explicitly acknowledged but centrally thematized through both a self-conscious probing of the novel's frame and a deliberate and parodic reliance on earlier texts, had the likeliest chance to survive with a renewed impetus.

Fundamental to this new literary energy was the emergence of the Abject Hero to serve at once as a principal narrative voice and a kind of obsessive intellectual/emotional problem of the Saturnalian dialogue-novel. What the Saturnalian dialogue came to enact was essentially the cry of *ressentiment* and the counter-cry of all the voices whose very existence had provoked and kept alive that *ressentiment*. And what figure, if not the Abject Hero, could articulate the self-regarding lacerations of *ressentiment* while entrapping in a true dialogue spokesmen of the very society that had formed, frustrated, and ultimately rejected him? I have argued that although the Abject Hero has an ancestry that derives directly from classical satire and owes a number of his typical characteristics to the Renaissance "wise fool" and "malcontent," he first came into focus as a fully realized figure in *Le Neveu de Rameau*'s dizzying subversion of traditional satiric topoi. That the full *novelistic* potential of the Abject Hero was not worked out in all its permutations until Dostoevsky is scarcely surprising since it is only in the narration/enactment of a cultural crisis that the Abject Hero becomes a compelling literary voice.

Dostoevsky undoubtedly saw the Russia of his day in terms of an imminent catastrophe, but his position differed from that of most of his contemporaries by recognizing that the individuals whose alienation and bitterness should have given them the clearest perspective on the degraded nature of society were actually its most characteristic products. Like distorting mirrors, his underground men only reflect back an inverted image of the hollowness that marks the bureaucratic time-servers or philistine reformers they scorn. A Davus, a Feste, a Malvolio, or even a Rameau would be quite content to change his own particular situation; none of them has much interest in using the perspective gained from his alienated vantage point to authenticate any global claims. But Dostoevsky's characters, from the Underground Man through all the sons in *The Brothers Karamazov*, demand nothing less than the right to remake the whole world as a necessary precondition of transforming their own predicaments.[61] They are at once abject and heroic, and if the scale of their simultaneous abjection and heroism is only visible in the unfolding of a densely textured novel, then it is equally true that their complexity is itself the result of the fullness of incident and conflicting voices of the novel form.

It is as though the collaboration between the novel's broad social canvas and the Abject Hero's leveling mockery recreated the communal marketplace of carnivalesque fiction that Bakhtin feared had been lost since the Renaissance,[62] but with the crucial difference that both the Saturnalian ritual and the relationship among its participants was transformed radically. In works like *Notes from Underground*, Dostoevsky took a decisive step in uncovering the latent potential of the Saturnalian carnival as a literary paradigm by drawing on it for both the characters and the structure of his novel. But if the family resemblance between Jean-François Rameau and the Underground Man has been recognized by at least some commentators, there has been a persistent reluctance to address the parallel kinship between the "gentlemen readers" and Diderot's *philosophe*. No doubt such reluctance is a tribute to Dostoevsky's ironic strategy of simultaneously discrediting both his narrator and that narrator's prudently rationalistic critics. However, not only does the conflict between the Underground

Man and his fantasized interlocutors take up, at a more hysterical pitch, the debate between *Moi* and *Lui*, but it is crucial to Dostoevsky's project for the reader to recognize aspects of himself in the tone of those interlocutors, to admit that the terms and values of the "gentlemen" with whom the Underground Man is caught in so futile and mutually contemptuous a quarrel, actually correspond closely to his own instinctive and communally approved assumptions. Our revulsion at the futility, self-destructiveness, and irrationality of the Underground Man's polemical confession is bound to echo the charges he already hurls at himself through the mouths of his imaginary interlocutors, and the long and impassioned record of responses to *Notes from Underground* demonstrates how difficult it is not to occupy a position already developed in full by one of the book's voices.

To occupy such a position is itself notably depressing, for two distinct, but closely related, reasons. The first is largely internal to the novel and arises from the Underground Man's success at mocking the philistinism of his opponents. Indeed, the only moments at which the Underground Man sounds almost persuasive come when he shows how bathetically misplaced is his opponents' faith in an always calculable, rational self-interest and concomitant historical meliorism. Readers today, who come to the text with the events of the intervening century inevitably in their consciousness, can only find this aspect of the Underground Man's critique all the more powerful and be correspondingly more uncomfortable when they find themselves sharing numerous presuppositions with the rationalist gentlemen. But at the same time many of these shared assumptions are so persuasive that it would be an act of sheer underground spite to deny one's accord. Appropriately enough, the chief among such points of agreement would be a sense of the utter inadequacy of spite as a response to intolerable conditions and an awareness of the extent to which the Underground Man himself embodies the vices he most despises in his environment. No doubt the urgency of distancing oneself from the Underground Man's position—and to that extent at least making common cause with his interlocutors—has become more apparent in light of the catastrophes of recent history, which have borne repeated witness to the terrors that ensue when a cult of pure irrationalism is held up as a "solution" to an over-bureaucratized, over-mechanized society.

The second reason for the reader's discomfort is what we may call a kind of genre effect since it depends on our familiarity with the tradition of which *Notes from Underground* is a part. We know that in a Saturnalian dialogue no one escapes the satire's corrosive mockery, and that knowledge makes us struggle all the harder to avoid being in any way identifiable with the text's characters—thereby, of course, exactly duplicating one of the novel's central obsessions. If the Underground Man's chief torment is his sense of entrapment in a literary-philosophical tradition, then it is equally true that a similar deterioration in originality marks the articulation of the contrary voices. The "gentlemen readers" represent a distinct degradation from *Moi*'s flexible and deeply committed—even if a little too smug and self-congratulatory—intellectual honesty, just as writers like Chernyshevsky or Buckle seem markedly vulgar and naive when their version of rational human development is compared with the complex lucidity of the *Encyclopédistes*. Thus, if *Le Neveu de Rameau* already made one squirm at the thought of sharing *Moi*'s moments of blindness and pomposity, then the prospect of hearing oneself rehearsing the arguments of any one of the "gentlemen readers" is bound to cause an especially nasty kind of injury to one's narcissism. In novels like *Notes from Underground* the very fact of being part of a Saturnalian tradition operates as a self-conscious strategy within the fiction, making both the narrator and the novel's readers victims of a common crisis of citationality, both rendered equally impotent to articulate a position without raising the dread that it is merely a vitiated version of an earlier and more potent formulation. The reader too now fears sounding, at best, like a kind of lesser *Moi* or, at worst, like the most hectoring and brutal of the book's fantasized interlocutors.[63] After all, much of what we know we know because we are such diligent readers, consumers of a philosophical and literary heritage we usually find impossible to live up to, let alone surpass, and from this perspective our dilemma becomes remarkably akin to the Underground Man's. It is scarcely necessary to add that this same voracious consumption of traditional texts is the minimum enabling act of the Saturnalian dialogue itself, which, as the parodic genre par excellence, depends entirely on the prior existence of the traditions it mocks. But unlike the comforting formulations in which such a parodic relationship is seen as freeing the mocker by the act of exposing the unintentionally ridiculous side of the respectable model, the works we have been looking at make amply clear that such an exposing is altogether different from an overcoming, and that laughter, at its most unsettling, does not free the mocker but instead, further implicates him in his comically painful predicament.

In chapter 1, I suggested that when the consciousness of his abjection became intolerable, a characteristic solution of the sufferer was to adopt the guise and accents of a monster, hoping through the respect such a creature inspires to forget both his own insignificance and the contempt he fears is actually his due (if only because contempt is what he mainly feels for himself). Dostoevsky is full of such abject and frightened characters, trying, mostly without success, to pass themselves off as monsters, and both the Underground Man and Ivan Karamazov are notably complex embodiments of that dilemma. But what if the world actually believed the imposture and took the abject creature at his word? What if it really did label, even legally designate, such a man as a monster? What if, moreover, the

Abject Hero found himself in a situation in which the borderline between abjection and monstrosity had, in effect, itself become obliterated? This, as we shall now see, is precisely the situation of Louis-Ferdinand Céline, narrator and principal character of the World War II trilogy *D'un château l'autre*, *Nord*, and *Rigodon*, a set of novels that seem to me the darkest vision of the Saturnalia in all of modern literature.

Five

L'Apocalypse à Crédit:
Louis-Ferdinand Céline's War Trilogy

> Estragon (suddenly furious): Recognize! What is
> there to recognize? All my lousy life I've crawled
> about in the mud! And you talk to me about scen-
> ery! (Looking wildly about him.) Look at this
> muckheap! I've never stirred from it! . . . You and
> your landscapes! Tell me about the worms!
> (Samuel Beckett, *Waiting for Godot*)

EARLY IN *The Brothers Karamazov*, Ivan tells his father that although Smerdyakov has the soul of a resentful lackey, his frustrated vanity and cringing
defiance make him a "prime candidate" for the role of social incendiary.
"When the time comes," Ivan predicts, the revolution will be initiated by
the Smerdyakovs of the world.[1] Dostoevsky clearly feared a left-wing uprising, inspired by doctrines imported into Russia from Western Europe. But
the *ressentiment* that drives the Smerdyakovs to their compensatory longings for power is as likely to find expression in right-wing as in Marxist
conspiracies, and the past century has born witness both to the prescience
of Dostoevsky's worst fears about Communism and to the lure of every
variety of Fascism and xenophobic race hatred.

In novels like *The Possessed*, Dostoevsky sketched the ideological foundation of a world characterized by the abandonment of all emotional inhibi-
tions to, and institutional restraints on, the violence human beings can
inflict on one another. But what remained prediction in Dostoevsky became a "normal" fact of existence during Louis-Ferdinand Céline's life
(1894–1961). Dostoevsky warned about the consequences once traditional ethics are discarded, but Céline actually lived through those consequences, voiced some of their most debased impulses, and wrote the most
penetrating chronicle we have of an era during which the abject and sordid
flourished as never before. Céline does not so much straddle as perpetually
rupture the margin between history and literature, and in his writings abjection spills over from the realm of ideas and fiction into the reality of
European history. In his trilogy, *D'un château l'autre*, *Nord*, and *Rigodon*,
Céline pushes the figure of the Abject Hero beyond Dostoevsky's usage by

locating him at the heart of a global war as destructive and vicious as the modern world has endured.[2]

The leakage between history and literature is so problematic in Céline because his novels lack the kind of careful framing devices that Dostoevsky took care to provide. The Underground Man is not the author of *Notes from Underground*, Dostoevsky is, and he even introduces an "Editor" in between the two to draw attention to the book's frame. But the Céline who both wrote and narrates the trilogy is also the author of the ferociously anti-Semitic pamphlets *Bagatelles pour un massacre* and *L'école des cadavres* and the eager Collaborator in the Franco-German alliance whose open letters to the pro-Nazi journals during the Occupation called for a "fanatical and total racism."[3] The voice to which we are listening in his books is the modern descendant of Diderot's parasite and Dostoevsky's underground railers, but because it is also the speech of a novelist with stunning comic power and literary inventiveness, the dilemma of how to react to his narrative becomes more acute than earlier expressions of an Abject Hero's *ressentiment*. Céline is like a Fyodor Karamazov with the skill to write his own tale and the wit to know that the most unsettling trick is to voice one's nastiest impulses as though they were only a macabre joke, all the while knowing them to be completely genuine.

In *Le Neveu de Rameau*, after listening to one of the Nephew's particularly unsavory anecdotes, *Moi* says to himself: "I didn't know whether to stay or run away, laugh or be furious."[4] He finds himself morally repelled but aesthetically fascinated by Rameau's performance, and much of *Le Neveu de Rameau*'s power comes from the ways it makes us consider the specter of an irreconcilable conflict between the two kinds of responses. Céline's works, written by a witness to a savagery beyond anything of which Rameau could have conceived, confronts us with the extreme version of this dilemma and makes that confrontation the essence of his Saturnalian dialogue with his readers.

Because the trilogy so obsessively returns to the question of its status between absolute fiction and authentic chronicle/reportage, and because the judgment of Céline's whole life is centrally at issue in the novels, my reading must engage these problems, even when doing so may seem to exceed the chapter's principal theme: Céline's recasting of the Saturnalia as a shabby apocalypse. But not to face these issues seems to me fundamentally dishonest, untrue both to Céline's writings and to the larger concerns of this study.

As we watch Céline play his own version of Rameau's or the Underground Man's gambit to engross by appalling, we register how the terms of the dialogue have been intensified almost, though not entirely, beyond recognition. By the end, not the least alarming of Céline's legacies is the thought that only through an exacerbation of its stakes to such an extreme pitch can the topos still succeed in unsettling us at all.

> The genius of misfortune
> Is not a sentimentalist.
>   (Wallace Stevens, "Esthétique du Mal")

Perhaps the best way to situate my argument is with two stories about a lost governorship, two fantasies, or even, in Céline's sense, *féeries*.[5] But these stories, unlike Céline's *Féerie pour une autre fois*, will be not so much *for*, but rather *from*, two different times and emotional registers.

From the very beginning of his adventures, Sancho Panza was obsessed with the ambition of someday obtaining a governorship. The desire was initially implanted in Sancho by Don Quixote himself, who urged his neighbor to serve him, "for some time or another an adventure might occur that would win him in the twinkling of an eye some isle, of which he would leave him governor."[6] From that moment on, Sancho had "a great desire to see himself governor of the isle his master had promised him,"[7] and the longed-for governorship functions as a minor but entertainingly persistent motif throughout part 1 of the novel. In the second part, though, the motif becomes a major event in its own right when the two adventurers meet a duke and duchess who have read part 1 of *Don Quixote* and know all about Sancho's longing. The aristocrats use their knowledge to initiate a fantastic series of entertainments at Sancho's expense. The squire is even tricked into thinking he has actually taken up a post as "Governor of the Isle of Barataria,"[8] but after much teasing, Sancho voluntarily renounces his title, admitting he simply isn't up to the job—even though he has shown himself to be as well suited as most "legitimate" rulers. Sancho may be both gullible and easily abused, but he is too innocent and good-natured to be inwardly humiliated, let alone abject, for long.

Late in 1944, Louis-Ferdinand Céline, reluctant doctor to a pitiful colony of French Collaborators, now hanging on as refugees in Nazi Germany, goes to visit Pierre Laval, the former Vichy Vice Premier and Foreign Minister, in his suite at the castle of Sigmaringen. Here, the ragged remnants of the Pétainist leadership and a few of their most compromised followers, who had fled France just ahead of the advancing Allied armies, are housed, miserably awaiting a fate over which they no longer have the slightest control.[9]

Céline himself has ended up in Sigmaringen against his will, ordered there by the Germans while they decide on his application for travel permits required to proceed to Denmark. There he expects to find both a

sanctuary and money from royalties deposited years earlier in a Copenhagen bank. Almost everyone in the Castle shares a similar fantasy about
reaching a safe haven since the disintegration of the Third Reich will soon
leave all its foreign lackeys defenseless against the anger of their own citizens. From July 10, 1940, when the French Senators and Deputies assembled in the casino of the spa town of Vichy voted by 569 to 80 to give the
eighty-four-year-old World War I hero Maréchal Henri Philippe Pétain
full power, through August 20, 1944, when the Vichy government was
removed under German orders, first to Belfort and then (September 8) to
Sigmaringen, Pétain and a shifting cabinet of Ministers, the most ambitious of whom was probably Pierre Laval, ruled the section of France not
under direct German occupation. They administered it with an increasingly slavish dependence on the German conquerors, often acting well in
advance of any directives from them, especially in the brutal suppression of
Jews, anti-Fascists, and other "undesirables."[10] The Collaborators of Vichy
were exceeded in their loyalty to the Nazis only by those living in Paris, and
one of the ironies of life in Sigmaringen is that it threw together two mutually suspicious gangs of Nazi sympathizers. The inanity of their quarrels
was finally unmistakable now that they were both defeated and under sentence of death from the victorious Gaullist troops.[11]

The old Hohenzollern fortress that Céline ironically insists on mis-
calling Siegmaringen throughout *D'un château l'autre* (to pun on the German word for victory, *Sieg*) nicely concretizes a picture of European history
in which all the towers are fake and only the cellars, built to conceal the
slaughtered victims, are real:

> How many holes, hiding places, dungeons had those princes, dukes, and
> gangsters dug? . . . in the muck, in the sand, in the rock? fourteen centuries of
> Hohenzollerns! [. . .] their whole history was under the Castle, the doubloons,
> the slain, hanged, strangled, and mummified rivals . . . the top, the visible
> part, all phony, trompe-l'oeil, turrets, belfries, bells . . . for the birds! [. . .] the
> real thing was underneath: [. . .] the skeletons of the kidnapped [. . .]
> the treasures of Florentine merchants [. . .] fourteen centuries of dungeons.
> (*C* 107/130)[12]

Historically considered, the scum of Europe's present are living on top
of the scum of its past. Although he and Laval supposedly cannot stand one
another,[13] and Céline cheerfully admits that he had publicly called Laval "a
crook, a no good, a traitor, and a Jew!" (*C* 241/280),[14] he now offers the
architect of the bankrupt Franco-German Collaboration the most precious
of gifts in a crumbling dictatorship: a capsule of cyanide with which to
forestall the public executioner. In return, and to transpose the tone of the
scene from a historical narrative to an episode in a sinister legend (a technique Céline employs throughout much of the trilogy), Laval offers to

grant Céline one wish. And though Céline, unlike Sancho Panza, has never manifested any such desire before, he now asks for the governorship of the islands of Saint-Pierre and Miquelon, largely because of their enormous distance from both Sigmaringen and Paris. Laval readily grants Céline's wish and gets Jean Bichelonne, the former Vichy Minister for Industry and Commerce, to witness the appointment. At least on paper, Céline has been miraculously transformed from a quasi-captive in a prison-town to governor of two beautiful and safe islands in the North Atlantic.

But Céline is no luckier in his quest than was Sancho Panza. There is no need to belabor the grim humor of Céline's paper elevation being offered as a *quid pro quo* for the gift of an easy death, but it is worth remembering that all three men in the scene emerge as consummate losers in what *Nord* calls "the 'Everything Goes' Casino of History" (*N* 313/13).[15] Either the cyanide or his courage must have failed Laval, since he fled from Germany to Spain and then to Austria, from where he was shipped back to France, tried, and executed in 1945.[16] Bichelonne, the sole witness to Céline's governorship, died even before the war ended, probably murdered in a Nazi hospital at Hohenlychen where he had gone for surgery. The freezing train ride from Sigmaringen to Hohenlychen and back, for which Céline joins a French delegation futilely hoping to attend Bichelonne's funeral service, is one of the most memorable of the darkly comic set pieces at the end of *D'un château l'autre*. By linking Bichelonne's death to his now permanently lost governorship, Céline mixes literary modes, combining elements of *commedia dell'arte* (the defrauded servant vainly crying for his wages), historical reportage, satiric travel guide, and the picaresque. At the book's close, welding his memory of Sigmaringen to a description of his present life in Meudon (a fusion, that is, of chronicle, autobiography, and black farce), Céline returns to the lost governorship, with the tone of the melancholy, unpaid attendant of classical comedy, glumly conceding that he will never get his reward: "maybe my qualifications will be contested . . . maybe they'll say I haven't got Saint-Pierre and Miquelon . . . that Laval is dead . . . and Bichelonne left no word, nothing in writing! . . . that there's no record at the Ministry of Colonies, and that my say-so isn't enough!" (*C* 293/339).[17]

But Céline, as he never ceases to complain, lost more than the promised governorship. After all the effort of persuading the Nazis to let him leave for Denmark and all the risks of the voyage across Germany to Copenhagen, he was unable to recover the gold that motivated the whole trip. Instead, he was greeted with fourteen months in the Vester Faengsel prison, nearly three years exile in Denmark, an *in absentia* court sentence of one year in prison, a fine of fifty thousand francs, confiscation of half his property, and a declaration that he is "en état d'indignité nationale."[18] After the amnesty of 1951, when he was able to return to Paris, he did so as a vilified and unwelcome reminder of one of the greatest humiliations in French history. That he should dare to write at all, Céline whines, is felt as an outrage by all those who wish he had joined such famous novelists of the Collaboration as Drieu la Rochelle and Robert Brasillach in their suicide or death sentence. In other words, the trilogy also functions like a twentieth-century version of Chateaubriand's *Mémoires d'Outre-tombe*, but instead of recounting vanished glories, Céline's text is a relentless and inconvenient reminder of an era everyone not only wished to forget but would like to pretend never took place.[19] Its teller is humiliated in the narrative present in which he lives, in the historical past that constitutes the core of his tale, and in the tone he and his antagonists/readers take toward his own destiny. He is abject three times over, and his entire narrative is a perverse effort, both to confirm the truth of his abjection and to lessen its sting by forcing the whole nation to share in it with him.

Throughout his post-War writings, Céline's deepest scorn is reserved for those who, like the majority of Frenchmen, switched loyalties when their self-interest so counseled and tried, beginning in 1944, to pass themselves off as Resisters from the outset. His own positions, he insists with pride, have never deviated, irrespective of who governed the country. But those positions were so bizarre and idiosyncratic that it is hard to image how Céline might have modified them successfully even if he were so inclined, except by retreating into total silence. In this regard, it is probably helpful to specify that Céline was more a pure racist and anarcho-pacifist than a committed Fascist in the classic French tradition of Maurras, Daudet, or Brasillach. He conspicuously lacked the "tempérament du droit," the deep reverence for the army, the love of hierarchy, order, and religious ortho-doxy, and the *romanità* of the proto-Fascist Action Française; he never fit in with the theoreticians or activists of any political grouping.[20] Like the Austrians who were eager to join the Germans in "cleansing" Europe of its Jews but showed no parallel zeal in risking their lives on the battlefront, Céline made a very good anti-Semite but a decidedly bad Nazi.[21] Fre-quently his racism was so extravagant it even offended what would other-wise have been a like-minded audience. In 1942, for example, *Les beaux draps* had the peculiar distinction of being banned by the Vichy govern-ment because of its open contempt for both Pétain and the whole French army. In this, the last of his pamphlets, Céline refused to echo the wide-spread right-wing explanation that France's catastrophic military defeat was due to "the corrupt, Jewish-financed Parliamentarians," attributing it instead to the abysmal incompetence of the generals and the cowardice of the soldiers.[22] Still more revealing, Lucien Rebatet tells how in 1942 the editorial board of *Je suis partout* had to reject an open letter from Céline because of its "délire raciste."[23] For *Je suis partout*, the most committed to the Nazi cause of all the Collaborationist journals, to refuse publication to someone of Céline's stature because the text was too "deliriously racist" is scarcely imaginable, and, as Rebatet recognized, the letter must have been intended as a deliberate, if obscurely motivated, gesture of defiance by Céline.[24]

In the trilogy as well, Céline's "délire raciste" is completely unpredictable in its choice of targets. Not only is Laval, as we have already seen, accused of being a Jew, but Hitler is called a "bastard Caesar, semi-painter, semi-ham actor, credulous stupid sly, semi-queen, and champion bungler!" (C 175/206).[25] According to *Nord*, the whole Chancellery in Berlin is populated by Jews "in close contact with Hitler" (489/200).[26] Berlin is described as full of Asiatics, and, as Patrick McCarthy notes, in the trilogy "the only character threatened by the laws on racial purity is [the cat] Bébert, who risks being put to sleep because he is 'without pedigree.'"[27] Flashes of insight into the regime through whose collapse he is living—like the observation in *Nord*: "in a moment you'll see [. . .] the National Socialist mystique! the murderers become commanders!" (N 691/423)[28]— coexist with outbursts like "the real hatred of the Germans, I might say in passing, was directed against the 'collaborators' . . . not so much against the Jews" (C 108/131);[29] or "the Chinks, the genuine Chinese, the hardcore, the ones that are going to occupy France [. . .] and there's more coming! lots more across the steppes . . . hordes and hordes! [. . .] the big thing is their blood! . . . it's only the blood that counts! they've got the 'dominant blood'" (R 926/260).[30] The tone of all these passages is so bizarre that they are impossible to make sense of except as either lunatic self-parody, sheer delirium, or perhaps most unsettling, as both at the same time. But if they are morally and tonally unfathomable, such pronouncements are also ideologically unstable enough to make evident how marginal Céline's racist fanaticism would be in any organized political movement.[31]

In *D'un château l'autre* Céline's description of the bickering, rank-and-privilege–obsessed egomaniacs in Sigmaringen makes ludicrous the main self-justification of the Vichy dictatorship. The principal claim of the French Right was that only some form of absolutism could do away with the internecine feuds, inefficiency, and political corruption of the Third Republic. Yet Céline shows us that all of these vices marked the Collaborationist crowd at least as much as the Parliamentarians they replaced. Moreover, every detail of life in Sigmaringen reveals the self-deception in which the Vichy leadership indulged. Their whole situation was grotesquely ironic since, as one historian puts it, they had insisted "so often and stridently that Gaullists were mere tools of foreigners," but by 1944 they themselves had "become the most hapless hangers-on of an enemy power they could not or dared not quit."[32] Céline makes their dependence on the whims of their German masters abundantly clear and is unsparing in his sarcasm at the pretensions of the Sigmaringen leadership to anything but a parody of real authority.

In literature, the closest precedent for Sigmaringen would be Kafka's *Schloss*, which also appears so grand from the outside but turns out to be populated by petty tyrants and frantic bureaucrats. Even the bizarre relationship between the officials of the *Schloss* and the Land Surveyor K. is remarkably similar to that between Céline and the officials of "his" Castle. Everything about Sigmaringen is fraudulent, but the fiction tries to persuade itself of its own reality by a pathetic insistence on ritual and hierarchy. Most of the characters in Sigmaringen vary only in the degree of their refusal to recognize how doomed they actually are. In this refusal, Collaborators like Alphonse de Chauteaubriant, who dream of hiding in an inaccessible Tyrolian valley to perfect "a bomb of concentration! of faith [. . .] a stupendous moral bomb," are matched by Germans like Otto Abetz, who spend their time making plans for a "super-colossal bronze statue of Charlemagne [. . .] Charlemagne and his valiant knights . . . [with] Goebbels as Roland" to be placed "at the end of the Avenue de la Défense" as a sign of a renewed and victorious Franco-German alliance (*C* 228–31/267–69).[33]

Whether his contempt is turned on the Collabos, the Nazis, the Jews, the Gaullists, or the "Resisters of 1945," the transitions in Céline's tone are so rapid and his language so inventively self-lacerating that it is hard to know how to respond, except to read it as simultaneously a dark farce and the outraged cry of an *un*licensed clown who wanted to be a prophet, failed miserably, and paid too high a price for the attempt. If, as I will argue later, to whitewash his incitements to hatred is thinkable only for a literary intellectual with the characteristic *déformation* of the profession, it is equally true that Céline's dazzling rhetorical leaps try to make us feel that there is something clumsily pedestrian in our expressions of moral outrage. Like *Moi* with Jean-François Rameau, we are simply too entertained to react to Céline's utterances with our normal defenses. Céline often uses the brilliance of his prose and his ready self-mockery to disarm the hostile reader in an approach remarkably similar to what Walter Benjamin described as the Fascist *culte de la blague*, the "joke" that served as a barely disguised means of propagating otherwise unmentionable themes.[34]

But when *D'un château l'autre* was published, few of the old Vichy survivors were amused by a *blague* aimed at them as much as at the triumphant "enemy." As a result of Céline's sarcasm, most of the veterans of the Collaboration were incensed by the novel, since it seemed to mock their "martyrs" as a gang of venal, hysterical, and squabbling politicians. Writing in the June 20, 1957 number of *Rivarol*, for example, Pierre-Antoine Cousteau blasted Céline for his cruelty in laughing at the defeated and disgraced men of Sigmaringen.[35] But Céline insisted from the outset that he found everyone equally repulsive, and the only difference he saw between the Vichy élite and their Gaullist conquerors was that defeat had made the former more circumspect. Such a view was unlikely to endear him to either side, and Céline clearly enjoyed placing himself in a position without allies or supporters. What he did insist on, in all of his works, is the worm's-eye view of history, the perspective from the mud, in which every bureaucrat, administrator, and general looks the same and from which every armed conflict is only a conspiracy of madmen to slaughter the helpless idiots who obey them. Rameau, we recall, insisted that "I am willing to be abject but not under duress."[36] But Céline makes us see that there is always more than enough duress to make one abject, that the human condition (need, fear, weakness, and mortality) and human temperament (violence and viciousness) are in essence lessons in duress. From his first writings up to and through the trilogy, Céline never shifted from his conviction that "the real iron curtain is between the rich and the down-and-outers . . . between people of equal fortune ideas don't count" (*N* 417/124–25).[37] What distinguishes both Céline and Rameau's Nephew, who voices the identical argument, from traditionally radical writers, is that the worm's-eye view has no room for the idealization of one's own kind either, no faith that a different class would behave otherwise. Only the negative, the critical judgment has a chance to be true. Thus, Céline writes in 1935 to Elie Faure that "'the people' in your sentimental sense doesn't exist. There are only exploiters and the exploited, and every one of the latter would like nothing better than to become one of the former. [. . .] The proletariat is a bourgeois who hasn't made it."[38]

Rhetorically, the equivalence of leaders from antithetical factions is illustrated at every turn. If Laval is portrayed as a grotesque and vainglorious bore, belonging roughly "between Nasser and Mendès [France]" (*C* 241/280), he is only similar to, and finally slightly less obnoxious than, his detractors and successors on the world's stage. Céline's enemies are all fundamentally in the same camp. Irrespective of their "official" political loyalties, it is their private wealth, royalty checks, or party offices that place them on the same side of the only divide that counts, the gulf between those with nothing in their bellies and those living in well-fed comfort on top of the social ladder: "ten years of misery, two of them in a cell . . . while they, Racine, Loukoum, Tartre, and Schweitzer were passing the hat one place or another, picking up the dough and the Nobel prizes! . . . enormous sums! stuffed, bloated like Goering, Churchill, Buddha! Superstuffed, plethoric commissars!" (*C* 10/9).[39]

Goering, Churchill, and Buddha are connected by the size of their bellies, a stock device of political caricature but especially plausible from someone who claims to have been starving since his days in the Passage Choiseul. But the bizarre conjunction of Racine, Gallimard [Loukoum], Jean-Paul Sartre [Tartre], and Albert Schweitzer is inspired solely by Céline's *ressentiment* at their international acclaim and economic success. What raises Céline's *ressentiment* to delirious proportions is its utter contempt for chronology: he is as capable of railing at a writer who died in

1699 as at a contemporary like Sartre. Céline's lists are among the most wildly inventive, and to my taste, at least, comic parts of the trilogy and in their verve they remind me of Joyce's lengthy catalogs in *Ulysses*. But unlike Joyce's, Céline's lists derive their energy almost entirely from jealousy, *ressentiment*, and paranoia; they are more psychologically than linguistically motivated, and what gives them an unmistakably abject note is the way they simultaneously mock and vent their own helpless envy.

In Céline's eyes, what makes all public figures ludicrous is their limitless vanity. Listen to a typical description, in which the opening phrase seems to signal the most intractable Vichy nostalgia only to be immediately and devastatingly undermined by all that follows. But the sarcasm directed at Pétain is expressly not allowed to validate the equally ridiculous pretensions of his conqueror, Charles de Gaulle:

> Say what you like . . . I can speak freely because he detested me . . . Pétain was our last King of France. "Philip the Last! . . ." the stature, the majesty, the works . . . and he believed in it . . . first as victor at Verdun . . . then, at the age of seventy and then some promoted to Sovereign! Who could have resisted? . . . A pushover! "Oh, Monsieur le Maréchal, how you incarnate France!" That incarnation jazz is magic . . . [. . .] Once Pétain incarnated France, he didn't care [. . .] you could cut his head off . . . he'd go right on incarnating [. . .] Charlot [de Gaulle] shooting Brasillach! he was in seventh heaven too! another incarnator! (*C* 124–25/149–50)[40]

Like the Germans who, according to *D'un château l'autre*, "had worked out a certain mode of existence for the French in Siegmaringen, neither absolutely fictitious nor absolutely real . . . a fictitious status, half way between quarantine and operetta" (*C* 224/262),[41] the trilogy oscillates disturbingly among genres having radically different commitments to the project of either historical verisimilitude or narrative coherence. The Abject Hero is himself fundamentally a maelstrom of mutually contradictory impulses, of wild swings among antithetical stances, and Céline's self-representation as the trilogy's Abject Hero/narrator constitutes an ingeniously economical solution to the dilemma of how to tell, within a single novel, all the divergent stories his thematic materials require. (Consider, for example, that in addition to the genres already mentioned, the trilogy also functions as a kind of modern prose epic containing both war and the fall of an empire, like the *Iliad*, and a long and arduous homecoming, or *nostos*, like the *Odyssey*. But it is an especially bitter *nostos* because for Céline, home means only further public humiliation and ignominy.)[42]

The technical decision to narrate the last days of the Collaboration from the underground perspective of an Abject Hero lets him justify, at the level of characterization and motivation, the very substance of his tale, the compulsion to speak about what everybody else wishes to forget. But unlike other works that attempt to confront the Collaboration, Céline is able to

speak from the inside with all the abjection of one of the defeated and
vilified losers. Like Rameau's exposure of the Bertin-Hus household's conspiracy against the *Encyclopédistes*, the shabbiness of the Vichy leadership
and the blindness of their self-delusions is rendered most powerfully by a
narrator who is one of their own camp. Céline's portrayal of himself as
detested by everyone and surviving without dignity or respect ("You're
despised? . . . You get used to it" [*C* 8/6]) gives his account a mordant
edge necessarily denied to the memoirs of the triumphant: "there are certain advantages in being cursed by all and sundry . . . especially, it dispenses
you with having to be agreeable to anybody . . . there's nothing more
emollient, stultifying, emasculating than the mania of wanting to be liked
. . . 'not nice!' . . . that does it, you're free!" (*N* 524/236).[43]

> Politics . . . has always been the systematic organi-
> zation of hatreds.
>   (Henry Adams, *The Education of Henry Adams*)

> We forgive the crimes of individuals, but not their
> participation in a collective crime.
>   (Marcel Proust, *Le Côté de Guermantes*)

Céline's trilogy often reads like a debased version of *Don Quixote*, and
its hungry and exhausted narrator pictures himself as the belated and
abject World War II version of Cervantes' "knight with the woeful counte-
nance," wandering across a landscape peopled by men with delusions far
crazier than his own.[44] But to the degree that the novel invokes such parallels, how can we not read everything in it as a sophisticated satire on the
phenomena it narrates, including, perhaps even primarily, the character of
the woeful narrator? Such a conclusion was, famously, the one reached by
André Gide when he described Céline's anti-Semitic pamphlet, *Bagatelles
pour un massacre*, as a parody, "une plaisanterie," satirizing standard racist
diatribes.[45]

In this context it is impossible not to reflect that unlike Don Quixote,
Céline was driven to scrambling from castle to castle, not because of his
reading, but on account of his own *writings*. The four pamphlets he wrote
between 1936 and 1941 (*Mea culpa*, *Bagatelles pour un massacre*, *L'école des
cadavres*, and *Les beaux draps*), but especially *Bagatelles pour un massacre*
and *L'école des cadavres*, made him a prime target for assassination or summary execution in the turbulent atmosphere of 1945–46. The pamphlets
have also, and rightly in my judgment, continued to haunt any engagement
with his work that seeks to sidestep a confrontation with them.

To understand the strategy of that sidestepping, it may help to think in
terms of a third fantasy, different again from the two versions of a lost
governorship with which this chapter began. This fantasy is not taken from

a novel, but is played out in the pages of one of Céline's most distinguished French advocates, Julia Kristeva, in her *Les Pouvoirs de l'horreur*. Kristeva writes with passion of Céline's stylistic virtuosity, of his novels' radical openness to the forces of textual dispersion and the disruptions of bodily excesses that French literature is supposed to have repressed since Rabelais. Then, at a pivotal moment in the argument, she asks a question that crystallizes an entire way of thinking about, or, in this case, avoiding thinking about, the enormous difficulties of finding terms within which to frame a convincing account of Céline: "Do not all attempts, in our own cultural sphere at least, at escaping from the Judeo-Christian compound by means of a unilateral call to return to what it has repressed (rhythm, drive, the feminine, etc.), converge on the same Célinian anti-Semitic fantasy?"[46] The most direct response is a simple "no," and, should a qualification be felt necessary, there is the clear counter-example of Joyce, whose texts satisfy most of Kristeva's desiderata even better than Céline's, but who remained not only untouched by, but programmatically opposed to, the *ressentiment* and racism on which Céline's prose draws.

But Kristeva's question also encapsulates a particular moment in the history of Céline's reception, a collective fantasy we might call the *"Tel Quel* Céline," in which the Fascist is, by a curious inversion, revealed as a liberator because of his *virtù* as a technician of language and the unconscious. Roland Barthes, for example, writing in the same tradition, can dismiss the whole issue of Céline's racist politics with a benign *obiter dictum*: "He made a mistake only because he looked at reality with a literary gaze. He transformed reality with his language."[47] No doubt the second sentence is true, although it is equally pertinent to every important writer and tells us nothing specific about Céline. The first sentence, though, strikes me as remarkable in its blithe disregard of anything that might legitimately make one view Céline's "mistake" as of more than trivial concern. The real transformation in both Barthes's and Kristeva's accounts seems to be less Céline's literary artistry than the critics' confidence in their power to effect his metamorphosis. What is strange is that anyone would wish to transform into so respectable and even anodyne a figure, a writer who derives much of his energy from his resistance to all such pieties, whose novels boast that "I live more on hatred than on noodles . . . but genuine hatred . . . no cheap imitation" (*C* 92/111).[48] Criticism of the *Tel Quel* sort tries to offer Céline a transformation even more bizarre than the one Laval promised him at Sigmaringen, but this time the donors did not have to pay quite so dear a price themselves.

There is a powerful current in Céline studies that seems to regard Fascism as fundamentally no more than a matter of literary style, not politics, or more accurately, as the apotheosis of politics-as-style. As such, it is rapidly retranslated into a subset of intellectual and aesthetic fashion, at which point Fascism's seductive glamor can be yielded to with a dismissal of the dully censorious bourgeois moralities that might be troubled by such a move. Yet as historians of the 1930s forcefully remind us, it was precisely as a question of style that Fascism first presented itself for consumption to the French intelligentsia who later provided the principal ideological underpinnings for the politics of Collaboration.

Any attempt to "aestheticize" Céline, to treat all of his writings as phantasmagoric/visionary texts with no relationship to, or influence on, the history of their era, seems to me profoundly irresponsible to *both* realms, that of writing as well as that of communal and public social existence. Ultimately, I am convinced, it is far less demeaning to condemn an author for his worst errors than to remove from him the capacity to err.[49] The consequences of reading the pamphlets in a moral vacuum are clearly audible in phrases like this one from Nicolas Hewitt's *The Golden Age of Louis-Ferdinand Céline*: consideration of these texts, Hewitt writes, "has often been unduly confused by partisan political considerations."[50] To be appalled by Céline's pamphlets is certainly a "partisan" position, but I am unable to long for a response to texts like *Bagatelles pour un massacre* and *L'école des cadavres* that would do away with all partisanship. Beyond a certain point, "impartiality" is just a professionally cultivated moral obtuseness that risks deadening any capacity to register the power of words. That Céline himself would have mocked such academic piety, and that all his writings aim precisely at shaking their readers out of their cultivated impartiality, only makes its invocation in this context all the more misconceived.

But if I see no grounds either to ignore or to aestheticize away the viciousness of works like *Bagatelles pour un massacre*, I am equally unpersuaded by arguments like George Steiner's that one's judgment of the pamphlets ought to serve as a touchstone determining a humanely responsible reading of Céline's whole oeuvre.[51] Accordingly, even though any extended analysis of the pamphlets would take us beyond the focus of this book, it seems to me essential to indicate at least in brief (1) how their internal logic simultaneously fulfills, and yet in crucial ways frustrates, the conventions of their genre, and (2) how the trilogy, while drawing on many of the same linguistic resources and technical innovations as the pamphlets, deliberately differs from them in conception and strategy.

The best place to begin is with the curious fact that, as Alice Kaplan's *Relevé des sources et citations dans "Bagatelles pour un massacre"* has documented, virtually every significant claim, pseudo-historical description, and cluster of associations in the pamphlet is cribbed, usually with no effort at any kind of transformation, from the numerous readily available anti-Semitic tracts Céline consulted.[52] What is curious about this is not Céline's practice but its unexpected consequence. The haphazard stringing together of citations from sources that themselves are mostly a hodgepodge of barely reworked commonplaces like the *Protocols of the Elders of Zion*,[53] results in a final text that is unmistakably Célinian. For all the plagiarisms Kaplan traces, no reader is likely to confuse *Bagatelles pour un massacre* or *L'école des cadavres* with the countless similar writings in circulation at the time. This is a matter of both their language and ideological position, in neither of which, for all his specific borrowings, Céline had much to learn from—or, equally important, to teach to—other propagandists.

But if it is true that none of the Vichy Collaborators or Nazi officials needed to learn their racism from Céline or required his assistance to implement their policies, the events of the Collaboration were sufficiently grim to make untenable the usual critical alibis, such as the "unreliable narrator," the persona of a delirious satirist, etc. (Imagine, for instance, reading Juvenal in a murderously homophobic and misogynist society, or Swift in a community of cannibals with gourmet aspirations, and it immediately becomes apparent that social context, not just the internal signals of the text, determines the way satiric invective is taken up by the reader.)

Considered purely as writing, there is no doubt that Céline's distinct technique, developed since *Mort à crédit*, of building paragraphs and even whole episodes through emotional associations and explosive outbursts, and establishing a narrative voice that unleashes its story as a metonymic catalog motivated by *ressentiment* was ideally suited, at the strictly *formal* as well as at the psychological level, to the demands of a species of writing like the racist pamphlets, constituted as these are by an itemization of the multifarious sins of one's enemies. A novel like *Mort à crédit* may not endorse any anti-Semitic views, and in the figure of Auguste, Ferdinand's pathetic father, it may even satirize such impulses,[54] but it creates both a rhetoric and a narrative structure that required only an intensification of its technically most distinctive devices to be ideally serviceable for the quite different ends of a racist call-to-arms. The pamphlets are a laboratory of stylistic combinations in which Céline tested and worked out many of the touches that led him from the prose of *Mort à crédit* to the more idiosyncratic syncopations of the trilogy: the increased emphasis on an explicitly antagonistic dialogue between narrator and reader, the dependence on metonymy for a blackly comic discursive hysteria, an increasingly private but readily comprehensible slang, and the invention of a whole series of onomatopoeic words and phrases to indicate both the narrator's state of mind and the way he registers phenomena from the outside world.[55]

But strictly stylistic analyses of the pamphlets are bound to seem intolerably skewed because the racist content of these works so clearly motivates their energy. In rhetoric, organization, and incorporated citations, *Bagatelles pour un massacre* and *L'école des cadavres* shrilly summon the whole nation to purge itself of its insidious Jewish infestation before it is too late. Although critics, who often seem to regard it as their chief task to plead like defense attorneys for their favorite author,[56] regularly note that, strictly speaking, the subject of the titles *Bagatelles pour un massacre* and *L'école des cadavres* is in the first case Céline himself and in the second France as a whole, that it is Céline who expects to be massacred for speaking the truth, and his country that will become a school of corpses if it allows the Jews to drive it into war against Germany, readers like H. E. Kaminsky in 1938, or George Steiner today, are deeply right, even if formally in error, when they label these books "reiterated calls to mass murder."[57]

But the very fact that a certain ambiguity can be generated by the titles of racist pamphlets, a sub-genre notoriously resistant to any form of uncertainty, points to a paradox at the core of Céline's long journey to the end of *ressentiment*. I do not know any writer with a greater flair for memorable titles, from *Voyage au bout de la nuit* and *Mort à crédit*, to, in their own macabre way, *Bagatelles pour un massacre* and *L'école des cadavres*, coinings which are, if nothing else, intensely evocative. But with all their admiration for Céline's linguistic verve, even such committed anti-Semites as Brasillach, Rebatet and the *Je suis partout* editorial team felt hesitant about recommending either text without considerable qualifications.[58] Part of their hesitation was due, as I have already indicated, to Céline's scorn of the entirety of the French right-wing leadership, from Pétain to Charles Maurras. But the degree of his contempt is astonishing even by Céline's habitually high standards. For example, in *L'école des cadavres*, Céline committed the outrageous provocation of linking "le latinisme" of Maurras with the Jewish style that had corrupted and weakened France. Not only does Céline call Maurras's theories "academic narcissism" and his personality that of a "furious schoolboy,"[59] but he goes so far as to wonder about the sincerity of Maurras's anti-Semitism and the racial "purity" of his style.[60] Pétain is treated even worse than Maurras. Céline has him speak in a grotesque Mitteleuropa accent supposedly characteristic of Jewish immigrants ("moi, Bedain! [. . .] Pour la Badrie des cadavres!") and unmasks him as a vainglorious butcher who, concerned only to benefit his Jewish masters, has nothing to offer France except another slaughter even bloodier than the one at Verdun where his reputation was made.[61] Considering that the Marshal was named virtual savior/dictator of France not long after such passages went into print, it is scarcely surprising that he was inclined to ban Céline's next polemical work, *Les beaux draps*, and that Céline, for his part, felt entitled to claim that he and Pétain despised each other.

Céline's hyperbole was simply too ideologically unanchored and politically unreliable for anyone to make use of, except by carefully editing out large portions of the text, and it is hard to see whom Céline hoped to reach, let alone persuade, by the cascade of vituperation that constitutes the pamphlets. In a fascinating interview with Patrick Modiano, Emmanuel Berl remembered the Céline of the 1930s as so bizarre he could never fit the mold of a dutiful propagandist:

> Céline said that anyone who had been to a lycée was, by that fact alone, already a Jew. For him, the archetypal Jew was Mallarmé and Racine. . . . He [Céline] is very violent [on the subject], but one is no longer very certain against what since, ultimately, a Jew was whoever didn't talk *argot*: the entire intelligentsia, etc. . . . He was more or less the only one left who wasn't a Jew.[62]

Céline's fantasy of being the sole remaining non-Jew does nothing to excuse his provocations to murder, and indeed is itself a hysterical intensification of the very fear that underlies traditional anti-Semitism—the anxiety that the Jews are powerful enough to infect the whole population. But unlike other such articulations, this kind of racist hysteria is, in Rebatet's words, too "delirious," to fit into any organized program. Perhaps the way to illustrate this point most economically is to look at a single, characteristic moment in *Bagatelles pour un massacre*.

After rehearsing countless times the stock clichés of the Jew as lascivious erotomaniac intent on violating every Aryan available,[63] Céline, as though in despair of ever triumphing over so sinister and ubiquitous a foe, suddenly wonders why he should even bother fighting the natural tendency of the French, which, he insists, is to delight in offering themselves to be sodomized by the potent phalloi of their conquerors. His countrymen have always rejoiced in being sexually used, first by the Etruscans and Romans, then by the Moors, and now by the Jews, until these too will yield their dominance to the even more potent Kirghiz and Mongol hordes.[64]

In the course of my research I have read a demoralizing number of racist tracts, but I have never come across one in which the group whom the author is trying to warn, and to which he himself belongs, is described in anything like these terms. The portrait of France as a nation of eager sexual slaves longing to be ravished by foreign penises is unlikely to have offered much in the way of useful propaganda to Pétain or the Collaborationist ideologues. In other anti-Semitic tracts, a healthy virility is attributed exclusively to the Aryans, while the Jews are portrayed, with no anxiety about the internal contradictions of the description, as simultaneously effeminate, homosexual, and driven by a desperate frenzy to rape females of other races. In *Bagatelles pour un massacre*, though, Céline completely reverses the stereotypes, and it is the French, of both sexes, who are described as passively opening themselves up for their sexual masters, ultimately welcoming even the Asian legions because their sexual demands are still more intense and brutal than those of the Jews.[65]

Even if, at other moments, Céline reverted to the more conventional dichotomies of racist propaganda, and asserted that any Aryan, no matter how degenerate, alcohol-besotted, or congenitally stupid, is worth more than a million Einsteins,[66] he immediately enumerated all the ways in which Aryan degeneracy manifested itself. The pamphlets are astonishingly dialogic, and in a strategy typical of Dostoevsky as well as Céline, but quite unlike conventional polemics, the various interlocutors/opponents are given adequate space to attack the narrator with a rhetorical vehemence and verbal inventiveness equal to his own. At several points Céline is directly accused of sounding and acting very much like a Jew himself and comes close to admitting the justice of the accusation[67] —a premise that would lead to the grotesque conclusion that since *no one* is left uncontaminated, the anti-Semitic warning of the pamphlets must be addressed to a completely Jewish world, the original writer-audience of one having himself finally gone over to the other side.

Although racism has a multiplicity of causes and internal rationalizations, and any single account is bound to be reductive, Céline's anti-Semitism is in noticeable measure a highly charged case of projective class and family *ressentiment*. His writings rage at the wretched existence of the petty bourgeoisie into which he was born. Their situation is permanently hopeless, but never hopeless enough to make them change their lives because they retain the illusion that still harder work, still stricter conformity to bourgeois values will "save" them from the shame of poverty. Hence, even if their existence is lived with a continual fear of bankruptcy and proletarianization, their complete identification with the mores of middle-class life makes affiliation with working-class, let alone revolutionary, political movements unthinkable. Céline's petty bourgeoisie has no real stature or dignity to lose—even *they* don't want to be who they are. In *Mort à crédit* we see how their presence "stank up the countryside," polluting nature as thoroughly and revoltingly as they do the city.[68] Initially, Céline describes the petty bourgeoisie as feeling themselves little more than contaminators of the world around them. But once he accepts the explanatory consolation of anti-Semitism, he has the partial vindication of knowing that though his class is made up of contaminated "stinkers," this is only because Others (the Jews, Freemasons, etc.) have succeeded in contaminating them first.[69] Even though he attributes these failures and humiliations to the maleficent powers of the Jews (and just as often Céline says that the repulsiveness of his own class, as indeed of all peoples, is innate), he never promises that eliminating the Jewish perpetrators will increase the dignity of petty bourgeois life. Céline is in the ideal position to take on the role of Abject Hero since he experiences his whole class and social world as irremediably abject. The problem with his racism is that there simply is no one on "his" side who possesses any compensatory virtues to balance the Jewish vices, so that the only reason for his struggle against the Jews is that, not being one of them, he will never be able to benefit from their monopoly of wealth and power.

Céline had the idea of a catastrophic Jewish menace fixed firmly in his consciousness. What he completely lacked was any corresponding sense of an Aryan "master race" destined to rule after the Jews had been eliminated. In Thomas Pynchon's rhetoric, Céline has an acutely developed "They-system" but lacks the matching "We-system" that every "creative" paranoid requires.[70] From Céline's perspective, though, such faith in a "We-system" is less a sign of creativity than of sentimentality, and it is an illusion by which he remains entirely untempted. His "racial brothers," he never hesitates to point out, regularly reveal themselves to be far more abject ("cent mille fois plus abjects") than the Jews—especially in the ways they have treated him![71] But because there is no "We," no group, race, or class for whom he has the slightest regard, victory is a nonsensical concept. Unlike most other polemicists, he provides no image of what the world would be like once the perceived evil had been overcome, nor does he show any particular pleasure when "his side" actually seems to be winning.

The absence of any feeling of solidarity with the "positive" hopes of the Collaboration enabled Céline to make the strategic shift from the pamphlets to the trilogy without, on the one hand, seeming to discard his earlier convictions out of expediency, or, on the other, finding himself permanently trapped in the role of Vichy apologist. Since the Pétainist slogan "Fatherland, Family, Labor" had even less appeal for Céline than the old republican "Liberty, Equality, Fraternity" that it was intended to replace, and since the only thing he admitted sharing with the other survivors of the Collaboration was the sense of victimization that had always been his literary stock-in-trade, Céline was prepared to exploit his experiences in the last months of the war in a way that acknowledged the pamphlets but avoided repeating their (by then even for Céline) too dangerous racist incitements.

> They had taken the most extraordinary pains to be
> the kind of people who *deserve* their ruin. . . . Scene
> upon scene, written on the run, in frantic haste—
> each ended in catastrophe, and immediately after it
> there began a new scene, enacted among different
> people and having nothing in common with those
> that preceded it but the *deserved* catastrophe with
> which they all ended.
>
>   (Elias Canetti, *The Play of the Eyes*)

Céline himself prepared the ground for the collective fantasy of his aestheticizing admirers. In the immediate post-War years, he sought above all to project the image of a pure technician of language. He enjoyed comparing himself to Cervantes, who also wrote his masterpiece after a stretch in prison, old and bankrupt (as early as 1955 Céline wrote to Gallimard asking to be included in the Pléiade volumes "entre Bergson et Cervantes"), and devoted an extraordinary effort to putting into circulation the legend of a craftsman of prose, working his three dots like his mother had worked her lace or the Impressionists had applied their local color, all equally indifferent to issues of content.[72] But he also counted on the certainty that no French reader of a novel published in 1957 about life in Sigmaringen—and written by a notorious ex-Collaborator—with a cast of characters that includes Pétain, Laval, and most of the other principal Vichy leaders, was going to ignore the book's thematic concerns.

Far from representing some implausible exercise in pure style, *D'un château l'autre* was precisely calculated to thrust Céline back into literary prominence. After trying to "lie low" for several years, Céline deliberately sought a scandal in order to get publicity for his new book.[73] For someone who genuinely loathed the literary world, Céline orchestrated the reception of his novel with great effort, giving at least eleven interviews or public statements to whet the public's curiosity between the start of June and the end of October 1957, when the novel appeared in print.[74] When *D'un château l'autre* was already in published, Céline kept offering wildly provocative public pronouncements, even going so far as to defend *Bagatelles pour une massacre* and *L'école des cadavres*.

Throughout the mid-1950s, Céline played a strange cat-and-mouse game, in which he repeatedly stressed that he was purely a stylist, that, like Cézanne, it is his "technique" alone that matters, not his subject. But he deliberately wrote about an episode in recent history that he knew would fascinate, enrage, and disgust all of his contemporaries exactly because of its subject.[75] In post-War France, it was decidedly not sexuality nor the pleasures of the body, depicted in all its carnivalesque excesses and excretions, that the culture repressed. But what *was* unmentionable, almost to the point of being a national taboo, was that most of the country had hailed Pétain as its savior after the disasters of 1940, had enthusiastically endorsed the Vichy regime for as long as it seemed to have any chance to survive, and had lent its (largely passive) support to the Resistance only after an Allied victory was certain. In *D'un château l'autre*, the Castle and its village function as a kind of microcosm of France itself, a France with which the contemporary readership has a significant stake in denying any link. By publishing *D'un château l'autre* Céline thrust before the unwilling eyes of the French nation a vivid chronicle of an era and regime no one wanted to see recalled. Like some sardonic return of the repressed, his novels compel readers to recognize and respond to a profoundly unwelcome version of their own history.

Since the trilogy is Céline's attempt to write an "Apocalypse à crédit," surpassing in sweep and intensity the familial and class savagery of *Mort à crédit*, the context in which the work was accomplished represented a fertile conjunction of problem and opportunity. The national amnesia surrounding the Collaboration matched, and largely motivated, the virtually total silencing of Céline by the literary establishment in the post-War period. His politics before and during the Occupation, the legal banning of his pamphlets, and the relative critical and commercial failure of *Guignol's Band* and *Féerie pour une autre fois* left Céline as expelled from the consciousness of the French world of letters as the Vichy era was from reflections on contemporary politics. Both seemed to belong to another and entirely unlamented age, so that in writing about the *temps maudits* of Sigmaringen, Céline, the literally and legally proscribed *poète maudit* of the Collaboration, had come upon the precise formal correlative to his own position. Since everyone else insisted that they were not implicated in the humiliations of the Collaboration, Céline was able to thrust himself forward as the sole authentic voice of that disgrace, the only witness who had not been intimidated or suborned into accepting the pieties of the post-War French social contract.

In the trilogy, Céline's paranoia, his need for an audience to shock and seduce, as well as his shrewd sense of literary strategy, all coalesce for perhaps the first time since *Voyage au bout de la nuit* to shape and give energy to his work. The crucial decision from which the whole of the trilogy proceeds was to abandon the role of unacknowledged national prophet, which had dominated the pamphlets, for the accents of a helplessly skeptical observer caught up in a calamity too senseless to be grasped by any individual. Céline insists that the ordinary Collabos in the town of Sigmaringen, unlike the ex-Ministers living in relative luxury in the Castle itself or the pampered heroes of the contemporary literary scene (whether left-wing like Sartre or conservative like Mauriac) were "all really serious intellectuals! . . . not the gratuitous, verbal kind . . . but ready to pay and paying . . . with Article 75 [a death sentence for treason] on their ass! . . . real lamppost fodder . . . flawless intellectuals . . . dying of hunger, cold, and scabies" (C 105/127).[76] This momentary sense of solidarity, even if it is marked by his usual sarcasm, is astonishing for its rarity. Usually Céline is at pains to emphasize the difference in quality and kind of his own suffering from anyone else's, going so far as to voice annoyance at the sympathy the right wing felt for the executed Robert Brasillach and the rest of the world for Anne Frank, because the attention paid to either might detract from his own claims to an exemplary martyrdom.

In *Féerie pour une autre fois*, Céline had fantasized that an inspired/delirious artist was able to call down a conflagration of bombs on Paris through a kind of sympathetic magic with the forces of destruction. But in the trilogy he emphasizes his complete helplessness before events. By taking on the role of passive and confused subject of forces beyond his comprehension or control, Céline rejoins a great tradition of war novels like *La Char-treuse de Parme*, *War and Peace*, and his own *Voyage au bout de la nuit*, in which the chaos of any individual's experience of war is a central theme. The trilogy tries to undermine all the larger teleologies of narration through which war and human history have been made comprehensible, including, most problematically, any moral distinction between the opposing sides in the conflict.

What swerves away from the classic Stendhalian or Tolstoyan vision, is the paranoid vanity by which Céline imagines everything that happens as simultaneously random and directed explicitly and malevolently against him. The acknowledgment of a certain fraternal sympathy for a group of freezing and wretched Collabos huddled together almost immediately dissolves into an account of the closing months of the War as a series of catastrophes whose principal, if not only, important victims are Céline and his travelling companions. But whenever the intensity of that egotism becomes unbearably suffocating, Céline is cunning enough to argue that (1) anyone trying to survive will feel much the same way, although later, once they have reached safety, they may well deny that feeling, and (2) his daily life as a spectacularly unsuccessful doctor in Meudon is so entirely an extension of his marginal existence in Sigmaringen that he has a valid claim to take his experiences as singularly blighted.

The trilogy is undoubtedly intended as an elaborate *apologia pro vita sua*, but the terms of that *apologia* are peculiar in the extreme, since they involve constantly infuriating, rather than pacifying, his accusers. The productive tension of the novels makes itself felt through his contradictory aims: on the one hand, Céline's need to present himself as a misunderstood and helpless victim, and on the other, his desire to flaunt his most unspeakable notions. While Céline the apologist seeks to excuse and minimize, Céline the writer, eager to keep his audience engrossed, if only with the bait of their own curiosity, tries by every means to remind his readers just how monstrous many of his opinions really are.

In the narrative present of the mid-1950s, in which most of the trilogy is actually set, Céline describes himself as the only Collabo-victim left, hated by everyone and betrayed by even his old Vichy acquaintances. Céline willingly accepts—indeed goes out of his way to create—the circumstances in which he can assume the role of universal scapegoat. But his way of expressing his predicament is so extravagant that it encourages a mock-tragic reading in which his own words are no more reliable than anyone else's. He insists, for example, that the one thing now uniting all Frenchmen, irrespective of their roles during the ideological battles from the 1930s to the 1950s, is a common loathing for, and desire to injure, Louis-Ferdinand Céline: "the little triumph of my existence, my tour de force, is getting them all . . . right, left, center, sacristies and lodges, cells and charnel houses [. . .] to agree that I'm the foremost living stinker!" (*N* 619/ 344)[77] But he goes still further and insists that even *during* the War he already was hated by all the different sides simultaneously—Collaborators, Nazis, and Gaullists alike—and provided, through his very detestability, a kind of negative rallying point for the whole nation: "I can be proud of having created throughout the most divisive period in French history the absolute unanimity of all Frenchmen on at least one subject: the need to murder me."[78] Ejected and rejected by everyone, Céline becomes the entirely abject—indeed, the national abject—who inspires the most violent reactions, akin to retching, in the population as a whole.

Everything about his story makes clear how simultaneously abject and self-congratulatory, wretched and proud of his achievements, the narrator really is. Céline is convinced that the constellation of his qualities and experiences gives him a unique authority to tell the "underground" version of the events he witnessed.[79] Abjection cuts across the conventional tonal choices of an *apologia* since it precludes real repentance just as much as it does genuine defiance. But equally pertinent, abjection is the most fitting correlative to the fundamental logic and daily practice of Vichy collaboration with the Nazi conquerors. In chapter 1, I said that the essence of abjection is to occupy the logically impossible space created by the intersection of the satanic and the servile, and this role is the most succinct description I can imagine both of the tone created by the Célinian narrator and the mentality of the Pétainist government, whether lodged in comfort in Vichy or in terror in Sigmaringen.

Céline, like the Underground Man, goes out of his way to outrage the reader—to outrage *any* imaginable reader—and yet, again like the Underground Man, he is cunning enough to present his worm's-eye view of events as more humanly true than those told from any other perspective. Even at the most basic, physiological level, Céline insists upon the truth of the "view from below," the sight, beyond shame or pride, of elemental human weaknesses and fears. Consider, for example, how often in *D'un château l'autre* Céline is called upon to perform a prostate examination, especially upon various German officials, and how his patients often break down and weep afterward, as though the probe into their anus had brought them close to a kind of bedrock, undisguised "honesty" beneath the pretensions everyone normally assumes. The body's weaknesses and pain are indifferent to ideology or decorum, and the carnivalesque body we see in Céline's fiction is more often racked by misery than transfigured by any ecstatic *jouissance*. (Consider, too, how nearly all of Céline's patients, from *Voyage au bout de la nuit* to the trilogy, are described as chronically and incurably ill from cancer, old age, or internal hemorrhaging.) Céline claims to narrate the shameful secrets and embarrassing scenes that implicate his whole generation, without having been bought and paid off by the privileged (whether of the Right or Left), whose possessions now include the collective memory of the nation.[80] Like a modern, more desperate version of Rameau's Nephew, Céline enacts a frantic struggle to survive amidst the hazards of extreme poverty, the contempt of everyone around him, and the constant risk of a physical collapse into hysteria and temporary unconsciousness.

What the Collaboration did for Céline, or better, its function in the trilogy, is to let him first assume, and then try to shake off, the monster's role. The Collaboration is a theme shocking enough to goad the reader into a Saturnalian dialogue with any narrator who would defend it. Céline, though, adopts the worm's-eye view not merely to justify himself and his politico-racial theories but also to indict the cruelty of war. The "perspective from below" thus has two contradictory purposes. On the one hand, it is intended to sustain a morally repellent *apologia* for Vichy and for Céline's own pro-Nazi pamphlets. On the other hand, his rage against the carnage of the war recapitulates the whole literary tradition of the voice from underground as privileged truth-teller, echoing motifs from contexts as diverse as Rameau's cry of "vanity" at the prospect of dying for one's country, and Shakespeare's Thersites, railing against Greeks and Trojans in *Troilus and Cressida*. I know how unpalatable a notion this may be, but I think that the logic of abjection could only continue to function powerfully in the shadow of a kind of monstrous collective crime with which the Abject Hero is associated but for which he is not directly responsible. To mobilize our sympathy for the fate of a racist Collaborator, to have us follow his journey into disgrace with the kind of attentive concern that a first-person narrative virtually compels—especially when it is able to make us laugh at the narrator's tonal pyrotechnics—is the ultimate test of the Saturnalian dialogue's capacity to mobilize our identificatory sympathy with a pariah. Only with the stakes raised so high could both participants in the Saturnalian dialogue be thrust back into their conventional stances in spite of their mutual revulsion at the element of repetition and exhaustion in the whole topos.

Céline's insistence on describing himself as simultaneously the monster and the martyred victim, although characteristic of his voice from the beginning, is, as he fully knew, unlikely to evoke the same kind of compassion in a book about the Collaboration as it did in *Voyage au bout de la nuit*'s descriptions of the First World War. It is not only that Céline really wants to be pitied—although he does wish this as well—but that he can now exploit the reader's indignation at his desire for pity in order to maintain the dialogue on which the novel depends. Céline has so inextricably intertwined the roles of wise fool and provocateur, monster and disenfranchised victim of hypocrisy, that one's responses change, page by page, sometimes even phrase by phrase, without the text ever letting one reach a settled judgment. Racist diatribes jostle against a melancholy nostalgia for the quais, riverside restaurants, and silent screen stars of his childhood, and these in turn are part of a fabric that speaks so deeply and with such conviction about the futility and horror of all wars that the ordinary categories of evaluation and reaction are constantly disturbed. Or, to put it in terms of its literary effect, our attention is constantly kept alert to the shocks that it will have to confront next.

> One needs to be more than a little bit dead to be
> truly droll!
>   (Louis-Ferdinand Céline, *Entretiens avec le*
>   *Professeur Υ*)

A concise way to bring into a single focus the issues we have discussed separately thus far is to ask a different and more conventional question of the trilogy: why is the chronology of Céline's war-time experiences narrated in so skewed an order? Céline's actual experiences in Germany occurred in the following sequence: the events in *Nord*, then those of the first part of *Rigodon*, followed by those of *D'un château l'autre*, and finally by those in the second half of *Rigodon*.[81] Undoubtedly, to observe a strictly chronological sequence would imply a greater comprehensibility and coherence than Céline wishes to claim. The scrambled narration thus mimes the confusion of the characters and denies any totalizing vantage point. Moreover, the order in which events occur to the narrator in the novels' present time dictates the order in which the past is recounted. In a formal sense, all of the books are set in the narrative present. But posed as a structural, not a psychological, issue, the question becomes: why decide to make the months at Sigmaringen (November 1944 to March 1945) the center of his first novel about the Collaboration and the fall of Germany? Four answers suggest themselves, each of which shows how calculated a venture *D'un château l'autre* really was. (1) Sigmaringen is the most concentrated of all the well-known places Céline passed through; the story of his stay there has an almost classical spatial and temporal unity. (2) The initial emphasis on a single, historically infamous setting, rather than on his random wanderings, establishes the trilogy more as a darkly comic tragedy than a picaresque tale. (3) By using the Sigmaringen episode as the center of his narrative, Céline could write new books going forward and backward in time from a single fixed point; however many novels he might write about the last months of the war, the cycle would be guaranteed a structural unity beyond the merely biographical. (4) The failure of *Féerie pour une autre fois* made Céline try for something especially shocking to regain an audience. Sigmaringen could do this in a way the farm of *Nord* or the train rides of *Rigodon* could not: it is the ideally provocative setting to inaugurate the trilogy because it can feature characters like Pétain, Laval, etc., about whom readers already had strong opinions.

The shocks Céline inflicts on his reader are a kind of parallel to, or revenge for, the shocks of his own experiences, from the childhood beatings described in *Mort à crédit* to the violent uprooting of people, earth, and entire cities under the saturation bombing that is heard as a menacing background rumble throughout the trilogy. Since *Rigodon*'s plot consists largely of chaotic train rides across Germany in the last days of the war, its description of a mountain of refuse and bricks, on top of which a giant locomotive has been catapulted by the force of a colossal explosion, so that the locomotive now squats upside down like some enormous metallic insect, is a particularly powerful visualization of the wreckage that Europe has become (*R* 833/151). But this is only one of a series of cinematic set pieces, matched in intensity by the description of the napalm burning of the Kiel shipyards and the total obliteration of Hamburg.[82] But for all their undeniable power as scenes of havoc transformed into a kind of poisonous beauty, the element of constant shock in Céline is predicated less on events than on attitudes and tones, and more specifically, on the unpredictable alternations of hostility and flattery, of sneering contempt and pathetic pleading, with which Céline assaults the reader.[83]

Still more than *Le Neveu de Rameau* or *Notes from Underground*, but continuing their literary tradition, Céline's works are entirely dialogic. In all three, the dialogism is experienced as pure rage, as the most abject of all dependencies and the most degrading of all entrapments. The anger and desperation in Céline's dialogues arises from a Pascalian certainty that "No one can stand anybody else's ego."[84] He echoes the *Pensée*'s "All men naturally hate one another" but extends Pascal's "The [very consciousness of a] self is loathsome" to the whole human race.[85] As though to underline the surprising connection, Céline insists that "I'm not at all unlike Pascal myself."[86] Although the mere existence of one's own ego is repugnant to others, Céline sees no alternative to making its demands the central preoccupation of one's life. Even to oneself, of course, one's ego regularly manages to seem rather repulsive, but the fundamental realization of *ressentiment*—that others are still more detestable—sets the only reliable limit to self-loathing. Yet these same others are indispensable to Céline for whatever identity still remains to him, since the categories of abject victim or monster are only imaginable from the vantage point of an outside judgment. Céline must have an interlocutor, just as Rameau needs *Moi* and the Underground Man requires the "gentlemen readers," and this subjection to a dialogic imperative is even more humiliating and impossible to evade than was his confinement in Sigmaringen.

Irrespective of his original intention in writing the racist pamphlets, by the time he composed the trilogy Céline was not trying to recruit, nor even to persuade, but simply to be "interesting," as a means of seducing the reader to pay attention to him. This is already a thoroughly abject role, but if fulfilling it required Céline to treat his own life alternately as a bitter path to the truth of human degradation and as a farcical *blague* with no significance whatsoever, then it was a price he was willing to pay—all the more so since Céline himself was essentially unable to distinguish between the two with any more certainty than his readers. Again, the best analogy is Fyodor Karamazov in Father Zosima's cell, wildly insulting everyone and goading himself to renewed fury and self-loathing with each hysterical outburst. Céline's sarcasms aim to thrust the reader into a role like that occupied by Pyotr Miüsov or the Underground Man's gentleman antagonists, prosperous "liberals" for whom a Karamazov/Céline embodies the basest level of human existence. But it is a position the reader, unlike Miüsov, tries to resist, since he has also read his Dostoevsky and knows how ignominious such a pre-scripted part inevitably becomes.

Céline's dependence on his readers is even more acute than that of his literary predecessors, and its novelistic elaboration is both more densely textured and more fully motivated. Unlike the Underground Man's Notes, for example, Céline's novel only *begins* after he has already been the subject of others' discourses—including, most significantly, the pronouncement of the court that had labeled him a traitor and a national disgrace. But the book also rings with the daily chatter of neighbors, journalists, publishers, etc., all of whom treat Céline as either a pathetic has-been or as a creature too repugnant to be allowed to continue living in Meudon at all.

These hostile voices are not merely the generic "you" of traditional dialogic opponents. In Céline's books the antagonist often has a specific habitat and name, and I know of no novels in which the Saturnalian debate is simultaneously so specific and so socially, biographically, and historically contextualized. Céline's novels echo like a carnival marketplace crammed full of shrilly competing voices, ranging from so-called "friendly" critics like Roger Nimier who tell him that he ought to give up literature for the far more lucrative art of writing comic books (*N* 507/219–21), to his publisher who keeps urging him to try to recapture the humor that made his first two novels so commercially successful, to journalists who telephone him hoping for some nasty outburst to scandalize and titillate their readers. Like many such belligerently jostling squares, it is a place that is a good deal less pleasant to inhabit than the sentimental fantasies our current populism would have us believe. Céline had no such illusions, and his description of his consciousness resembles nothing so much as an overly mobbed fairground, in which only the most intense and manic tones can keep pace with those of everyone else clamoring to be heard: "For more than twenty-two years madness has been hot on my trail. [. . .] She's tried a million raucous noises, an unbearable uproar, but I raved louder than she ever could."[87] The uproar ("vacarme") is the overflow of both his own hysteria and the madness of a world that he has watched hurl itself from Verdun to Sigmaringen, from world depressions to global conflagrations, from apocalypse to apocalypse.[88]

What is unique to the dialogism of Céline's trilogy is how thoroughly it is motivated by his material situation and how carefully Céline links the dialogic structure of his narrative to the books' thematic concerns. For example, Céline the refugee-Collaborator tries to agree with everyone who might hurt him, talks surprisingly little, and then only when forced to. He rails, rages, and attacks only with the voice of the novelist-doctor safely back home in Meudon. In both cases, the motive is survival, but it requires antithetical strategies in the last months of the War and the mid-1950s. The split creates two distinct voices: a largely passive Céline who chooses silence as his best self-defense and an active, provocative and polemical "forgotten" author who *needs* to be loudly outrageous to be heard.

If Céline, like his literary predecessors in abjection, is entirely dependent on his interlocutors/readers, and if, like all earlier Abject Heroes, that very dependence is the surest sign of his distance from the monster he both pretends to be and is regularly charged with incarnating, Céline nonetheless has found an aspect of his need for dialogue that had never been thematized before. He requires readers desperately, not only for inward, emotional/psychological reasons, but as purchasers of the only (barely) marketable commodity he has left: his words. Céline's dialogism has a degrading specificity that is at once entirely economic and completely textual. The costs of his exile, trial, and sentence have left him worse than bankrupt. He is heavily in debt to his publisher, and since his books no longer sell, he has no way to repay these advances, let alone reach any degree of financial security. Céline keeps stressing the specific hazards of being an unpublished, unpopular, and impoverished author: in the chain of circulation linking writer, publisher, and reader, Céline, the writer, unlike the other two, is the only one for whom a rupture in the chain would lead to total destitution. In a particularly effective crystallization of this motive, Céline actually pleads with his reader to go out and *buy* his novels instead of taking them out of the library or borrowing them from a friend. In *Nord* he admits his distress at *D'un château l'autre*'s relatively poor sales: he needs every penny of the paltry royalties his writings bring in. The reader's silence is thus not merely an ontological threat but a concrete and immediate economic punishment.

Like Rameau, Céline realizes he had better keep his interlocutor entertained if he hopes to eat that night, even if that requires mobilizing and pandering to his well-nourished listener's contempt. It is difficult not to be amused when one thinks how Marxist theoreticians stress the material basis of literary creation and consumption, and yet, so often their actual examples of such economic determinations seem tepidly indirect and metaphorical. A perfect instance of their argument lies readily at hand, but since it is in the work of a racist Collaborator and anti-Communist, it cannot be cited as evidence. Céline's trilogy is the most specifically materialist work of literature that I know, always acknowledging its status as a product of labor produced for sale, with the lion's share of the profits going not to the author-worker, but to the publisher-owner of the means of (re)production. All the professional/trade aspects of producing a book are explicitly—and comically—thematized in the trilogy, from discussions with his secretary, who, he tells us, hasn't really cared for any of his novels since *Voyage au bout de la nuit* (*N* 649/378), to quarrels with his copy editor who wants to regularize parts of Céline's text and thereby destroy his prose rhythm (*R* 925/259). Even his identification with Cervantes is mimicked and given explicit utterance by a rival publisher, Gertrut de Mornay, who is eager to steal Céline away from Gallimard. To Céline's protest that he is too old and ill for another masterpiece, Mornay rejoins: "'No, no, Céline . . . you're full of vigor [. . .] take Cervantes!' [. . .] eighty-one . . . Don Quixote!" As the dialogue continues it becomes clear to Céline that everything, from his own personal vanity to literary history as a whole, are mere counters in the endless quest of publishers to extract more surplus value out of their writers: "That's the dodge all publishers pull when they want to stimulate their old nags . . . they tell you Cervantes was a stripling . . . at eighty-one! 'And disabled worse than you, Céline!'" (*C* 36/40).[89]

Céline's awareness of how badly he needs readers for physical as well as psychological survival helps account for the tone of aggrieved wheedling and aggressive vituperation with which he both resists and acknowledges his dependence:

> Maybe I'm going to bore you . . . something funnier? . . . more titillating? [. . .] All I care about . . . you know that . . . is giving you a laugh [. . . .] the story of our mishaps may strike you as monotonous . . . when you have so many things to do, or just sit down with a drink at your TV . . . movie stars, grunt-and-groan, heart surgery, tits and twats, two-headed dogs [. . .] and then me coming along asking you to buy my handiwork! . . . too much to expect! (*C* 43/50; *N* 454/164)[90]

There is no place for such frustrated acknowledgments in the earlier novels, since their dialogism never became an explicit, let alone explicitly economic, concern. In this shift, the link between the trilogy's dialogism and its historical themes becomes particularly clear. It is, as he never stops reminding us, precisely for having written *Bagatelles pour un massacre* and *L'école des cadavres* that he had to flee to Sigmaringen, just ahead of "Leclerc's army [. . .] and its chop-chop Senegalese!" (*C* 106/128)[91] and that after the war he returned home as a pariah who must live on his editor's increasingly reluctant advances against ever more dubious future royalties.

The catastrophes that drove him from Sigmaringen to prison and back to Meudon (another of the many ironic meanings of "castle to castle") is the story he is compelled to tell, having exhausted both himself and his imagination simply surviving the voyage. He is also careful to present himself as too modestly conscientious a clinician, too reluctant to collect bills from his few patients, most of whom are even poorer than he, and too indifferent to social appearances to make a decent living as a doctor. The precise syncopation of the passages describing life in Meudon lets us overhear the insults aimed at Céline, as though we were watching a scene in a slapstick movie, and we can't help being won over since it is almost impossible to be judgmental about a person at the moment he is making one laugh.

> I've had at least ten garbage cans swiped [. . .] people have stopped calling me "Doctor" . . . just plain "Monsieur" . . . pretty soon they'll be calling me "you old bum!" [. . .] a doctor without a maid, without a housekeeper, without a car, who hauls his own garbage [. . .] just think it over . . . And in the meantime, while you're thinking it over, if you'd buy one or two of my books, it would be a help. (*C* 12/11)[92]

All the money from his earlier books vanished long ago, so he is really writing about Sigmaringen and the end of the Collaboration in order to make back some of the income he lost because of it. He is writing, in other words, about exactly what ruined him and in so doing compelled him to write. The continuing emphasis on the present turns the historical narrative into the direct causal explanation for his immediate circumstances, thereby both justifying the novels' existence as literary artifacts and validating Céline's sense of himself as a historical victim, able, implicitly and explicitly, to accuse his accusers. Céline enjoys playing the reluctant author, forced by circumstances to take up the task he has come to despise. He regularly announces that if it were not for his enormous debts to Gallimard he would never put another word down on paper. But his defiance is only an attempt to cloak more shameful motives under the plea of *force majeure*. No doubt the plea is valid up to a point, but poverty is far from being the trilogy's sole begetter. It does, however, serve to remind us how often the carnivalesque is triggered not by an outpouring of abundance but, on the contrary, by the most pressing of wants.

> Why do I write? I'll tell you: to make the others
> unreadable."
>   (Louis-Ferdinand Céline, "Interview with
>   Pierre Audinet")

Jean-François Rameau admits how haunted he feels by his predecessors, how tormenting is the knowledge that he can never equal their accomplishments. But in Céline the torment is, if anything, still greater, even though it is rarely acknowledged. For the most part, Céline criticism has taken at face value his pronouncements of indifference to the work of all but a few earlier novelists—most of whom, like Henri Barbusse, are simply not significant enough to threaten his prestige. But I believe that Céline was engaged in a continuous, and even in his own eyes, unsuccessful rivalry with Marcel Proust for the title of France's pre-eminent twentieth-century writer, and that the Saturnalian mockery of the trilogy is also an attempt to sustain a quarrelsome dialogue with *A la recherche du temps perdu.*

I am aware that such a comparison may seem far-fetched to many readers, all the more so since we are only beginning to recognize the extent to which Céline's books are embedded in a conscious competition with the entire tradition of the French novel. Although arguing this case in detail would take us too far from our central concern, I at least want to suggest that the subversive laughter in Céline's writing is often a deliberate taunting of his most celebrated modern predecessor.

When Céline says an artist must be able to "find the secret of Time [. . .] but the music of Time changes and is never the same from one century to the next—only it's death that makes this music and death only—*you have to pay dearly for it*—it's dreadful and sad," the link between temporality, death, and writing is unmistakably Proustian in articulation as well as subject.[93] So too, I believe, is a book like *Mort à crédit*, where the characteristic Célinian mockery of Proust's style and themes cannot disguise the confession of a rivalrous kinship.[94] Céline, like Proust, is riddled with *ressentiment* against Time as an irreversible succession leading to death and permanent loss. Although their responses to the fundamental injury inflicted by temporality differ, there is more angry scorn in Proust and more nostalgic revery in Céline than we usually acknowledge. Whether the squandered past is envisaged as happy or wretched is ultimately less significant than its ambiguous status as the moment of initiation/subjection to the depredations of history. Proust and Céline are the two great French novelists of *ressentiment* against "time and time's 'It was.'" Both men made a fantasized, re-imagined version of their lives the primary obsession of their writings, and each was determined to fix his own radically solitary version of the truth of his experiences, no matter how it violated the expectations of his social world. But they pursued their search in antithetical circumstances and contrasting idioms, and the bitter narrative voice remembering a wretched past that Céline first developed for *Mort à crédit* is, I believe, his sarcastic "response from below" to what he saw as the pampered complexities and overwrought sentences of *A la recherche du temps perdu*. The fact that Proust was wealthy, half-Jewish, homosexual, and a graduate of the élite lycée Condorcet, categories that in Céline's imagination were more or less synonymous, no doubt contributed to his resentment of Proust's canonization. But Céline also admitted that Proust was "a great writer, [perhaps] the last one . . . He is the great writer of our generation,"[95] and sensed that *A la recherche du temps perdu* was the only twentieth-century French novel with a better chance to endure than his own work. His challenge to Proust was that of an embittered rival trying to find any ground upon which he could reclaim at least a smattering of success.

The opening into memory of *D'un château l'autre* enacts the rivalry in a particularly vivid and condensed way, paralleling in the form of grim humor the *petite madeleine* of Proust's "Ouverture." One of the most technically skillful aspects of *D'un château l'autre* is how Céline keeps teasing the reader with the promise/threat to "tell the truth" about Sigmaringen, only to pull away, until suddenly the illness-delirium (the hallucination of Charon's bark) overwhelms his resistance and compels him to narrate the events of 1944–45. The brilliantly staged nocturnal set piece of Charon's boat, *La Publique*, as an old *bateau mouche*, transporting the executed and exiled Collaborators to Acheron, but only after Charon himself cleaves their heads open one last time with his gigantic oar, is narrated as a kind of wild challenge to Proust's fortuitous dunking of the *madeleine*. I especially like thinking that if one accepts my analogy, then the grim barge-captain who clubs his passengers over the head would stand as the Célinian equivalent to Marcel's Tante Léonie, a conjunction that would not at all be outside the imaginative range (and rage) of an author whose notion of domestic happiness we already know from *Mort à crédit*.

Both scenes trigger the torrent of recollection that then forms the thematic content of the rest of the work. Earlier, I mentioned the simple pun by which Céline transformed the historical Sigmaringen to the novel's Siegmaringen. But the misspelling of the Castle also suggests that the book's journey is from the actual Sigmaringen to the phantasmatic Siegmaringen, the ghost-town of doomed Collaborators created by Céline's prose. There is a splitting, initiated by Céline's encounter with *La Publique*, of both the setting and the characters from their historical existence into a realm of imagination, as though, when Charon splits open his passengers' skulls, he signals their final passage from living beings to novelistic creations.

Céline had already fantasized about the day he would meet everyone "in Charon's boat, enemies, friends, all with their guts around their necks!" (*C* 15/15).[96] But when he really does see the haunted death-ship it comes as a totally unexpected and terrifying vision. Unlike his wish-fulfillment boat, *La Publique* is not transporting his present-day enemies, but rather the tortured and long-dead bodies of old acquaintances and friends from the Vichy years. The result of so uncanny a vision is a total collapse into fever and delirium.[97] And yet the delirium only makes the memory of the war years that he already carried within himself more urgent and vivid; it does

not release a hitherto inaccessible past. In a deliberate attempt to appropriate one of the central Proustian images for his own work, Céline compares
his novels' capacity to recapture the past to a "magic lantern" (R 731/28).[98]
But when it does surge up within him, the past, unlike Proust's, does not
return in any lucid and stable order or with any greater meaning. There is
no more comprehension now, in memory, than there was the first time
around. Unlike Marcel, Céline remembers and records his past to *refute* the
version others are circulating (his mother in *Mort à crédit*, his political enemies in the trilogy). He insists on all the bitterness, degradation, and abjection of his existence to establish *his* truth in the face of the lies of the Other.

In his earlier novels, Céline's grim version of childhood is meant to reject
familial lies, pieties, and corrosive nostalgia (symbolized within the novel
by his mother and intertextually by Proust). In the trilogy, Céline wants to
correct the official mythology of France created by the Gaullists, their historians, their press, and their judiciary. But this implies that if only these
Others (first his mother, then the official judgment of the French nation
itself) would not implicate *him* in their distortions and falsifications, he
would not have to write at all and could sink back into the silence and safety
he says he most craves. What he simply cannot tolerate is to *let himself* be
silenced and thereby yield the last word to his opponents. Art for Céline is
not a means of personal salvation or an access to a transcendent vision. The
lesson of Charon's *bateau mouche* is only that life progresses from the beatings one received as a child to the final beating that retroactively confirms
one's death. Even this ultimate brutalization must be paid for in cash.
Charon requires his fare with the same cold ruthlessness that his publishers
demand their manuscripts or his utility company its monthly payment. The
unfolding of the whole trilogy, Céline's travels through Germany, his time
in Sigmaringen and in Zornhof, the sight of the fire-bombed cities, etc., is
the real historical equivalent of the journey to the end of one's dying that
Charon offers his passengers.

The memory Charon unlocks in Céline is of a time when he was forced
on a whole series of trips as violent as any with which the daemonic barge-
captain can now threaten him, and it is typical of Céline that if, in the first
few moments, his meeting with the ghosts of the old Collaborators should
evoke wonder and sympathetic curiosity, that sympathy lasts only long
enough for smoldering rancors and another round of accusations to burst
forth. He is no more at home among the specters of *La Publique* than with
the Gaullists, Communists, or Opportunists. It is as though he needs to
establish both his complete isolation from and victimization by everyone
before he is finally driven to present his story, aware all the while that the
most his tale can earn him are the coins he will need the next and last time
he sees Charon again.

The subconscious has gotten used to the light
like bacteria that after a while
get used to a new antibiotic.
A new underground is being established,
lower than the very lowest.
  (Yehuda Amichai, "Travels of the Last Benjamin
  of Tudela")

Even in a confrontation with the dead, Céline seizes the role of the pariah whose words cause the most offense to his listeners and attract the most (negative) attention to himself. The attention must be hostile because that is the only kind Céline trusts to be sufficiently intense, focused, and committed enough never to waver. Love, except for his wife Lili's and that of their animals, will always be too shifting, but hatred is the one steady and reliable emotion. So poverty and rage combine to motivate Céline's words, and to motivate them *ab initio* as a counter-narrative, a version told against those in circulation already. But thereby his account is doomed to remain both logically and chronologically dependent on what it responds to, and its every word is aimed at an already articulate and often vividly personalized antagonist. Céline's dialogue is not just with the prior voices that have driven him to speech. Because his words will give rise to new responses, his text is constituted by the anticipation of reactions it will evoke as well as by a refutation of those already uttered. His words are dialogic at both ends of their temporal trajectory, being aimed at what has already been said and at what will be said in the future. But even the term "ends" is misleading. Although there is a temporal element to the intention of the stories, there can be no end to the process, as each new moment only exacerbates the crisis and generates a new set of charges and counter-charges. Céline's vituperations against his readers are an attempt to *terminate* an intolerable dialogue, the nightmare of a cycle of mutual recriminations, renewed and rebutted forever; Céline's wheedling tones, his effort to entertain, shock, elicit pity from, and even charm his readers are an attempt *to keep alive* an indispensable dialogue, a cycle of words without which his existence as an artist, a witness, and a monster would cease. Trapped between mutually exclusive needs, Céline is caught in so irreconcilable a set of positions that even the hope for success can only raise anxiety, since to achieve one aim would guarantee a catastrophic failure in the other.

  The novels advance as much through the kaleidoscopic oscillation in the aim and tone of their dialogues as through any thematic progression. And since that dialogue is both the expression and the very basis of Céline's abjection, the trilogy has found a way to make abjection the foundation of its entire narrative structure. For formal, even formalistic, reasons then,

D'un château l'autre, *Nord*, and *Rigodon* represent the ultimate stage of the Abject Hero as a literary figure and of the Saturnalian dialogue as the tawdry music of *ressentiment*.

But even after it is clear how desperately Céline seeks to fix the attention of the reader he is busy insulting, it is often difficult to admit that these insults are themselves one of his most effective lures. I am not suggesting that there is inherent masochism in the dialogic situation, although it is as well to admit how compelling narratives can be that make us confront our absence of mastery. There is an undeniable fascination in watching how a novelist like Céline pushes the always potentially tense relationship between author and reader to its rhetorical extreme and makes the rivalrous nature of that relationship central to his books' unfolding. Céline knows that one of the reasons we keep reading him is out of a scarcely acknowledged excitement to see how far he will go. We are again engaged in a contest formally similar to, but much more intense than, *Moi*'s debate with Jean-François Rameau, in which the Nephew's outrageousness provided the *philosophe*'s chief inducement for conversing with him. Now, though, in a development inaugurated by Dostoevsky, it is we, the readers of the trilogy, who assume the tone of normative reason and conventionally sanctioned judgments formerly voiced by the Enlightenment sage. By absorbing the reactions of the reader as one of its constituent elements, the dialogic situation has become fully internalized into the structure of the novel. But in the interval between *Le Neveu de Rameau* and *Notes from Underground*, and then between Dostoevsky's work and *D'un château l'autre*, everyone's sensibility, the reader's as well as the Abject Hero's, has coarsened and become accustomed to harsher fare. So both because of his inherent verbal brutality and because the reader demands no less, Céline, as a dialogic narrator, feels compelled to offer increasingly more strident pronouncements. But to the exact degree that his most repugnant notions are offered up as an inducement to keep the reader entertained, responsibility, and even complicity, for those same notions also fall on the reader.

Throughout the trilogy, Céline plays fast and loose with this problem, claiming that everyone, reader and critic alike, wants him to be even nastier and more monstrous than he already is. His publishers encourage this idea, and tell him that the failure of *Féerie pour une autre fois* was due to the absence of sufficiently racist diatribes: "I was expected to be provocative, to grind up some more Jews, to run myself back into the slammer! and for good!" (*C* 45/55).[99] As a general plea, this kind of defense is hardly convincing. But considered as an insight, not just into Céline's practice, but into the entire literary tradition that we have been examining, from classical antiquity through Diderot and Dostoevsky, until its culmination in Céline's trilogy, there is a disturbing element of truth in the claim. Our entire cultural heritage, of which these texts are a notable part and which they helped in no small measure to shape, endorses at least a restrained version of Céline's abusiveness by giving it the prestige of, if nothing else, an "authenticity" that the rest of us are too settled, too conventional, and too cowardly to express. In provoking such underground *ressentiment*, are we not encouraging and thrilling to a voice ready to risk uttering out loud what we ourselves feel and believe (in part), but are unwilling to take the consequences of saying? Are we not to an unsettling extent the "customers" whose "needs" meal-cadging parasites like Jean-François Rameau or roy-alty-hungry authors like Louis-Ferdinand Céline try to satisfy? And if so, is the kind of appalled laughter these books provide one of repugnance or of recognition?

The Céline of the trilogy is the consummate literary incarnation of the Abject Hero, so driven by *ressentiment* that his only motive for staying alive is to learn from the daily obituary notices that he has outlived those he loathes, and so tormented by his memory/vision of an unbearable truth about humankind that he is driven to expose it again and again to the public gaze, knowing both how dubious are his own motives for doing so and how little the public will appreciate his gesture. What Céline found between writing *Voyage au bout de la nuit* and the trilogy, or, more accu-rately, what history "gave" him, was the scenario of a tawdry and sordid cataclysm whose poet he was born to become: the devastation of a conti-nent without dignity or grandeur, grotesque even at its most horrific, and experienced, to appropriate his own earlier formulation, as an "Apocalypse à crédit."

Céline spent a lifetime pondering the function of the licensed clown in contemporary culture. He concluded that "anything goes, you can do what you please as long as you're a fully recognized clown! as long as it's per-fectly clear that you belong to a Circus . . . you don't? . . . that's bad! No tent? The ax!" (*C* 18/19).[100] By definition, the Abject Hero can never enjoy the security of belonging to an established party or "Circus" for long, just as he can never be on the winning side—if only because of his own ruinous attraction to the futile and disreputable. For Céline there has never been a conception of "winning" that didn't seem absurd from the outset. What he created in the trilogy is something like the scorched-earth policy of abjec-tion. The ax to which Céline refers is the one he always longed to wield against his enemies but that he thinks they succeeded in wielding against him instead. But it is also the weapon his novels create to slash out at the very topos from which they derive their structure. Caught between the already paid-for shelter of the "Circus," from within which no Saturnalia is possible, and the ravages of a global war whose destructiveness mocks any Saturnalian leveling, abjection has no more carnivalesque language to call purely its own and no new revelations to authenticate the claims of its worm's-eye view. The masterless clown, as we shall see in the final chapter, has merged too readily with the motiveless murderer, and the borderline between the servile and the satanic is transgressed too often and too "normally" for its literary presentation to inspire the anxious laughter of fresh insights or astonishment.

Six

These Children That Come at You with Knives: Charles Manson and the Modern Saturnalia

nerves wired with the prophecies
of one more West Coast lumpen Raskolnikov.
  (Moses Elch Brugger, "Revolutions Before")

Psychopaths like myself emerge when societies are
about to change.
  (Ira Einhorn, Campaign Speech:
  1971 Philadelphia Mayoral Election)

WHEN Ivan Karamazov finally testifies at his brother's trial for patricide, he is less interested in clearing Dmitri of the charge than in convicting everyone else in the courtroom of longing to commit the act for which they now feign such repugnance: "Who doesn't desire his father's death? . . . My father has been murdered and they pretend they're horrified. . . . They keep up the sham with one another. Liars! They all desire the death of their fathers. One reptile devours another."[1] But Ivan is far from alone in his demoralizing realization. After all, fourteen-year-old Lisa Khokhlakova had told Alyosha much the same thing, in an even more malicious tone than Ivan would later use: "Listen, your brother is being tried now for murdering his father and everyone loves his having killed his father. . . . Yes, loves it, everyone loves it! Everybody says it's so awful, but secretly they simply love it. I for one love it."[2] It is true that the spectators at Dmitri's trial show no desire to applaud Ivan's insight into their natures. But, no doubt, the prospect of confessing that they, like the Karamazovs, are all "reptiles" in addition to frustrated father-killers helps to dampen their enthusiasm, or perhaps they, unlike both the narrator and intended audience of *The Brothers Karamazov*, had not read enough Diderot or de Sade (or indeed early Dostoevsky) to recognize a universal truism when it was shouted at them.

In this context, it is striking to remember the ease and tone of assured, speculative daring, so utterly unlike Ivan's hysteria or Lisa's nastiness, with which Diderot's *philosophe* was able to advance a similar theory, and even to go beyond Ivan by explicitly acknowledging the sexual motive of patricidal impulses. The very fact that in *Le Neveu de Rameau* it was the *philosophe*, rather than the anarchic parasite, who said, "If the little savage were left to himself and kept in his natural condition, combining the undeveloped mind of an infant in the cradle with the violent passions of a man of thirty, he would wring his father's neck and go to bed with his mother,"[3] is an index of the confidence with which Diderot felt able to voice his most unsettling theories. Part of his confidence, though, is grounded in the certainty that there will always be a "father" in some form (social as much as biological) sufficiently powerful to compel the "little savage" to repress his desires, and the sanguine future whose possibility is theoretically envisaged is in practice (because of the father's intimate knowledge of that possibility) effectively foreclosed.

But in *The Brothers Karamazov* patricide does happen, and in books like *The Possessed* Dostoevsky is concerned to show that the uncontrolled violence he fears is the logical consequence of Enlightenment liberalism, not of its reactionary antagonists. From a Dostoevskian perspective, there is nothing paradoxical in the fact that it should have been the *philosophe*, rather than Rameau, who uttered the famous aphorism about murder, and he would have read Diderot's untroubled phrasing as a sign of intolerable, but entirely typical, complacency, rather than of intellectual daring. The characteristic worldly suavities of the *Encyclopédistes* could not but ring very differently in an epoch when their most unfettered imaginative flights had degenerated into the commonplaces of street-corner pamphlets. Dostoevsky saw in the radical tracts mainly an appeal to the worst promptings of *ressentiment*, disguised in the accents of a humane revolution; in their rhetoric he diagnosed a grotesque fusion of the destructive scorn of Diderot's out-of-work parasite with the sense of intellectual superiority and universal skepticism of the worldly *philosophe*. Thus joined, these initially antithetical strains produced, as a sort of parody of a Hegelian synthesis, the murderous obsessions of figures like the "young student of lower-middle-class origin, who has been expelled from the university, and who lives in dire poverty, [who] succumbs—through thoughtlessness and lack of strong convictions—to certain strange, 'incomplete' ideas that are floating in the air, and . . . resolves to kill."[4] Dostoevsky's novels raise the stakes of the Enlightenment's conception of human nature by dramatizing the consequences when abstract theories become the ideological justification for, and psychological goad to, immediate action. Throughout *The Diary of a Writer*, Dostoevsky insists that the revolutionaries of his time are motivated almost entirely by envy and fanaticism.[5] But he also recognizes that *ressentiment* becomes more venomous the more it senses an opportunity to extract a measure of revenge against the world. Amidst circumstances in which all of the restraints both *Moi* and *Lui* took as permanent *données* of communal existence were beginning to fray, the temptation to follow one's darkest urgings was proving increasingly irresistible.

In all these cases, what is so intriguing is how powerful the literary fascination of that *ressentiment* and rage has remained until today; how we, unlike the audience at Dmitri's trial, thrill to Ivan's charge, and how ready we are to find in the feverish accusations of a whole succession of tortured underground men the native accents of our own deepest, although (so the convention runs) repressed and unacknowledged, natures.

Already in the Renaissance, in Shakespeare's magical land of Illyria, there is no one, either on stage or in the stalls, to side with Malvolio when he seeks in vain to quiet Sir Toby Belch and Sir Andrew Aguecheek. By the logic of the genre as a whole and of *Twelfth Night* in particular, although Belch's and Aguecheek's jokes are singularly unfunny and their characters ignoble, the audience must second their mocking question: "Dost thou think, because thou art virtuous, there shall be no more cakes and ale?"[6] In Diderot's Café de la Régence, internal authority is distributed more equitably. Each speaker is allowed to score a series of local triumphs, and neither emerges from the dialogue unscathed, let alone victorious. But it is only honest to admit that from the start it was Jean-François Rameau who fascinated, and thus largely seduced, the work's readers: it is the Nephew's contemptuous undermining of the Enlightenment sage's certainties, rather than the *philosophe's* attempted defense of his beliefs, that has given *Le Neveu de Rameau* its explosive force. Diderot's manuscript only bears the title "Satire 2de," but by naming it *Le Neveu de Rameau*, posterity rightly marked, if not the text's, then at least its own center of interest and arousal. Analogously, for all the Underground Man's irrationality, seediness, and spite,—indeed largely because of these very qualities—it is hard to find any commentator on *Notes from Underground* ready to confess that he shares the earnest beliefs of the novel's "gentlemen readers." One has the feeling that were these "gentlemen" to read Dostoevsky, they too would refuse to recognize where their real kinship of mind and temperament lies and would begin to applaud the Underground Man's speeches.

In spite of their specific differences, in each Saturnalian confrontation we find ourselves expected to have an identificatory sympathy with whichever voice claims to embody anarchy and rebellion, the voice that strives to topple the normative or prudential reasoning on which the text's social order and hierarchy of values is shown to rely—values that are presumed to hold sway in the readers' world as well. It is the authority claimed for these values, not merely the weakness of their specific representatives, that is mocked, for its blindness to human nature and human needs. In particular, reliance on prudential, rational, and anti-apocalyptic modes of cognition is despised, and that contempt is expressed in tones of increasing shrillness. (This is a more paradoxical development than it may at first appear, if only because any reading of history would suggest that prosaic rationalism has hardly been the dominant motive in human affairs. Indeed, given the notable success, at both the political and ideological levels, of the extremist and utopian strains in our thinking, it is the champions of normative quotidian rationality, not their polemical antagonists, who ought to exhibit the *ressentiment* characteristic of impotent failure.)[7]

In what is probably the most arresting of all the textual developments of the Saturnalian dialogue, we see the reader's emotional identification with the voices of rage and thwarted rebellion ever more thoroughly compelled by the structure and tone of succeeding works at the same time that the dangers of that role are ever more explicitly argued. Readers of *Le Neveu de Rameau* are not forced by the inner logic of the text to choose between *Moi* and *Lui*, and they can find in each a welcome counterbalance to the demands of the other. But in *Notes from Underground* the "gentlemen readers" have nothing left to offer us, and the novel makes it difficult not to feel the same contempt for their platitudes that the Underground Man himself flaunts. The clearest index of the development I am tracing is the formal shift from Diderot's dialogue proper to Dostoevsky's first-person novel, but this mutation is itself already a consequence of a more indirect and disturbing cause. Dostoevsky, in the famous cry of *The Possessed*, was certain that "the fire is in the minds of men and not in the roofs of houses,"[8] and he believed that only the prior corruption of Russia's intelligentsia, their eager surrender to the lure of conspiracy and violence, could have led so many of them to the acts of senseless brutality characteristic of the epoch. His fear of an imminent social catastrophe, fueled by *ressentiment*, false pride, and incoherent utopian fantasies, marks all of his important post-Siberian political and cultural writings.[9]

But if Dostoevsky predicts the terrible future unleashed by any political movement motivated largely by spite and frustated ambition, he makes it extraordinarily difficult not to find that movement's victory inevitable, if for no other reason than the paltriness or implausibility of its antagonists. No one has shown more clearly than Dostoevsky the psychological inscape of temperaments like Raskolnikov's or the revolutionaries of *The Possessed*, or foreseen with greater lucidity the murderous consequences when they erect into a system "those certain strange, 'incomplete' ideas that are floating in the air." For each Ivan, his Smerdyakov, and for each Stavrogin, his Pyotr Verkhovensky; but only in an entirely different imaginative register, that of the "miracle story," is there a believable Sonya for each Raskolnikov or a Zosima for the Karamazovs. As Dostoevsky himself sometimes feared, his Lizas, Sonyas, and Zosimas are too monochromatic, too fixed to serve as the convincing ethical and religious correctives they are intended to embody, and as a result, it is hard to refute those critics who have accused Dostoevsky of being in part on the side of the very demons he would cast out. But the issue has nothing to do with the novelist's unconscious desires or motivation; it concerns instead the more vexed problem of literary representation and genre expectations. Particularly disturbing is the characteristic way Dostoevsky orchestrates all of his major novels: the pressures of a claustrophobic entrapment erupting into scenes of increasingly hysterical confrontation. Such a pattern is central to the unfolding of his narratives, so that in their fundamental logic, Dostoevsky's novels already embody precisely those traits of feverish urgency and daemonic paranoia whose disastrous consequences in the political realm he is determined to expose.

In Dostoevsky's judgment, the rage to disorder, to overthrow a flawed society, is more often a product of *ressentiment* and wounded vanity than of a scrupulous moral consciousness. And he is relentless in his diagnosis of the fusion of self-aggrandizement and self-loathing, of the sense of one's infinite potential and actual insignificance, that fuels the radical conspirators' *ressentiment*. Too sharp a sense of one's own victimization usually leads to a compensatory urge to tyrannize over others, and the man of *ressentiment*, if given a chance, will prove a bully both to himself and to others, whether his frustration is confined to a cramped room like the Underground Man's apartment or vented in political cells like those of the nihilists in *The Possessed*. In moving from the one to the other, Dostoevsky has not so much changed his emphasis or broadened his perspective as he has shown the kinship between two intimately related consequences of the same psychological disturbance.

If Diderot is able to give both voices in his dialogue equal weight, it is only because, although he knows the blindness and compromises of his own camp, he also feels that its victory is already assured, and that, on balance, it is a victory very much in the general interest. Rameau's values undercut all the positions for which Diderot spent his life fighting, but he is scarcely a threat to the social and political triumph of those ideals. Neither *Moi* nor Diderot himself could see that the world inhabited by both the *Encyclopédistes* and their opponents was close to being toppled, if not by men like Rameau, then at least by their more energetic descendants, and that the debates of the Café de la Régence were soon to be replaced with the tumbrils of the Place de la Bastille and the cellars of the Lubyanka. Still less could he foresee that the death sentences ordered by subsequent revolutionary and reactionary Terrors would be formulated in the rhetoric of his own Enlightenment doctrines (the supremacy of the public good) but stoked by a *ressentiment* like Jean-François Rameau's. The purges sanctioned in the name of an increasingly catastrophic series of experiments in utopian civic transformation inflect with a new and savage undercurrent the way we hear the famous ending of *Le Neveu de Rameau*: "He laughs best who laughs last."[10]

Dostoevsky had few illusions about the stability of his social world, but as most of the conservative ideologues of his own age realized, he was a thoroughly unreliable ally, since he despised many of their aspirations almost as much as those of their antagonists. Dostoevsky often resorted to a strategy dangerously akin to the Bolshevik formula of "heighten the contradictions." He hoped to bring his readers to the brink of accepting the religious vision of a Sonya Marmeladova or a Father Zosima by making plain the bankruptcy of all other positions, including especially both the Westernizers' liberal rationalism and the revolutionaries' tyrannical utopianism. But in their fundamental structure, Dostoevsky's books often incarnate the tendencies he most deplores. His novels grip us largely by exposing—and exploiting—the lacerations and hysteria of his major figures, and for all the embedded criticism of their self-justifying doctrines, it is those same figures who focus upon themselves our identificatory energy. Because the narrative practices and psychology governing Dostoevsky's novels are violently at odds with their ideological intentions, those readers who have continued to be hypnotized by the Underground Man, by Raskolnikov, and by Ivan Karamazov are not just careless in their responses. Rather they, like Dostoevsky, are captivated anew by the literary glamor of the satanic rebel at the very moment that this figure is being mocked and trivialized. To deconstruct the satanic and reveal it as abject turns out to be insufficient to undermine it. The satanic character, as Ivan's Devil shrewdly argues, probably even survives best in a modern society by undergoing such a deconstruction—one that incorporates a certain irony into its typology—and Dostoevsky's genius lies more in knowing how to mobilize the fascination of the daemonic than in his programmatic efforts to undermine it. Part of the reason why Dostoevsky so deeply needs the allure of the satanic, even if in the attenuated form of abjection, is that he intends the Abject Hero to show up the moral and intellectual blindness of the novels' philistine rationalists. The accuracy of the Underground Man's charges against the "gentlemen readers," like Ivan's and even Fyodor Karamazov's mockery of liberal Westernizers, is never in doubt. At the same time, though, the motives compelling them to make these denunciations are stripped of any self-congratulatory pretensions and revealed in their full shabbiness. This kind of double usage—on the one hand, the Abject Hero must function as an entirely commendable satiric voice against a noxious set of opponents, while, on the other, he becomes the principal target of the novel's own satiric vision—requires a constant series of precarious adjustments in order not to seem fundamentally incoherent, and often the strain of that balancing act is too great even for Dostoevsky's uncanny dexterity.

But if Dostoevsky's practice marks an extreme pitch of internal tension in the Abject Hero's contradictory textual functions, the dilemma is only in part uniquely his. The entire tradition on which Dostoevsky drew, and whose resources he, more than anyone before him, successfully appropriated for the novel, nourished the confusion I have detailed. The Bakhtinian concept of a "genre memory" is a useful way of crystallizing this problem, since it emphasizes that every specific genre carries with it a certain way of understanding and seeing the world, as well as a constellation of distinct formal characteristics, strategies, and expectations, based on both prior exempla and on the genre's logically available potential. According to P. N.

Medvedev and the Bakhtinians, "one does not first see a given aspect of reality and then shape it to a given set of conventions. Instead, one sees reality 'with the eyes of the genre.'"[11] Although I believe that Dostoevsky deliberately sought ways to expand the Saturnalian dialogue's formal characteristics and its particular angle of vision on the world, the genre memory itself would have exerted its own pressures that simultaneously enabled and complicated his task. Simply put, the dilemma is how to be fully inside a tradition and marshal all of that tradition's resources with the paradoxical intent of criticizing its cardinal terms; how to be constrained by the affective power of a topos while struggling to eradicate its appeal. But in Dostoevsky, the whole struggle is waged in order to prepare the way for the one higher category—the religious—which can never be introduced effectively into the narrative exactly because the Saturnalian story has no room for it in its rhetorical or logical space. Genre memories, all the more powerful for being so long-lived and subterranean, are powerful enough in Dostoevsky to flood material from a radically different register: they function like underground voices to subvert and discredit all the novel's positive affirmations. Dostoevsky did not so much fail to solve a problem—one in which it is clear that formal and thematic cruxes are equally implicated—as build his oeuvre on the inevitable coming-to-ruin of successive attempted solutions. Each of these attempts, by a kind of local genre memory effect, draws on, challenges, and extends the partial solutions of its predecessors, so that despite their immediately apparent and sharp differences, all of Dostoevsky's works seem like increasingly complex drafts of a single, never realized, and impossible novel.

   If Céline's books, pushing Dostoevsky's bitter carnival into the twentieth century, represent the ultimate realization/explosion of the Saturnalian dialogue, it is not only because abjection is so completely the center of their experiential universe but also because they return to the tradition without wanting to transcend or escape its limitations in any way. Céline seeks only to intensify the effects of the genre's grim irony, not to use it as a ladder to a higher dispensation. Indeed, Céline programmatically rejects any notion that such another realm exists, except as one more delusion to be mocked by the Saturnalian text. Céline embraces the leveling nihilism of his abject vision, and he does so with just the kind of anarchic and excessive laughter that has been the genre's single most characteristic and enduring trait. Because he entirely accepts its terms, he also accepts the constraints of the Saturnalian dialogue without the constant inner struggle against the convention that marks Dostoevsky's novels. Undoubtedly, this resistance to the limitations of the form is one sign, among many, of Dostoevsky's massive artistic superiority to Céline. But in a macabre way, Céline was "luckier," insofar as his best writing is nourished by an uncanny conjunction of the constraints of his form and his imaginative needs: his instinctive "at-homeness" at the heart of the Saturnalian rage found an exactly appropriate setting in the sordid history of the Collaboration, the fall of Vichy France, and the disintegration of Nazi Germany. There is nothing in his narrative beyond the reach of his form, no surplus of perception or aim that is not amenable to being incorporated into the trilogy's savagely carnivalesque structure.[12] For Céline every experience unfailingly teaches the same negative lesson and every journey ends in the identical darkness: choice comes into play only in the ways one either learns, or seeks to evade, that truth. And by so entirely acquiescing to the condition of an empty horror momentarily held at bay by the sheer energy of his rant, Céline has, as it were, both outdone his predecessors and brought the topos to its fullest narrative realization thus far.

> Though we may be able to sit underground forty
> years without speaking, when we do come out into
> the light of day and break out, then we talk and talk
> and talk.
>   (Fyodor Dostoevsky, *Notes from Underground*)

In spite of such clear, and often powerfully effective, successors as Thomas Bernhard's *Wittgenstein's Nephew* and *Woodcutters*,[13] William Burroughs's *Naked Lunch*, Hubert Selby's *Last Exit to Brooklyn*, and many of Rainer Werner Fassbinder's films, no work yet has gone beyond Céline's presentation of a modern Saturnalia. But the impression of a generic stasis is not attributable to a failure of invention in more recent artists. Rather, it is a consequence of Céline having located his work with total internal conviction at the heart of as all-encompassing a cataclysm as we are likely to be able to survive. The consonance of theme, technique, and occasion endows his trilogy, bizarre as the term may seem, with an almost archetypal kind of literary "decorum," an aesthetic integrity that is, in the formal sense, strictly classical and impossible to surpass.

But the appeal of a convention to other writers is rarely lessened by such considerations, even though the results, in most cases, do little more than demonstrate the risks of a too formulaic, too easily attempted, appropriation.

Although it is hardly necessary to confirm this point with a litany of instances, consider, as a kind of microcosm, two famous examples of such writing. Albert Camus's *La Chute* (1956) is structured with almost embarrassingly scrupulous fidelity to prior novelizations of the Saturnalian dialogue. Its allegorically self-named speaker, Jean-Baptiste Clamence (a futile *vox clamantis in deserto*, or in his own words, "an empty prophet for shabby times"),[14] cries out his sins in the wilderness of post-War Amsterdam in order, at the end, to ensnare the confessional guilt latent in his interlocutor. Like Ivan Karamazov, Clamence, in accusing himself, accuses not just his immediate partner in the dialogue but all of humanity. But his trap isn't nearly cunning enough, nor is the reversal from penitent to judge sufficiently disconcerting to elicit the moral discomfort and bleak laughter that it so strenuously intends.

What is most interesting about *La Chute* is how its very lack of success makes evident both the precise formal conventions of the modern Saturnalian dialogue and its thematic obsessions. From his opening speech to his fellow Frenchman, Clamence goes through a complex process of revelation and denial, punctuated by rhythmic variations on the words "judge," "justice," and "justified," until the climactic exhibition, in his room, of van Eyck's stolen panel "The Just Judges."[15] He accuses himself of an increasingly grave declension of turpitudes, hypocrisies, and cowardices, in order, finally, to earn the right to say, "But just think of your life, *mon cher compatriote!* Search your memory and perhaps you will find some similar story."[16]

This five-day Saturnalia often reads like a cinematic version of a classical drama, and it constantly aligns itself with its canonic predecessors in the tradition. Clamence's injunction to his interlocutor/reader to recognize the similarity between them is an essential gesture in all such works, constituting "the moral lesson," unlikely as the phrase may appear, of the genre as a whole. From Davus's growing defiance ("It is you I'm talking about")[17] to the Underground Man's insistence that the "gentlemen readers" and he share the same vices, the abject ironist is determined to collapse the boundary between himself and his dialogic partners, to bring them into the arena as participants, not spectators or judges. *La Chute* keeps signaling its debts to *Notes from Underground*, but the fact of generic indebtedness never figures in the consciousness of the two characters. It is as though Clamence's real "fall" is not his refusal to have helped the young suicide on the Pont des Arts, but his ignorance about the fact that all his crucial experiences, including especially his anguished guilt, are simply repetitions of the Underground Man's prior story.[18] And if we recall that the Underground Man himself suffered primarily from an awareness of the utter belatedness of his whole existence, his lack of any authentic suffering not determined by literary models, then we see that Clamence is a shadow of a shadow, a reflection of a character who already felt himself only a reflection, "ready made . . . stolen from the poets and novelists."[19]

Clamence seems entirely unaware of his fundamental belatedness, and thus he slips doubly below the Underground Man, who made that realization the core of his dilemma. Nothing in *La Chute* indicates an understanding that exactly here, in the theme of a fall from the fall, of an infinitely regressive mirror of derivations, is there an occasion for an "originally imitative" agony. The novel continues to take entirely seriously, as though it were newly minted, its hand-me-down inheritance. Yet, by a kind of echoing that in this context resembles a return of the repressed more than a literary homage, Clamence's situation and phrasing continually return to, without ever daring to name, *Notes from Underground*. Like the Underground Man, Clamence explains his withdrawal into the role of "judge-penitent" as the delayed results of a traumatic encounter years earlier with a young woman, an encounter whose details we are teasingly assured will eventually be revealed. And like the motif binding the two sections of *Notes from Underground* (the second of which is entitled "Apropos of the Wet Snow"), *La Chute* ends with an image that evokes St. Petersburg as much as Amsterdam: "Look, it's snowing! . . . Amsterdam asleep in the white night, the dark jade canals under the little snow-covered bridges, the empty streets, my muffled steps. . . ."[20]

Ultimately, Clamence's narrative efforts are directed not so much toward compelling his interlocutor—and reader—to acknowledge a common human guilt as toward providing an adequate occasion for a strictly rhetorical performance, the lengthy rehearsal of his theory of confession as an act of aggressive unmasking:

> Inasmuch as one couldn't condemn others without immediately judging oneself, one had to overwhelm oneself to have the right to judge others. Inasmuch as every judge someday ends up as a penitent, one had to travel the opposite direction, and practice the profession of penitent to be able to end up as a judge. . . . The more I accuse myself, the more I have a right to judge you. Even better, I provoke you into judging yourself, and this relieves me of that much of the burden.[21]

If there is no particular reason to accept these *obiter dicta*, nothing indicates the narrator's, or indeed the text's, awareness of a contrary position. Although Clamence's speech is always addressed to and structured by, his interlocutor's words, the novel is never really dialogical. As though Camus realized that Clamence's experiences provided simply too little foundation for so massive and marmoreal a set of pronouncements, the novel is at pains to bring in the additional literary/theological authority of a Dantean Inferno ("Have you noticed that Amsterdam's concentric canals resemble the circles of hell?")[22] and the historical horror of the deportation and slaughter of Amsterdam's Jewish community ("I live in the Jewish quarter . . . the site of one of the greatest crimes in history").[23] Both evocations, in their different ways, fail to endow the story with the kind of surplus intensity for which they were summoned, and it is a nice moral point whether Camus's attempted literary appropriation of the Holocaust is not more dubious than any of the iniquities ever perpetrated by Jean-Baptiste Clamence.[24]

There is, nonetheless, a particularly revealing moment, almost at the exact midpoint of the novel, in which Camus's narrator provides the valuable service of explicitly articulating what we can, with justice, take as the grounding assumption of all such novels: "we rarely confide in those who are better than us . . . we confess to those who are like us and who share our weaknesses."[25] What is fascinating is how indispensable such a premise is to motivate the novel's unfolding, while, at the same time, outside the particular literary convention at work, there is no reason to agree with Clamence's pronouncement. On the contrary, virtually every religion has some form of ritualized confession/declaration of one's obliquities to a listener whose superior wisdom or purity makes him the ideal auditor, precisely because, linked to the capacity to comprehend, is a parallel power to forgive and release from guilt. But in a Saturnalian dialogue, no such position can be tolerated since it would confirm just those principles of hierarchy, order, and non-equivalence that the Saturnalia exists to contest. The emergence of any moral authority would halt the carnival at its most promising moment. When voices claiming to speak in the name of either rational or transcendent values do appear in a Saturnalian text, they come into its purview only to be challenged and shown up as no better than those they would either condemn or pardon (an act that itself can only follow a prior judgment of guilt).

In passages like the one I quoted, it is the reader whose supposed assumptions of superiority are brought into the text and held up to derision. Since we are listening to the identical words as Clamence's interlocutor, the novel forces us to occupy the role of that character's extra-textual double. Clamence's confession, as well as his claim that we all share his corruption, is thus addressed primarily and centrally to us. The logic of Clamence's lengthy declaration at the book's end is intended to universalize the theme of humanity's guilt, but his speech is completely dependent on the generically fixed characteristics of the invariably guilty listener. We are always guilty, because that is our function as readers, just as it is the function of the abject characters always to make us aware of our guilt, thereby ensuring that the carnival is indeed "without footlights," that is, without uninvolved spectators. The surprising thing, surely, is how ready we are to pretend to be surprised by these reversals, how we have been so well trained by the convention that we take up without rebellion what is, by any account, a decidedly predictable and obtuse part.

Our readiness to assume the role of straight man to the Abject Hero's mockery—and to congratulate him the more unrelenting his attacks and the deadlier his aim—may be surprising, but it can hardly be blamed on a deficient memory. Unlike, for example, the reader hypothesized by Stanley Fish's implausible *Surprised by Sin*, the Saturnalian text does not rely on a forgetting of the lesson of the prior work as soon as one turns to its successor. On the contrary, the only way the dialogues we are discussing can function is if, at some level, we recall the tradition in which they participate and thus, coached by the genre memory, are already prepared to applaud the "surprises" we know lie in store for us. The difficulty of creating an adequately resonant and convincing fictional occasion for such a strategy helps account for the feeling one often gets of a simplistically manipulative rehearsal of stereotypes. *La Chute* is an all-too-deliberate attempt to make use of the Saturnalian topos to provide the sinews of both its structure and theme. But as an instance of exactly the opposite problem, consider for a moment what happens when genre memories exert such automatic control over a book that it becomes a catalog of the most familiar and shop-worn Saturnalian effects, massed together without any reflection on their provenance. This seems to me true of a whole press of recent fictional celebrations of the madman's or criminal's "deeper insights" into our culture's hypocrisies, among the most popular of which is Ken Kesey's *One Flew over the Cuckoo's Nest* (1962).

In a contemporary novel, it is a safe assumption that the moment we encounter the world of a mental hospital, with its psychiatric doctors, nurses, and patients, then for strictly generic reasons, as well as in obedience to the moment's popular culture, all of the book's medical officials will be at best incompetents and, more likely, conformists and conformity-inducing philistines. The nurses, in particular, will be brutal tyrants of dubious sexuality, and those inmates not drugged or terrified into catatonic stupor will embody the forces of resistance, authenticity, and wisdom for whose triumph we, as readers, have been trained to cheer. I suspect that the reason *One Flew over the Cuckoo's Nest* attracted such a devoted audience, both as a novel and later as a film directed by Milos Forman, was its perfect joining of the most accessible clichés of the era's popular culture with the formal narrative devices of the literary carnivalesque. This conjunction is seductive enough to make aspects of the novel acceptable that might otherwise offend its enthusiasts, such as the astonishingly sexist treatment of a figure like the villainous Head Nurse Ratchet, the none-too-delicate variation on the "noble savage" motif in the character of Chief Bromden, and the linkage of heroism, personal integrity, and voracious sexual demands in the character of the book's chief anarch, Randle Patrick McMurphy (who, it is worth remembering, got himself transferred to the Oregon asylum from prison, where he was serving time for statutory rape).

Astonishingly, Kesey's narrative succeeds in persuading its readers that it is taking the enormous risk of defying all conventions at the very moment that it is fulfilling each imperative of its own fixed tradition without the slightest deviation or self-questioning. An actual madhouse may seem to promise a witty instantiation of the Saturnalian marketplace, but its potential cannot be fulfilled by substituting a simple reversal of who is crazy and who is sane for a questioning of the fundamental categories themselves. Without such questioning, all that remains is a particularly cunning pretense whereby the rhetoric of anarchic rebellion has been marketed as the most desirable of all leisure-industry goods, whose consumption feeds, above all else, its audience's self-congratulatory impulse. It is probably difficult for any writer to resist the temptation of an excessively receptive readership, but novelists like Kesey seem to me to be "user-friendly" to a fault.[26] Céline, who longed in vain to see his books turned into money-making films, would have loved such success, but the very fidelity of his art to the genuinely disturbing strains in the Saturnalia made such an accommodation impossible. Dostoevsky, though, would have found the symbiosis between the artist, audience, and theme of *One Flew over the Cuckoo's Nest* quite unsurprising and would have interpreted it, no doubt, as a sign that the Gadarene swine had replaced the golden calf as the age's new fetish.

But, the objections will no doubt run, we read stories differently from the ways we react to and evaluate challenges in other spheres of our lives, and to conflate the popular success of *One Flew over the Cuckoo's Nest* or the critical esteem of *La Chute* with our quotidian expectations and values is clearly an act of consummate naïveté—the one accusation that terrifies literary critics today more than any other since we stopped holding *autos-da-fé* for doctrinal heresies. And yet I continue to wonder, thinking still of Ivan's courtroom outburst, about another speech by a defendant in a curious and complicated murder case, a defendant who, in the realm where cultural history and popular mythology intersect, has attained, at least for the moment, the kind of emblematic significance that we think of as preeminently literature's role to articulate:

I have stayed in jail and I have stayed stupid, and I have stayed a child . . . and then I look at the things that you do and I don't understand. . . . you say how bad, and even killers, your children are. *You* made your children what they are. . . . *These children that come at you with knives, they are your children. You taught them. I didn't teach them.* . . . the Family were just people that you did not want, people that were alongside the road, that their parents had kicked out, that did not want to go to Juvenile Hall. So I did the best I could and I took them up on my garbage dump. . . . I know this: that in your hearts and your own souls, you are as much responsible for the Vietnam war as I am for killing these people. . . . I can't judge any of you. . . . But I think that it is high time that you all start looking at yourselves, and judging the lie that you live in . . . you can project it back at me . . . but I am only what lives inside each and every one of you. My father is the jailhouse. My father is your system . . . I am only what you made me. I am only a reflection of you. I have ate out of your garbage cans to stay out of jail. I have wore your second-hand clothes . . . I have done my best to get along in your world and now you want to kill me, and I look at you, and then I say to myself, You want to kill *me*? Ha! I'm already dead, have been all my life. I've spent twenty-three years in tombs that you built. . . . It's all your fear. You look for something to project it on, and you pick out a little old scroungy nobody that eats out of a garbage can, and that nobody wants, that was kicked out of the penitentiary, that has been dragged through every hellhole that you can think of, and you drag him and put him in a courtroom. *You expect to break me? Impossible! You broke me years ago.* . . . I may have implied on several occasions to several different people that I may have been Jesus Christ, but I haven't decided yet what I am or who I am. . . . Is it *my* fault that your children do what *you* do? *What about your children?* (He rises, leaning forward in the witness chair) *You say there are just a few? There are many, many more, coming in the same direction. They are running in the streets—and they are coming right at you!* [27]

These lines are from a speech delivered in Department 104 of the Los Angeles Hall of Justice, in open court but without the jury present, by Charles Manson on Thursday, November 19, 1970, four months after the beginning of his trial for the multiple murders at the Sharon Tate and LaBianca residences. *The People v. Charles Manson, Susan Atkins, Patricia Krenwinkel, and Leslie Van Houten* has assumed iconic status as a kind of negative morality tale, a particularly favored candidate for the much-canvased role of symbolizing "the end of the sixties." [28] The individual elements of the "Manson Family" story contained, both singly and in the way they came together, the most archetypal—and hence accessible—characteristics of a daemonic carnival, spilling out from the urban underground and desert wastelands into the houses and lives of the Los Angeles community, and from there into the nightmares of the national imagination. The story combined the motifs of promiscuous sexuality and drug use, adolescent rebellion, and glamorous figures from the film and music industries with a core of random and unprovoked savagery astonishing even in the volatile climate of 1969. As a contemporary account pointed out, in the morally numbed and numbing idiom of its time: "Clearly, Charles Manson already stands as the villain of our time, the symbol of animalism and evil. Lee Harvey Oswald? Sirhan Sirhan? Adolf Eichmann? Misguided souls, sure, but as far as we know they never took LSD or fucked more than one woman at a time." [29]

The very term "Family," as used by Manson and his followers, seemed like a ferocious parody of the "tribal" identity adopted by many of the hippies and political radicals, as well as the kind of anodyne, asexual television families of the preceding era, like "The Adventures of Ozzie and Harriet," "The Danny Thomas Show," and "Father Knows Best." [30] The incomprehensible spectacle of a swarm of mostly female disciples completely committed to carrying out the commands of so unprepossessing a messianic leader, one who, considering his background (semi-literate jailbird), appearance (Manson is only five feet, two inches tall), and prospects (a failed musician, failed car thief, and failed pimp), might have seemed particularly *un*fascinating, only helped to heighten everyone's curiosity. But if these details guaranteed that the story of the Manson Family murders could be immediately circulated and interpreted by virtue of its almost excessive legibility, the savagery of the carnage at the Tate and LaBianca houses was a warning sign of just how high the cost of "breaking down" the footlights between spectators and revelers had become.

If Charles Manson helped to "end the sixties," it was because he *should* have been a fictional character in some apocalyptic fantasy novel and not an actual resident of a particular place and era, sending out gangs of disciples to butcher total strangers. What the Tate/LaBianca murders showed was that in America too the consequences of succumbing "to certain strange, 'incomplete' ideas that are floating in the air" were lethal. Only here it no longer required even the confused reading of a Raskolnikov or an Ivan Karamazov to lead to murder. In his testimony, Manson himself emphasizes his near-illiteracy as evidence of his life-long victimization by society. But in the Family's detailed exegesis of the songs on the Beatles' *White Album*, a paranoiac over-interpretation of a few lyrics by a popular rock group, the jargon of the moment—with its rhetorical yearning for an "eve of destruction" and a generalized rage at the politics and military policies of the Nixon government—sufficed to trigger a whole series of killings.[31]

I am ready to admit how hard it is to argue, let alone to prove, that the Manson Family story is a contemporary instantiation of the convention whose development we have been tracing so far primarily as a literary phenomenon. But the kinds of analyses that enabled the "Family" to interpret a song like "Helter Skelter" as a call to armed insurrection and race warfare is only a somewhat vulgarized variant of the arguments used by the conspirators in *The Possessed* to justify their violence and by Raskolnikov to legitimize his fantasies of himself as a superior being forced by sordid circumstances to commit murder. The fact that the Manson killings actually happened in Los Angeles, rather than in so appropriately novelistic a setting as St. Petersburg, far from indicating any incommensurability between the stories, seems to me only to make more haunting the specter of their interdependence.

The narratives we read and our strategies of interpretation are not so different in what the Underground Man called "the most abstract and intentional city in the whole world"[32] from what they are at the Spahn's Movie Ranch, where the Family lived when they set out for 10050 Cielo Drive in August 1969. The dramas of St. Petersburg helped shape the future in which they are interpreted, and the inner debates and violent resolutions of Raskolnikov or the conspirators of *The Possessed* continue, even if in the version of a lumpen and parodic degeneracy, to help set the terms of authenticity and spontaneity by which latter-day "geniuses" orchestrate their plunge into the daemonic. A murderer like Manson, whose monstrosity is born out of a fusion of abjection and *ressentiment*, need not be able either to name his condition or know anything of its history. He can incarnate the role so perfectly without any formal knowledge, because his whole culture has fed him the appropriate cues and provided a context in which his existence as simultaneously a monster and an abject dependent is as predictable as the Underground Man's or Raskolnikov's in the moral climate of Dostoevsky's St. Petersburg.[33] At Dmitri Karamazov's trial, the town prosecutor said, "they [the Europeans] have their Hamlets, but we, so far, have only our Karamazovs!"[34] Of course, through the very comparison, Dostoevsky is implicitly praising his own book as much as registering a historical falling-off in the speculative imagination of Russia's nineteenth-century "revengers." But I want to continue both the declension and the genealogy Dostoevsky proposed, and suggest that Russia may have had its Raskolnikovs and Karamazovs, but we, in America, will have to make do with our own Charlie Manson.

> What sickness is it that keeps sending me kids and
> followers? It's your world out there that does it. I
> don't solicit any mail or ask anyone to come and
> visit me [in prison]. Yet the mail continues to ar-
> rive and your pretty little flowers of innocence keep
> showing up at the gate.
> (Charles Manson in the early 1980s, *Manson in
> His Own Words*)

In Thomas Mann's *Doctor Faustus*, Adrian Leverkühn sardonically muses, "the nineteenth century must have been an uncommonly pleasant epoch, since it had never been harder for humanity to tear itself away from the opinions and habits of the previous period than it was for the generation now living."[35] For a certain kind of Saturnalian imagination in which the longing for an all-engulfing carnival functions as a kind of call-to-arms, and in which the "genius" is figured as a seer stung into visionary rage by the banalities and injustices of quotidian social existence, Leverkühn's contemptuous historicization has the truth of the self-evident. The nineteenth century bequeathed a paradigm to us whose governing certainty was, to continue quoting *Doctor Faustus*, that there is no inspiration that "has nothing to do with hell" and that "the artist is the brother of the criminal and the madman."[36] The unhappy corollary to this argument, its "underground" recasting as it were, became authoritative almost as quickly and with perhaps even more effectiveness: if the artist is akin to the criminal and the madman, then the criminal and the madman are in turn also artists. It is this paradigm within whose terms much of the modern imagination continues to be inscribed. Only it still remains easier to commit a crime than a masterpiece, and so if the one proves unattainable the other is surely within the reach of any sufficiently hardened will.

It is true that *ressentiment* and the fantasy of a utopian moment free from all burdens, divisions, and renunciations have existed from the beginning of our culture's self-representation. To put it more strongly, although the leveling rage of the Saturnalia and the truculent refusal to manifest the cultural imperatives of *gravitas* and self-command have been imagined traditionally as the repressed and secret Other of the dominant culture, that repression was only the thinnest and most transparent of disguises. The disguise was never intended to hide the existence of the underside, but to mask the fact that it already lay within, indeed at the very core of, the culture's most self-idealizing moments. But in the nineteenth century, as Dostoevsky understood more clearly than anyone else, the voices of abject rage ceased even pretending to the status of outside or marginalized positions, and fed by increasingly powerful injections of *ressentiment*, they sought to present themselves as enunciators of the "sole truth" on which both society as a whole and the consciousness of its most gifted members rested. The underground was reinterpreted not as an alternative or disruptive space but as the true foundation of the entire cultural edifice. And it is this constellation of tropes that our era has absorbed so deeply that it has become a central element of the stories consumed by illiterates as much as by college students, by professors as much as by prisoners waiting for parole, and by unwanted kids like Charles Manson, abandoned in a succession of juvenile homes, as much as by the communes of the counter-culture from which most of "the Family" were recruited.

Manson was first a great listener to, and later an "inspired" teller of tales, and his career enacts a terrifying example of the kind of leakage between literary genres and life on which Céline's trilogy is based. "The Family" dreamed of ruling a wide area of the desert around Death Valley, much as Sancho Panza and Céline each dreamed of winning the governorship of an island. And I suppose that if we want an image of the sort of administration the Manson Family would have instituted, Jonestown, Jim Jones's suicidal community in the jungle of Guyana, provides a likely enough model.[37]

I want to return now to Manson's courtroom speech, in order to probe some of the similarities between his position and the issues we have seen hitherto raised in what were apparently purely literary contexts. The jury that would determine his fate was not present during Manson's testimony. But in spite of the risk to his own defense, he refused to take the stand again in front of the jury, saying, "I have already relieved all the pressure I had."[38] Thus, his speech functioned primarily as a performance, to be heard and interpreted by an audience, rather than as a strategic element in the trial as such. What the speech invokes, and the reason for its power to disturb so strongly, is the full repertoire of Saturnalian mockery, abject whining, and *ressentiment*-driven social criticism that we have grown used to hearing and applauding in the relative safety of our most "daring," rebellious," and "subversive" novels. Over and over again—and at least since Rabelais, numbing repetition has been a crucial part of any Saturnalian discourse— Manson insists on two cardinal points: (1) Since he spent almost all of his life, beginning at age twelve, in various forms of social institutions, from foster families to juvenile detention centers to adult prisons, whatever he has become cannot be blamed on him; he is, in fact, entirely a creation of a corrupting and humanly destructive social system. (2) How can society blame him for turning the children who followed him into murderers? They were only under his influence for a few months, as opposed to the years they were under the tutelage of parents and teachers. Who, then, is at fault for the way they ultimately developed?

But these two points, fundamental though they are, lead Manson directly to several unexpected, and at times uncannily guileful, corollaries:

1a. Charles Manson himself remained, in a crucial sense, a permanent child, since his time in the juvenile homes and jails had never given him a chance to grow up and learn how to cope in the larger world.

1b. The death penalty with which he is threatened is meaningless because societal neglect and brutality had killed him years earlier—indeed, well before he had ever known a real life.

1c. The Charles Manson that the newspapers, prosecutors, and public officials denounced as a Monster was actually their creation, a projection of their fears of the whole youth sub-culture that seemed to be growing increasingly out of their control, and more interestingly, a projection of their hidden desire for just such a Monster as a source of titillation and economic profit.

1d. The various claims about *his* claims to inspired authority are merely further attempts to confine him, no different from the inmate number he received in prison. His own sense of identity is more fluid than any single label or name can encompass.

2a. If Manson and his followers constitute a "Family," this is only because its members had been neglected and abandoned by their natural protectors. The orphan in him matched and called out to the orphan in them.

2b. Instead of concerning itself with the well-being of its weakest members, the dominant society (what the jargon of the era called the "Establishment") devoted its energy to the insanity of the Vietnam War and the devastation of the planet's ecology.

2c. The "sick" rage and anger that this "Establishment" itself unleashed upon the earth was only being answered by the "righteous" anger of the young, who had never been offered persuasive adult models or emotionally satisfying choices in their years at home.

Any reader of the depressing sub-genre of "jailhouse literature" quickly becomes used to a series of more or less similar efforts at self-exculpation, in which it is always the Other, always someone else or society as a whole, that is to blame. Céline's description of his time in the Vester Faengsel prison offers a fascinating parallel to Manson's courtroom speech, not least because Céline, too, was accused of being an inhuman Monster, who was, if not the chief instigator, then at least an eager supporter, of a crime far more heinous than any committed by the Manson Family. More generally, Manson's speech is so pertinent to the problems with which we have been concerned throughout this book because he manages to unite with such concision virtually every major trope of the abject and bitter side of the carnivalesque tradition. Starting from the frantic oscillation between his self-representation as a weak, helpless, and even pathetic failure and his gradually increasing self-aggrandizement as a man of global insight and messianic destiny, proceeding through his self-righteous counter-attack against a society he sees as far more destructive and savage than anything of which he is accused, and culminating in an Ivan Karamazov–like invocation of all the abused and neglected children who are the community's true victims, Manson's deployment of generic topoi to turn his self-defense into an indictment of the moral legitimacy of his accusers is considerably more sophisticated than Jean-Baptiste Clamence's. Unwelcome though such a thought might be, there are times when I cannot help being struck by the thematic and temporal coincidences between Manson's speech of November 1970 and the 1975 publication of Michel Foucault's *Surveiller et punir*, with its spectacularly successful and endlessly imitated account of our "carceral society."[39] That both Manson's apocalyptic fervor and Foucault's complex and sophisticated arguments participate, in their different ways, in a specific historical moment, one which, outside of certain tendencies in academia, seems to me in relative decline, is not surprising. The astonishment comes from Manson's unexpected rhetorical skill in weaving so many powerful—if commonplace—fragments of an on-going cultural argument into the texture of his plea.

But beyond any chronological contiguities, the figures to whom Manson's discourse seems to be hearkening back, although unintentionally, are the Raskolnikovs, the Ivans, and all the other Underground Men of Dostoevsky's novels. And here I am thinking not only of the evident parallels in the ways they construct an obsessively formal itemization of their grievance against society and link this to an undisguised self-pity but also of the gruesome similarity in the consequences (whether actual, as in Manson's case, or novelistically imagined, as in Raskolnikov's) of their theoretical positions. The murder of two women, or the beating to death of an old buffoon by his illegitimate son/lackey, are deliberately depicted as simultaneously sordid, daemonic, and petty in order to highlight the pettiness of the impulse mastering their perpetrators and the sordidness of the daemonic ideology used to justify such deeds. The killings at the Tate/La-Bianca households were interpreted by much of the American "underground" community as a symbolically shattering event because they darkened the entire theoretical horizon, the utopian optimism and self-righteousness, of the counter-culture that had nurtured and, for a while, openly celebrated the Family. In a gesture of characteristic sensitivity, the most widely publicized underground white radical group of the era, the Weathermen, began to praise Manson as a "revolutionary hero" after his arrest, because he had "offed some rich pigs." The "Liberation News Service," an underground version of the "Establishment's" wire services like UPI and AP, circulated the Weathermen's declaration of support for Manson. They even coined a particularly hideous slogan, "Manson Power— The Year of the Fork," to commemorate the fork that the killers left sticking in Leno LaBianca's stomach.[40] But unlike the still popular romanticization of Dostoevsky's abject murderers, I doubt that today even the most polemically determined "strong misreaders" remain as enthralled by Manson and his followers as they continue to be by the glamor of their Dostoevskian novelistic prototypes.[41]

But, as we have already seen, the *negative* aspects of the Dostoevskian Abject Hero's critique—his condemnation of the smugness and moral indifference of civil society—is never entirely undercut by the revelation of his own ignominy and corruption. Contemptible in his efforts at self-justification, as a mocker of the normative platitudes of his day he is not without persuasive force. In Manson's speech as well, there is an uncanny drifting into and out of focus of the rage of a pure psychopath and the wounded perception of an underground anarch, ready to articulate the truly disturbing knowledge by which everyone in the room must have been haunted, murderer and shocked audience alike: the knowledge that, ultimately, when a group of a society's children can come at it with knives, ready to murder without a second thought, and when a sizable element of the popular culture of the day can find their actions fascinating, if not deeply thrilling, then the instigations of a single daemonic leader may offer a necessary, but never a sufficient, explanation. On trial in Department 104 was the acting out of the insight of the *philosophe* and the parasite in *Le Neveu de Rameau*, and it was scarcely more than the post-Dostoevskian psychoanalytic truisms about human nature and the dynamics of the modern family that this particular Family turned into literal practice.

Even the accounts given by Manson and his followers of why the case attracted so concentrated and uninterrupted a degree of attention contained a disagreeable element of truth. Like their leader, the other members of the Family maliciously insisted on playing up to the prurience of the public's gaze in order to make unmistakable how much it was titillated by what it condemned and fascinated by what it feared. As recently as 1989, one of these women, Sandra Good, still claimed that the whole trial and its attendant publicity were merely "pandering to the public's taste for vicious thrills."[42] Consonant with the contradictory status of all counteraccusations by such figures, her rebuke is justified insofar as it addresses the voyeurism of many of those who followed the case and entirely irrelevant as an exculpatory plea. Like the citizens of Skotoprigonevsk in *The Brothers Karamazov*, the spectators and journalists at Manson's trial "pretend they're horrified. . . . They keep up the sham with one another. Liars! They all desire [at least vicariously to participate in orgies of sex and murder]. One reptile devours another."[43] Manson's paradoxical emphasis on his own triviality and insignificance while repeatedly demonstrating his unbroken dominance over his disciples was based on his premise that he served only as a receptacle for everyone else's fantasies and projections; and vertiginous as this kind of reasoning may be, in an age when the yearning for an apocalypse was so widespread that it sustained what amounted to a major industry in literature, music, and cinema, it is hard to deny some justice to Manson's claim.

More curious still is that Manson's power over the popular imagination has not entirely abated, even after twenty years of imprisonment. The principal national newspapers continue to print a surprisingly large number of articles in which Manson is invoked or in which members of the original Manson Family are directly involved. Ed Sanders's 1971 book on the Family has recently been reissued in an "expanded and updated" version (1989); a new "as-told-to" autobiography of Manson was published and widely reviewed in 1981; a play about Manson in prison, *Mae Day: When Myths Collide (and don't apologize)* by Henry Steele was successfully staged in San Francisco throughout August 1989; and in July 1990 *The Manson Family*, a new "multi-media music drama" by John Moran, in which the composer "wants to show the Manson family characters as representatives of the same archetypes you find in Greek tragedy" had its premiere at Lincoln Center's Alice Tully Hall.[44] Robert McGrath, the director of *The Manson Family*, explained his New York production thus:

> I liken it [the Manson killings] to the story of the Bacchae. If you think of Manson as Dionysus and the Manson girls as the women of Thebes, it's amazing how it all follows . . . there's something fascinating about the Manson story that captures our imagination in the way that stories of other serial killers do not. . . . The Family believed that they were with God then. For them, God wasn't something you heard about on Sunday when you hedged your spiritual bets and went to church. He was right there with them.[45]

In 1991, Stephen Sondheim's off-Broadway review "Assassins" made Manson's most dedicated disciple, Lynette ("Squeaky") Fromme, a principal character in a musical with her own "show-stopping" number, "a sumptuous ballad" titled "Unworthy of Your Love" about her devotion to Manson.[46] In Germany, the writer Heiner Müller ends his famous piece *Die*

Hamletmaschine with a speech by a figure who is a combination of Ophelia and Squeaky Fromme: "When she walks through your bedrooms carrying butcher knives you'll know the truth."[47] Even the crucial phrases from the Family's murders can resonate in surprising contexts, like the newspaper headline "Helter Swelter," which the director Spike Lee created to signal a nerve-racking, and ultimately murder-provoking heat wave in his 1989 film *Do the Right Thing*. And Manson himself, probably correctly, saw the popular television program, "Charlie's Angels" as a "take-off on me and my girls."[48] No doubt, part of the reason for this continuing fascination is an easy attempt to play upon, and potentially exploit, a particularly tired "myth of the sixties," but the very fact that one abject killer remains so readily evokable and imaginatively accessible an icon is itself a compelling cultural phenomenon.

If Manson draws on, distorts, and appropriates the whole tradition of the *ressentiment*-filled and abject outsiders determined to seek vengeance for their own past suffering and society's iniquity, he is clearly stepping into a role that is instantly recognizable and that elicits a powerful level of response among people who themselves would never act in a criminal, let alone in a murderous, way. And if there is any truth to Manson's claim that he was only the reflector of his interlocutor's unconscious wishes, then it is surely at the most eerily readable level of all—that is, his public identity as a Monster. Genre memories work as powerfully in mass culture and on the consumers of its narratives as they do in great literature, and, perhaps most unsettling of all, as they also do in the dead souls of the homicidal. If "Helter Skelter" continues to be a kind of shorthand for a singularly brutish plunge into murder, it is only because the basic notion of just such an immersion holds a compelling place in our culture's imagination. In Joseph Conrad's *Lord Jim*, Jim is told that the only way to overcome his earlier failure is to test himself in the most extreme and trying circumstances possible—"to the destructive element submit yourself. . . . In the destructive element immerse"[49]—and, as Dostoevsky had already predicted, it is not that far from the celebration of authenticity, risk, and spontaneity to envisaging murder as the final confrontation with "the destructive element" in each of us.

Already in the motif of Manson as a reflector of the Other's desires, there is an oblique but terrifying echo of one of the central forms of our culture's conversation with and about itself, that of psychoanalysis, since this is precisely the function that classical Freudian theory assigned to the relationship between analyst and analysand. (Jacques Lacan even specifies that for the transference to occur in a therapeutically significant way, the analyst must make himself, rather than a "living mirror," an "empty" or "dead" one).[50] And if we consider how rich the vocabulary of psychoanalysis is in images of sadism and rage, of abysmal self-loathing and ecstatic self-adulation, all formally and logically irreconcilable but existentially equally present in the same emotional configuration, indeed establishing in their very irreconcilability the fractured core of who we are, then Manson's emblematic appeal may seem, if not less alarming, then at least less arbitrary. Certainly an era that has made the issue of transference and countertransference between therapists and patients fundamental to much of its speculative probing ought to find too many, rather than no, points of comprehension in accounts of the interaction and power rituals of the Family.

> The mad are predators. Too often lately they har-
> bor against us. A novel heresy exculpates all
> maimed souls.
>   (Geoffrey Hill, *Mercian Hymns*)

> I longed to kill without casuistry, to kill for my
> own benefit, and for that alone! I would not lie
> about it even to myself!
>   (Fyodor Dostoevsky, *Crime and Punishment*)

At least since the French Revolution much of our finest writing and many of our most powerful accounts of the human psyche have been based on a view of humanity that posits an impulse to murder and dominate as constitutive of consciousness itself. What the Underground Man still regarded as exceptional to himself—and found in that singularity the sole source of pride left to him—has become a commonplace of every would-be sophisticated self-description. Earlier in this chapter I admitted the vulnerability to a skeptical denial of my link between the Manson Family and the literature of abjection and *ressentiment*, but it is worth pointing out that a structurally analogous heterology has haunted the speculations of numerous other writers as well. A particularly powerful instance, because it issues from so authoritative a figure and is pronounced in so absolute an idiom, occurs in Primo Levi's outburst in his last extended meditation on his Holocaust experience, *The Drowned and the Saved*:

> I do not know, and it does not much interest me to know, whether in my depths there lurks a murderer, but I do know that I was a guiltless victim and I was not a murderer. I know that the murderers existed . . . and still exist . . . and that to confuse them with their victims is a moral disease or an aesthetic affectation or a sinister sign of complicity; above all, it is a precious service rendered (intentionally or not) to the negators of truth.[51]

This book is also the first in which Levi's anger is permitted to crack the surface of his prose, and in which the calm lucidity that had determined the tone of narratives like *Survival in Auschwitz*, *Moments of Reprieve*, and *The Reawakening* is deliberately fractured by an overflow of outrage and anxiety at the signs of dangerous incomprehension and historical forgetfulness surrounding him. Levi's outcry is a principled and complete rejection of the whole logic and psychology on which Ivan Karamazov's comments about the audience at his brother's trial are based; it is, in equal measure, a rejection of a central strand in psychoanalytic thinking, and, in a strong sense, of a major portion of the modern literary imagination. As such, it deserves to be heeded for the firmness of its refusal and for its unblinking reminder of the absolute differences that theory may elide but that lived human experience has shown to be all too pertinent. His warning against the "aesthetic affectation" of those whose theories risk comforting the torturers by confusing them with their victims is essential for a contemporary intelligentsia that at times seems to flourish most when it exhibits the most dexterity in finding arguments for such a confusion. Levi's vehemence, clear in the very rhythm of his sentences, reveals how isolated he feels in rejecting the fashionable psychological *topoi* of his epoch, and how much energy is required to combat the eradication of the distinctions on which any moral judgment must be based and in whose absence no such judgment—indeed no sense of a coherent morality at all—can continue to make sense.[52]

But mixing categories and undermining the ground on which ethical judgments are founded is precisely the function of the carnivalesque, and Levi's outcry accurately registers the painful loss in humanity that results from a thorough-going Saturnalian rejection of all hierarchies of value. Such otherwise dissimilar discourses as Ivan Karamazov's, the Célinian narrator's, and Charles Manson's originate in apparently incommensurable realms, but each is expressly intended to collapse the barriers between actor and spectator, sage and buffoon, and finally, victim and murderer.

Because Manson so explicitly aligns himself with the longing for a global Saturnalia—and that is literally what "Helter Skelter" meant to the Family and what the Tate/LaBianca murders were intended to trigger—he seems to me the most appropriate figure with whom to end this study, one who, perhaps better than any other, threatens to bring back (into our) home just what we have been so ready to celebrate and welcome in the fictions we read and teach. Manson is the ideal contemporary incarnation of the Abject Hero because his combination of shabby whining, defiant rage, and murderous cunning are all given spectacular license by a historical moment and culture, an epoch that demonstrated with remarkable fidelity the melancholy truth of Adorno's dictum about the relationship between madness and society: "And how comfortless is the thought that the sickness of the normal does not necessarily imply as its opposite the health of the sick, but that the latter usually only present, in a different way, the same disastrous pattern."[53]

I have quoted these lines once before, but want to repeat them now at the end of this book, if only because it is so appropriate to register here, for the last time, how powerfully they crystallize the problem whose inscape I have tried to endow with historical and textual density. But it is necessary to stress, too, that the insanity of a Manson can coexist perfectly well with both the numbing banality of his talismanic images (the Beatles as sources of messianic inspiration, himself as a Christ figure, etc.) and the canniness of his self-defense. To return to Adrian Leverkühn's diagnosis of the latent conformity at the heart of the spectacularly excessive: "there is an apocalyptic tradition which passes on to these ecstatic men visions and experiences to a certain extent already framed, however odd it may seem psychologically that a raving man should rave in the same pattern as another who came before him: that one is ecstatic not independently, so to speak, but by rote."[54] Or, in the shrewd formulation of Roy Porter's *A Social History of Madness:* "Even the mad are men of their time."[55] In the helplessness that such banality lays bare, as much as the whining plea for understanding, some of the abjection of men like Manson makes itself felt, but as case after case demonstrates, in the right setting, abjection can be as powerful a motor of devastation as the most unmixed and daemonic over-reaching. The problem to which I keep returning, however, and the one to which this study has tried not so much to find a "solution" as, on the contrary, to give a sharper edge, are the mechanisms by which, in the midst of our absolute difference, we absolutely participate by taking up our role as fascinated straight men.

We are closer in our habits and needs to Malvolio than to *Twelfth Night*'s midnight revelers, closer, even if not nearly as speculatively wide-ranging, to the Enlightenment intellectuals Jean-François Rameau scorns than to the nimble parasite, as eager for vicarious sensation as the audience Ivan Karamazov calls "reptiles," and in our own lives and attitudes not as different as we would probably wish from the Underground Man's "gentlemen readers." But in each case, it is the carousers, the parasites, the tortured ex-seminarians, and the voices of spite who trigger our identificatory curiosity. And this is not simply because they are our Others, acting out the repressed wishes we share but cannot bring to the surface. Instead, it is because so much of what we have read and admired, of what we have been taught to think and feel, and of what has become part of the fundamental categories by which we understand our culture and our own psyches is implicated in our not admitting where our interests lie and with whom our identification—were we less self-deceiving—might be expected (at least in part) to reside. Céline and Manson are dear to me, bizarre as that phrase may seem, because they make such self-congratulatory self-deception impossible, because, in their different ways, they show us where the celebration of what we are not could lead as soon as we leave our comfortable studies or crowded lecture halls. We are obviously not forced to choose between the soulless banality of the St. Petersburg bureaucracy and the horror of Manson's invocation of an apocalyptic "Helter Skelter," nor between the self-satisfied advice of an Enlightenment rationalist and the Célinian incitement to hysteria and *ressentiment*. But I am troubled by how easily the knowledge of our own compromises and renunciations, of our cowardices and repressions, tempts us to fantasize about a condition of pure authenticity, in which all these self-betrayals and cultural accommodations are cast aside for the immediacy of our unfettered desires. The political consequences of such fantasies, whenever they have been mobilized and harnessed by a mass movement, seem to me to have been genuinely horrific, unleashing a disastrous torrent in which little except a kind of numb brutality could survive.

Perhaps the sharpest way to formulate this situation is to insist that in our culture it is neither sexuality nor the darkest urgings to violence and domination that are repressed. Exactly these issues constitute an enormous, if not actually the major, portion of our cultural conversation about the human psyche. What *is* repressed, though, is the force of the prosaic, the counter-authenticity, if you will, of the texture and rhythm of our daily routines and decisions, the myriad of minute and careful adjustments that we are ready to offer in the interest of a habitable social world.[56]

Yet, at the same time, I also want to keep in focus an implicit underside of Adorno's aphorism: how comfortless is the thought that the sickness of the mad does not necessarily imply as its opposite the wisdom of the ordinary, but that each often presents, in different ways, fragments of the same crisis. And so, although I intend the argument of this book polemically, even now, at the end, I find myself unable to come down entirely on one side or the other of the debate whose changing contours I have been tracing.[57] In spite of the discomfort that many literary critics still feel at the notion of an ethical conclusion, I have been searching for just such a closing, but find that, like my chosen texts, my formulations keep coming out in a split or, to put the matter more generously, a dialogical way.

To side exclusively with the voices of conformity in our texts would violate the dialogues in which they figure merely to erect a "Positive Hero" (and often a positively unpleasant one), to offset the "Abject Heroes" whose vicissitudes have been my principal concern. But since the Abject Hero and his normative interlocutor only exist in a mutually defining relationship, the absence of any positive model one can take seriously makes it extraordinarily difficult to formulate a persuasive argument against the carelessly romantic view of the abject Other. The problem is all the more acute precisely because our culture already includes this carelessly sentimental romanticization as one of its foundational paradigms. It does so, I suspect, for three related reasons, each of which is, within certain limits, both valid and probably even necessary: (1) As a containment strategy that allows potentially destructive forces a certain measure of controlled freedom lest they erupt with sufficient force to destroy the entire network of social relations (the Saturnalia as a form of strictly licensed and limited liberty intended to preserve the dominant culture). (2) As a source of novelty and new thrills to keep vivid the imagination of a citizenry otherwise at risk of finding intolerable the demand for a public *gravitas* and pedestrian rationalism (the Saturnalia as a form of exotic escapism, primarily for the master's emotional and psychological pleasure). (3) As a way to acknowledge the heterogeneity of human motives, temperaments, and urges (the Saturnalia as the social embodiment of a psychological anthropology).

Nonetheless, each of these reasons is potentially dangerous as well:

(1) The containment can easily break down, as in the bloody carnival riots and pogroms that kept recurring throughout the Middle Ages and the Renaissance.[58] Historically, there have been too many such breakdowns not to raise a justified anxiety—too many moments when the Saturnalian marketplace becomes the Underground, and the Underground spawns violence like that practiced by the Fascist militia, the Cagoule in Vichy France (*ressentiment* endowed with full social authority), or by Manson's Family (*ressentiment* and abjection remaining oppositional but deriving group support and encouragement from popular culture).

(2) The novelty can become so seductive that it begins to replace the normative, from which it was originally envisaged as only a temporary escape. In this development, the apparently banal decencies of communal seemliness and private self-restraint are stripped of all cultural prestige and no longer appear worth the effort of maintaining.

(3) The recognition of psychological heterogeneity can become a refusal to hierarchize one's own needs. What may follow from this refusal is a theoretically grounded undermining of all ethical categories, so that no criteria remain by which the relative value of actions can be judged. At the extreme, the culture's intelligentsia fall victim to Primo Levi's diagnosis of "moral disease, aesthetic affectation, or complicity with murder," and it begins, in principle, not to be able to distinguish between killer and victim.

In an age still so enamored of a Romantic paradigm according to which it is the outsider and the outcast who represents the most exciting possibilities, the defense of the quotidian, prosaic world, with its undramatic practices and values, is bound to seem like an imaginatively narrow decision. Nonetheless, I believe it is the rhetoric of revolutionary apocalypse indulged in by a large contingent of Western academics and intellectuals that is the truly conventional gesture, in ready harmony with the pieties of the day. If this study has tried to restore the sense of an edge to the bitter carnival, and to emphasize the risks inherent in the topos of the Saturnalian dialogue, it is in order to compel us to think more honestly about what is at stake when we make identificatory and cultural evaluations in and through our tales.

Imagine, for a final moment, that the two men whose conversation in a bar or a bus station we overheard in chapter 1 have crossed paths again, perhaps even deliberately, as part of an annual encounter to see how each has fared in the interval. Physically, nothing much about either one has changed. One is still thin and edgy, his face nervously scanning the horizon for signs of danger or easy prey, his hand ready either to strike out or to take up a beggar's curve, depending on the kind of resistance it encounters; the other has left both the library and the university gym for the day, and appears, if not more prosperous than when they last met, somewhat more fashionably dressed and certainly more fit. And once again, the first begins his familiar whine of self-accusatory self-congratulation, ready to mix tales of woe and triumph, in order either to dazzle his interlocutor with the nimbleness of his wit or to terrify him with the ferocity of his rage. Only this time, when the interlocutor interrupts him, it is to shout, "You know, you're right, after all. I have been rereading those books you keep plagiarizing, and have come to the conclusion that even if everything you say is second-hand, compared to my own boring life yours has a great deal to offer. Even if you still feel so anxious and depressed, your experiences keep changing moment by moment and have more dramatic flamboyance than the deadening regularity and total predictability of my days." I suspect that this kind of interruption would infuriate our abject complainer even more than any of the former ways his speech was cut off and re-framed, especially since he never had the chance to tell his interlocutor that he, too, had recently found a teaching position at a local college and was busy preparing a syllabus on his abjection and belatedness.

I suppose the "moral" of this book is itself a final question: Who, at this stage in the history of our dialogue, is the true Abject Hero? When both speakers are in agreement that it is the very marginality of the abject, the victimization of the supposedly dispossessed failure, that has captured for him the full attention, rewards, and even admiration of the community of fascinated "straight men," who then still remains who can rightfully lay claim to Lebedyev's wonderful cry from *The Idiot*?

> It's just like me saying "I am abject, I am abject!" . . . Words and deeds and lies and truth are all mixed up in me and are perfectly sincere. Deeds and truth come out in my genuine penitence, I swear it, whether you believe it or not; and words and lies in the hellish (and always present) craving to get the better of a man, to make something even out of one's tears of penitence.[59]

Notes

Introduction
Murder and the Utopian Moment

1. Albert Robbins, "Blinded by the Light: The Einhorn-Maddux Murder Case," *The Village Voice*, July 23, 1979, pp. 1–31.

2. The most useful compilation of information on Ira Einhorn and Holly Maddux is Steven Levy's book *The Unicorn's Secret: Murder in the Age of Aquarius* (New York: Prentice Hall, 1988). Einhorn's own voice can be heard best in his book, named after its Library of Congress catalog card number, *78-187880* (Garden City, N.Y.: Doubleday and Co., 1972) and in the essay, "Change, Media, Communication," his contribution to an anthology called *The Prophetic Generation: Fourteen Essays on the Aquarian Age*, ed. Edward Rice and Jane Garmey (Rensselaerville, N.Y.: Catholic Art Association, 1970, pp. 86–104). Greg Walker's piece, "Holly," in *Philadelphia Magazine*, December 1979, pp. 144–51; 262–73, provides a useful index of the confusion Einhorn's arrest caused in the Philadelphia community. Walker also incorporates a lengthy interview with Einhorn, who never wavers from the claim that he is a victim of a massive, government-organized conspiracy to silence him.

3. Peckham's phrase, with its no doubt too easy reversal of Wallace Stevens's line "Oh! Blessed rage for order" from "The Idea of Order at Key West," was given its widest circulation in Morse Peckham, *Man's Rage for Chaos: Biology, Behavior, and the Arts* (Philadelphia: Chilton Books, 1965). In his acknowledgments, Peckham included Ira Einhorn among the brief list of people thanked for "their valuable criticism and suggestions" (p. xii).

4. Denis Diderot, *Le Neveu de Rameau*, ed. Jean Fabre (Geneva: Librarie Droz, 1963), p. 76: "L'atrocité de l'action vous porte au dela du mepris." The peculiarities of spelling and accentuation are those of Diderot's manuscript, as edited by Fabre. All subsequent references to *Le Neveu de Rameau* will be from this edition.

5. Diderot, *Le Neveu de Rameau*, p. 90: "c'est ce que nous apellons des especes, de toutes les epithetes la plus redoutable, parce qu'elle marque la mediocrité, et le dernier degré du mepris."

6. Michael André Bernstein, "The Abject Hero: A Study of *Le Neveu de Rameau* and Its Literary Posterity" (B. Litt. thesis, Oxford University, 1971).

7. Ira Einhorn, "Change, Media, Communication," p. 95.

8. Levy's *The Unicorn's Secret* quotes numerous examples of Einhorn's willingness to laugh at himself—but only if doing so would deflect the force of someone else's mockery by appearing to share in it. Einhorn's humor at his own expense served as one more, and not the least effective, of his aggressive weapons (see pp. 114–15).

9. Peter Stallybrass and Allon White, *The Politics and Poetics of Transgression* (Ithaca: Cornell University Press, 1986), pp. 5 and 191.

10. For a detailed history of this phenomenon in the visual arts, see John M. MacGregor, *The Discovery of the Art of the Insane* (Princeton: Princeton University Press, 1989). Robert Harbison's *Deliberate Regression* (New York: Alfred Knopf, 1980) is a more polemical exploration of similar themes, focusing primarily on the works of major artists and philosophers.

11. Illustrations of this tendency could be multiplied indefinitely. But as a typical exemplum, consider Norman O. Brown's "Intellect is sacrifice of intellect, or fire; which burns up as it gives light," or his longing "to bring this world to an end, in a final conflagration, or explosion, bursting the boundaries" (*Love's Body* [New York: Random House, 1966], pp. 188 and 177). Interestingly, both R. D. Laing's and Norman O. Brown's popular acclaim came well after the publication of books in which they already had presented similar, if less luridly phrased, theories. In earlier works they had relied on consecutive argumentation rather than the pseudo-Nietzschean aphorisms that marked their subsequent prose. Thus, for example, Laing's *The Divided Self*, which originally appeared in 1960, only became retroactively popular in its mid-1960s reprinting, and Norman O. Brown's *Life against Death: The Psychoanalytic Meaning of History* (1959) was similarly "resurrected" a decade later. But for the audience that celebrated *Love's Body*, the earlier book seemed only an excessively intellectual precursor text. Unhappily, that judgment appears not to have been significantly altered in the intervening years. The University of California Press announced the October 1990 reprinting of *Love's Body* by calling it a "meditation on the condition of humanity and its long fall from the grace of a natural, instinctive innocence [made] available once more for a new generation of readers." Eldridge Cleaver's *Soul on Ice* (New York: Ramparts Book/ McGraw Hill, 1968), on the other hand, seems to have vanished from popular consciousness, but its initial success was enormous and unchecked by the slightest alarm at the brutality of its sexual and social assumptions.

Chapter One
I Wear Not Motley in My Brain: Slaves, Fools, and Abject Heroes

1. William Shakespeare, *Twelfth Night*, ed. C. T. Prouty (Baltimore: Penguin, 1958), 1.5.88–89, p. 43. All further references are to this edition and are cited in the body of the text.

2. In *Shandyism: The Character of Romantic Irony* (Oxford: Blackwell, 1978) pp. 4–5, Peter Conrad sees this splitting as a general strategy in Shakespeare's comedies: "Satirist and clown stalk one another uneasily. . . . The satirist envies the fool's license. . . . The liberty the fool is granted as his only weapon against the slights of wise men, the satirist demands as a special charter." In *Ursprung des deutschen Trauerspiels* (Frankfurt: Suhrkamp, 1963), p. 135, Walter Benjamin posits the existence of a "daemonic fool," a kind of sinister twin to the licensed jester, through whom the Renaissance worlds of tragedy and farce could merge into a single spectacle. Benjamin goes on to speculate that Shakespeare drew upon the "daemonic fool" as the basis for characters like Iago and Polonius, but unfortunately he never extends his discussion of the "daemonic fool" much beyond this tantalizing hint.

3. Diderot, *Le Neveu de Rameau*, p. 61: "Il n'y a point de meilleur role aupres des grands que celui de fou. Long tems il y a eu le fou du roi en titre, en aucun, il

n'y a eu en titre le sage du Roi. Moi je suis le fou de Bertin et de beaucoup d'autres, le votre peut etre dans ce moment; ou peut etre vous le mien. Celui qui seroit sage n'auroit point de fou. Celui donc qui a un fou n'est pas sage; s'il n'est pas sage il est fou; et peut etre, fut-il roi, le fou de son fou."

4. Horace, *Satires, Epistles, and Ars Poetica*, ed. and trans. Henry Rushton Fairclough (Cambridge: Harvard University Press/Loeb Classical Library, 1929), 2.7, ll. 39–43. All future references to Horace's *Satires* are from Fairclough's edition, and will be cited in the body of the text in the form 2.7.14 to indicate Book 2, Satire 7, line 14.

5. Quoted in Niall Rudd, *The Satires of Horace* (Berkeley: University of California Press, 1982), p. 190. Rudd notes that, "in the Cynic-Stoic tradition the idea of the fool as a slave goes back to Diogenes . . . and Zeno" (p. 299, n. 45).

6. Mikhail Bakhtin, *Rabelais and His World*, trans. Helene Iswolsky (Cambridge: MIT Press, 1968), p. 11.

7. For a more detailed discussion of these issues, see Samuel Kinser's recent study, *Rabelais's Carnival: Text, Context, Metatext* (Berkeley: University of California Press, 1990).

8. Bakhtin, *Rabelais and His World*, p. 7.

9. By now the critical term "belatedness" has become linked, for better or for worse, with the theory of poetic inheritance developed by Harold Bloom. I have discussed my disagreement with Bloom's poetic Oedipology elsewhere, but even though I think his conception fails to account for the many kinds of relationships that have existed between major poets and their predecessors, it does offer a useful way to think about how the Abject Hero views his position vis-à-vis the "wise fools" of the satiric tradition. The struggle for imaginative supremacy that Bloom chronicles among lyric poets seems to me far truer as an account of the desperate efforts of the latecomers in modern Saturnalian dialogues to convince themselves and their interlocutors of their originality.

10. William Empson, *The Structure of Complex Words* (New York: New Directions, 1951), pp. 105–24.

11. Louis-Ferdinand Céline, *Rigodon*, vol. 2 of *Romans*, ed. Henri Godard (Paris: Bibliothèque de la Pléiade, 1974), p. 842: "à ça que l'homme est parvenu, son immense progrès, oecuménique, pluratomique, tout le monde dans l'arène, plus un seul voyeur aux gradins!"

12. Denis Diderot, *Eléments de physiologie*, vol. 9 of *Oeuvres Complètes*, ed. J. Assézat and M. Tourneux (Paris: Garnier, 1875–79), p. 418: "Mais l'ordre générale change sans cesse; comment au milieu de cette vicissitude la durée de l'espèce peut-elle rester la même?" For more specialized studies on this theme, see Emita B. Hill's two essays, "The Role of 'le monstre' in Diderot's Thought," *Studies on Voltaire and the Eighteenth Century* 97 (1972): 147–361; and "Human Nature and the Moral Monster," *Diderot Studies* 16 (1973): 91–117. Jay Caplan's *Framed Narratives: Diderot's Genealogy of the Beholder* (Minneapolis: University of Minnesota Press, 1985) also contains a valuable discussion of the monster in Diderot.

13. Jean Starobinski, *1789: The Emblems of Reason*, trans. Barbara Bray (Charlottesville: University of Virginia Press, 1982), p. 136.

14. Ibid., p. 198.

15. Walter Benjamin, *Illuminations*, trans. H. Zohn (New York: Schocken, 1969), p. 4.

16. Diderot, *Le Neveu de Rameau*, p. 72: "S'il importe d'etre sublime en quelque genre, c'est surtout en mal. On crache sur un petit filou; mais on ne peut refuser une sorte de consideration a un grand criminel. Son courage vous etonne. Son atrocité vous fait frémir. On prise en tout l'unité de caractere."

17. I owe this succinct definition to Katharine Streip whose "Laughter and *Ressentiment* in Twentieth Century Narrative" (Ph.D. dissertation, University of California, Berkeley, 1991), will be the first rigorous study of how ressentiment and humor interact in contemporary writing.

18. Julia Kristeva, *Powers of Horror: An Essay on Abjection*, trans. Leon S. Roudiez (New York: Columbia University Press, 1982), pp. 4–5.

19. Ibid., p. 4.

20. Ibid.

21. For a more sympathetic, but still shrewdly skeptical, analysis of *Powers of Horror*, see Juliet Flower MacCannell's essay "Kristeva's Horror," *Semiotica* 62, nos. 3/4 (1986): 325–55. The best critique in English of Kristeva, written from a Marxist perspective, is in Stallybrass and White, *The Politics and Poetics of Transgression*. For them, Kristeva's privileging of carnival is a characteristic bourgeois gesture: "When Kristeva returns to the carnivalesque scene as the potential site of political subversion she confuses the projection of bourgeois desire with the destruction of its class identity. The bourgeoisie . . . is perpetually rediscovering the carnivalesque as a radical source of transcendence. Indeed that act of rediscovery itself, in which the middle classes excitedly discover their own pleasures and desires under the sign of the Other, in the realm of the Other, is constitutive of the very foundation of middleclass identity" (p. 201).

22. The essays edited by Edward Dudley and Maximillian Novak, in their collection *The Wild Man Within: An Image in Western Thought from the Renaissance to Romanticism* (Pittsburgh: University of Pittsburgh Press, 1972), underline the power of this archetype.

23. Philip Roth, *Zuckerman Bound* (New York: Farrar, Strauss and Giroux, 1985), p. 655.

24. Stefan Collini, "Speaking from Somewhere," *Times Literary Supplement*, April 15–21, 1988, p. 427.

25. Ibid.

Chapter Two
O Totiens Servus: Horace, Juvenal, and the Classical Saturnalia

1. Friedrich Nietzsche, *Jenseits von Gut und Böse*, in *Werke in sechs Bänden*, ed. Karl Schlechta (Munich: Carl Hanser, 1980), vol. 4, sec. 223, p. 686: "zum Karneval großen Stils, zum geistigsten Fasching-Gelächter und Übermut, zur transzendentalen Höhe des höchsten Blödsinns und der aristophanischen Welt-Verspottung. Vielleicht, daß wir hier gerade das Reich unsrer *Erfindung* noch entdecken, jenes Reich, wo auch wir noch original sein können, etwa als Parodisten der Weltgeschichte und Hanswürste Gottes—vielleicht daß, wenn auch nichts von heute sonst Zukunft hat, doch gerade unser *Lachen* noch Zukunft hat." I have used

Walter Kaufmann's translation: *Beyond Good and Evil* (New York: Vintage Books, 1966), p. 150.

2. As an example of such an affirmative reading of Nietzsche, consider Michel Foucault's essay "Nietzsche, Genealogy, History," in *Language, Counter-Memory, Practice*, ed. D. F. Bouchard (Ithaca: Cornell University Press, 1977), pp. 139–64. I realize that Foucault is scarcely ever regarded as an affirmative writer, but his attitude towards the liberating power of carnival laughter seems to me much more celebratory and optimistic than Nietzsche's own.

3. Another problematic aspect of the passage is Nietzsche's use of the term "Hanswürste Gottes" (God's buffoons) as the principal remaining hope for mankind's "original" future. In *Götzen-Dämmerung*, Nietzsche repeatedly refers to his great intellectual antagonist, Socrates, as a "Hanswurst," in a context that makes the negative implications of the word unmistakable. Socrates is described as a buffoon because his dialectic method threatened to undermine aristocratic authority and thus bring about exactly the sort of Saturnalia Nietzsche finds contemptible: "Überall, wo noch die Autorität zur guten Sitte gehört, wo man nicht 'begründet,' sondern befiehlt, ist der Dialektiker eine Art Hanswurst: man lacht über ihn, man nimmt ihn nicht ernst. Sokrates war der Hanswurst, der sich *ernstnehmen machte* [Wherever authority still belongs to customary practice, where one does not 'argue through' but commands, the dialectician is a kind of buffoon: he is laughed at, not taken seriously. Socrates was the buffoon who succeeded in getting himself taken seriously]" (Nietzsche, *Götzen-Dämmerung*, in *Werke in sechs Bänden*, 4:953).

4. Friedrich Nietzsche, *Menschliches, allzumenschliches*, in *Werke in sechs Bänden*, vol. 2, sec. 213, p. 572: "Wie kann der Mensch Freude am Unsinn haben? . . . Das Umwerfen der Erfahrung ins Gegenteil, des Zweckmäßigen ins Zwecklose, des Notwendigen ins Beliebige, doch so, daß dieser Vorgang keinen Schaden macht und nur einmal aus Übermut vorgestellt wird, ergötzt, denn es befreit uns *momentan* von dem Zwange des Notwendigen, Zweckmäßigen und Erfahrungsgemäßen, in denen wir für gewöhnlich unsere unerbittlichen Herren sehen; wir spielen und lachen dann, wenn das Erwartete (das gewöhnlich bange macht und spannt) sich ohne zu schädigen entladet. Es ist die Freude des Sklaven am Saturnalienfeste."

5. Friedrich Nietzsche, *Also sprach Zarathustra*, in *Werke in sechs Bänden*, vol. 3, pt. 4, sec. 12, p. 558: "alle Lust will Ewigkeit-,/-will tiefe, tiefe Ewigkeit! "

6. Bakhtin, *Rabelais and His World*, p. 7.

7. Ibid., p. 8.

8. Enid Welsford, for example, devotes very little space to Rabelais, but finds that in *Twelfth Night* "Shakespeare transmutes into poetry the quintessence of the Saturnalia" (*The Fool: His Social and Literary History* [Garden City, N.Y.: Doubleday, 1961], p. 253).

9. Roger Chartier, "La Fête en question: Retour sur un colloque" and "Des fêtes de l'Ancien Régime à la fête révolutionnaire: Problèmes de lecture," in *La Fête en question*, ed. K. R. Gürttler and M. Sarfati-Arnaud (Montreal: University of Montreal Press, 1979), pp. 1–4 and 35–56.

10. See, for example, Emmanuel Le Roy Ladurie, *Carnival in Romans*, trans. Mary Feeney (New York: G. Braziller, 1979); Kenelm Burridge, *New Heaven, New Earth: A Study of Millenarian Activities* (Oxford: B. Blackwell, 1969); and Sylvia L. Thrupp, ed., *Millennial Dreams in Action* (New York: Schocken, 1970).

11. For a useful essay on the connection between carnival and drama that draws heavily on Bakhtin, see Michael D. Bristol, "Carnival and the Institutions of Theater in Elizabethan England," *ELH* 50, no. 4 (1983): 637–54.

12. René Girard, *Violence and the Sacred*, trans. Patrick Gregory (Baltimore: Johns Hopkins University Press, 1977), esp. pp. 118–42.

13. Robert C. Elliott, *The Power of Satire: Magic, Ritual, Art* (Princeton: Princeton University Press, 1966), p. 80.

14. Walter Burkert, *Greek Religion*, trans. John Raltan (Cambridge: Harvard University Press, 1985), pp. 258–59. For Burkert, the purpose of such license is deeply conservative: "It is precisely by the most natural and self-evident things being placed in question that their continuity is assured. . . . Immortal, everlasting gods guarantee continuity; ritual means determination. Even the festivals of dissolution and upheaval lead to the confirmation of the existing order. Important antitheses which reflect the history of mankind are acted out . . . and thereby the everyday order of authority and labor proves the only one that is permanently possible. And yet the wishful version of a golden age is conjured up, alternatives with their risks and possibilities are kept alive, so that the one-dimensional and total adaption of man to his role is prevented" (pp. 245 and 259).

15. Cf. Chartier's comment: "la fête est aussi un langage où peuvent se dire et se donner à voir les tensions qui traversent une société" (*La Fête en question*, p. 2).

16. For a good summary of recent opinions on the origins and rituals of the Saturnalia, see H. H. Scullard, *Festivals and Ceremonies of the Roman Republic* (Ithaca: Cornell University Press, 1981), pp. 205–7.

17. Aristotle, *Rhetoric* 3.17.1418. I have used *The Rhetoric of Aristotle*, trans. Sir Richard C. Jebb, ed. John E. Sandys (Cambridge: Cambridge University Press, 1909), p. 194, but have somewhat modified Jebb's translation in the version quoted here.

18. It is precisely this kind of liberty to which Martial appealed in defending his verses from the charge of obscenity:

Versus hos tamen esse tu memento
Saturnalicios, Apollinaris:
Mores non habet hic meos libellus.

[But remember, Apollinaris, these poems are meant to be read in the spirit of the Saturnalia: this little book doesn't voice my personal morals.]

(Epigrams 11.15.11–13)

I have used Walter C. A. Kerr's edition of the *Epigrams* (London: W. Heinemann, 1930), 2:246–49, but have somewhat modified Kerr's translation.

19. Robert C. Elliott, *The Shape of Utopia* (Chicago: University of Chicago Press, 1970), pp. 18–25.

20. See especially Mircea Eliade, *Le Mythe de l'éternel retour* (Paris: Gallimard, 1969) and *Le Sacré et le profane* (Paris: Gallimard, 1965) for two influential expressions of this tendency.

21. For a detailed discussion of this question, see Erwin Panofsky, *Studies in Iconology* (New York: Oxford University Press, 1939) and R. Klibansky, E. Panofsky, and F. Saxl, *Saturn and Melancholy* (London: Nelson, 1964). Panofsky

shows how ambiguous a figure Saturn was. The antitheses he embodies range from extremes of physical materiality to complete mental abstraction and from sloth and dullness to intelligence and pure contemplation, all based on the original, Hesiodic reversal of fecundity into impotence. Although Panofsky does not make this connection, his account suggests parallels between Saturn and Vertumnus, since both presided over, and were tutelary spirits of, manic extremes and uncontrolled fluctuations. Walter Benjamin's *Ursprung des deutschen Trauerspiel* brilliantly deploys the figure of a melancholic Saturn in its analyses.

22. Virgil, *Opera*, ed. R.A.B. Mynors (Oxford: Oxford University Press/Oxford Classical Texts, 1972), Ecloga 4.6, p. 10.

23. Ibid., p. 262. The translation below is by Robert Fitzgerald, *The Aeneid* (New York: Random House, 1983), p. 202.

24. For this account of Horace's career, see W. R. Johnson's foreword to Burton Raffel's *The Essential Horace* (San Francisco: North Point Press, 1983), pp. vii–xiii. Horace's description of his inglorious flight at Philippi is from *Odes* 2.7.10, in *Odes and Epodes*, ed. and trans. C. E. Bennett (Cambridge: Harvard University Press, 1927), p. 122. For a skeptical discussion of the historical accuracy of Horace's description of his battle experiences and an analysis of the famous phrase "relicta non bene parmula," see Eduard Fraenkel, *Horace* (Oxford: Oxford University Press, 1957), p. 11.

25. P. A. Brunt, "The Army and the Land in the Roman Revolution," *Journal of Roman Studies* 52 (1962): 75.

26. Rudd, *The Satires of Horace*, pp. 36–37.

27. Ibid., p. 37.

28. W. R. Johnson, *The Essential Horace*, p. x.

29. In context, Furet is speaking of the French Revolution. I do not mean to suggest that the situation in Augustus's Rome was similar to that in republican Paris, but rather that his account seems accurate as a description of how every new government established through the violent overthrow of its predecessor strives to confirm its right to power. Furet's lines are quoted in Alan Forrest, "Life-Cycle of a Circle," *Times Literary Supplement*, November 1, 1985, p. 1226. Richard Jenkyns's description of Augustus' use of the arts as political instruments directly relates the success of Imperial policy to similar attempts in later cultures: "It was by political propaganda expressed through poetry that both Augustus and Elizabeth [Queen Elizabeth I of England] imposed upon posterity the idea of themselves as presiding geniuses of a culminating age." See Jenkyns, *Three Classical Poets: Sappho, Catullus and Juvenal* (London: Duckworth, 1982), p. 182, n. 21. The centrality of political undercurrents in the verse of the major Augustan poets, even when they were writing on seemingly quite different themes, is powerfully demonstrated in the collection of essays assembled by Tony Woodman and David West, *Poetry and Politics in the Age of Augustus* (Cambridge: Cambridge University Press, 1984). In *Propertius, "Love" and "War": Individual and State under Augustus* (Berkeley: University of California Press, 1985), Hans-Peter Stahl describes the tensions between literature and politics in the Augustan elegy and traces the struggle of poets like Propertius to express a "personal voice in a publicly uniform and therefore homogenizing environment" (p. 3).

30. R.O.A.M. Lyne, "Augustan Poetry and Society," in John Boardman, Jasper Griffin, and Oswyn Murray, eds., *The Oxford History of the Classical World* (Oxford: Oxford University Press, 1986), p. 596.

31. The counter-example of Ovid, whom Augustus personally banished for life to Tomis, a wretched village on the coast of the Black Sea, indicates how poetic genius alone could not save a writer of the "wrong" sort. The severity of Ovid's punishment suggests that his poems, with their steady undercurrent of irony directed at the whole Augustan ethos, were in good measure responsible for the Emperor's harshness. In "History: Ovid and the Augustan Myth," Nial Rudd argues that Ovid's erotic poems, by their themes and tone, enacted a semi-deliberate mockery not only of Augustan values but of the Imperial family itself and thus helped to ensure the poet's miserable fate. See Rudd, *Lines of Enquiry: Studies in Latin Poetry* (Cambridge: Cambridge University Press, 1976), pp. 1–31.

32. I have not done a systematic count of all the uses of *invidia* as an explanation for his opponents' motives in Horace's work, but the following examples, although far from exhaustive, will give some sense of how important Horace felt envy was in explaining human behavior: *Satires* 1.3.61, 2.1.77, 2.6.48; *Odes* 2.20.4, 4.3.16; and *Epistles* 1.14.37–38. In the last passage, the word itself does not occur but the idea is strikingly presented: "non istic obliquo oculo mea commoda quisquam / limat, non odio obscuro morsuque venenat [Where you live, no one with eye askance detracts from my comforts, or poisons them with the bite of secret hate]." When Horace envisages his own future immortality in *Odes* 2.20.1–5, he cites a final victory over the *invidia* of his enemies as one of its principal benefits: "Non usitata nec tenui ferar / pinna biformis per liquidum aethera / vates, neque in terris morabor / longius *invidiaque* maior / urbes relinquam [On no common or feeble pinion shall I soar in double form through the liquid air, a poet still, nor linger more on earth, but victorious over envy I shall quit the towns of men]" (*Odes and Epodes*, trans. C. E. Bennett, p. 165, emphasis mine).

33. In an important essay, "The Roman Socrates: Horace and His Satires," in *Essays on Roman Satire* (Princeton: Princeton University Press, 1982), p. 29, William S. Anderson argues that the "Horace" of the *Sermones* must be understood as a persona created by the satires, who cannot be interpreted coherently by an appeal to the poet's biography: "Horace produced a Socratic satirist probably quite unrepresentative of himself; and this satirist, the speaker in his *Sermones*, is one of the greatest achievements of Horatian poetry." But for all its persuasiveness, Anderson's point must be considered only a necessary corrective to the facile assimilation of the author to the speaker of the verses, rather than a barrier against exploring tensions created within the poems themselves. Part of Horace's mastery consists in the ways his *persona* succeeds in alternately evading or triumphing over the pressures of the poet's actual circumstances. If the poems strive to create a certain voice and viewpoint, they do not do so with uniform success. Both the fissures in the representation and the moments of curious overemphasis on seemingly trivial points require their own kinds of explanation. My reading of Satire 2.7, for example, seeks precisely to uncover some of the cost—technical as well as emotional—of Horace's effort to maintain the *persona* of a "Socratic satirist."

34. For an enlightening discussion of this point, see, D. R. Shackleton Bailey, *Profile of Horace* (Cambridge: Harvard University Press, 1982), pp. 20–22.

35. In Satire 1.10.40–43, for example, Horace mentions "Davus" as the typical slave-trickster of the comic stage, who helps to fool the old father for the sake of the play's lovers. Again, in Satire 2.5.91–92, Horace has Tiresias advise Ulysses, "Davus sis comicus atque / stes capite obstipo, multum similis metuenti [Act like the Davus of the comedy, and stand with head bowed, much like one [pretending to be] overawed]." Later satirists continued Horace's own borrowings from Roman comedy by calling the slave in their poems Davus as well (e.g., Persius's Fifth Satire, 161ff.).

36. The description of Volanerius's mania may contain another elegantly indirect reminder that the poem is a Saturnalian text, since the holiday was a time when gambling in public was allowed.

37. Rudd, *The Satires of Horace*, p. 138.

38. Rudd's description here seems to me entirely accurate, and could be applied to Diderot as well as to Horace: "Horace had a genuine respect for men of homogeneous character. He recognized their potential heroism, and could formulate the ideal in memorable terms. . . . But he evinces no affection for such men, and it is clear that he himself was made of quite different stuff" (*The Satires of Horace*, p. 199).

39. Amy Richlin, *The Garden of Priapus: Sexuality and Aggression in Roman Humor* (New Haven: Yale University Press, 1983), p. 178.

40. In *The Garden of Priapus*, p. 192, Richlin shrewdly points out that Horace's advice on suitable sexual partners is itself a product of anxiety, not about sexuality per se, but about issues of wealth and control.

41. Rudd, *The Satires of Horace*, p. 192.

42. See also Cicero's *Paradoxa Stoicorum*, ed. A. G. Lee (London: Macmillan, 1953). The fifth of Cicero's six essays takes as its theme the proposition "Omnes sapientes liberos esse et stultos omnes servos [All wise men are free and everyone without wisdom is a slave]" and rehearses many of the same motifs that Horace draws upon in his satire. For example, Edward P. Morris's edition, *Horace: Satires and Epistles* (Norman: University of Oklahoma Press, 1974), p. 234, notes that the satire "follows in part the same line of reasoning [as Cicero's *Parad.* 5], using in vss. 89ff. the illustration of the lover enslaved by a woman and in vss. 95ff. the illustration of the infatuated admirer of works of art, almost precisely as they are used by Cicero." Criticism often treats the discovery of a canonic source as a sufficient answer to questions of interpretation. But no matter how complete such an inventory may be, listing echoes and borrowings cannot settle the issue of why an author chose a particular model at a specifiment in his own text. Here, for example, Horace's decision to make Davus's accusations recapitulate all of the typical comic vices in so arbitrary a fashion raises, rather than resolves, difficulties in the satire's structure and tone.

43. In *Le Neveu de Rameau*, *Lui* describes his rebellion against the demands of the Bertin household by saying, "On useroit un pantin d'acier a tirer la ficelle du matin au soir et du soir au matin [You'd wear out even a steel puppet if you kept pulling its string day and night, night and day]" (p. 65). Originally, however, in Satire 2.7, Davus applied the puppet image to Horace, not to himself, and the transformation in the thrust of the simile is a perfect index of the ways in which an "abject hero" differs from a "licensed fool."

44. It is fascinating to note here that although Diderot obviously enjoyed the whole idea of a Saturnalian license, he was unwilling to grant Davus his liberties when the issue turned to art. In the *Salon de 1767*, Diderot again quotes from Horace's Satire 2.7, and cites both the original Latin and his own translation of lines 95–98. But this time, unlike in *Le Neveu de Rameau*, he does so to defend the idea of taste and refinement against the slave's mockery. Diderot, the connoisseur, calls Davus's accusation foolish and insists that taste in painting, as in literature, must be acquired by diligent study (Denis Diderot, *Salons*, ed. Jean Seznec and Jean Adhémar [Oxford: Clarendon Press, 1963], 3:241).

45. One can compare the vividness of Horace's image here with Lucretius's didactic manner of expressing a similar idea:

hoc se quisque modo fugit, at quem scilicet, ut fit,
effugere haud potis est, ingratis haeret et odit
propterea, morbi quia causam non tenet aeger.

[In this way, each man struggles to flee from himself: yet despite his will he clings to the self, which, we may be sure, in fact he cannot escape, and hates himself, because in his sickness he knows not the cause of his malady.]

(De rerum natura 3.1068–70)

I have used Cyril Bailey's edition and translation of *De rerum natura* (Oxford: Oxford University Press, 1947), p. 356.

46. Horace, *Satires, Epistles and Ars Poetica*, p. 228, n. b.

47. For two valuable discussions of the place of dialectical argumentation in Stoicism and the relationship of this kind of mental training to ethical considerations, see, A. A. Long, "Dialectic and the Stoic Sage," and G. B. Kerferd, "What Does the Wise Man Know?" in *The Stoics*, ed. John M. Rist (Berkeley: University of California Press, 1978), pp. 101–24 and 125–36.

48. In this regard, it is fascinating to see the change in Horace's relationship to his patron during the poet's later years. In the First Epistle, Horace refuses Maecenas's request that he continue writing lyric poetry, but he does so with great tact, arguing that it is time now to devote himself to philosophy. By the time of the Seventh Epistle, however, Horace insists upon his right to remain in the country in spite of Maecenas's plea that he hurry back to Rome, and this time the poet asserts his personal independence with surprising aggressiveness, even going so far as to declare his readiness to return everything Maecenas had given him if that is the price of freedom. The offer has been seen as a "manly and dignified reply" (*Satires, Epistles and Ars Poetica*, p. 293), but to me it seems singularly crude, since it is clear that Maecenas would never stoop to accept the return of any of his gifts, and at this stage in Horace's career he is secure enough not to require any further patronage. D. R. Shackleton Bailey makes the interesting point that Maecenas himself "seems to have lost ground with the Emperor following the execution of his brother-in-law Varro Murena in 22. After the publication of the first Book of Epistles his name disappears from Horace's writings except for one affectionate reference in the fourth Book of Odes. Maecenas's message to Augustus in his will, 'Remember Horatius Flaccus as you remember me,' may not have been entirely innocent of *sous-entendu*" (*Profile of Horace*, p. 56, n. 25). I am unconvinced by Shackleton Bailey's last supposition, but there is no doubt that once he was able to establish his

full independence, Horace took a distinctly different tone toward Maecenas than he had adopted earlier. The change is sufficiently striking to make Horace's initial claims that his regard for Maecenas was innocent of all calculation more than a little suspect.

49. Juvenal, *The Satires of Juvenal*, in *Juvenal and Persius*, ed. G. G. Ramsay, Loeb Classical Library (Cambridge: Harvard University Press, 1940), 1.1–2, p. 3. I have cited Peter Green's translation from the Penguin edition of *The Sixteen Satires* (Baltimore: Penguin, 1967), p. 65, because in spite of its relative prolixity, it seems to me to capture Juvenal's tone more successfully than a rendering like Ramsay's ("What? Am I to be a listener only all my days? Am I never to get my word in / I that have been so often bored by the *Theseid* of the ranting Cordus?"). But neither translation places sufficient stress upon the aggressive anger in Juvenal's strategically placed *reponam* at the end of the opening line.

50. Juvenal, *Satires* 1.79: "Though nature may deny me [talent], indignation will prompt my verse."

51. Freud first uses the phrase in "The Taboo of Virginity" (*The Standard Edition of the Complete Works of Sigmund Freud* [London: The Hogarth Press, 1957], 11:199). He returned to it again in "Group Psychology and the Analysis of the Ego" (18:101) and in "Moses and Monotheism" (23:91).

52. Elias Canetti, *The Play of the Eyes*, trans. Ralph Manheim, (New York: Farrar, Straus and Giroux, 1986), p. 16.

53. Juvenal, *Satires*, 1.170–71, p. 16. E. J. Kenney's "The First Satire of Juvenal," *Proceedings of the Cambridge Philological Society* 188 (n. s. 8) (1962): 29–40, shows how close the end of Juvenal's first satire is to Horace's Book 2, Satire 1.

54. Juvenal, *Satires*, 6.162–64, p. 96.

55. Ibid., 166–68, p. 96.

56. E. J. Kenney's "Juvenal: Satirist or Rhetorician?" in *Latomus* 22 (Fall 1963): 704–20, argues that the poet was concerned only to exercise his verbal craftsmanship in traditional Roman rhetoric, not in social reform.

Chapter Three
Oui, Monsieur le Philosophe: Diderot's *Le Neveu de Rameau*

1. Plautus, *Persa*, in *The Plays in Five Volumes*, trans. Paul Nixon (Cambridge: Harvard University Press/Loeb Classical Library, 1924), 3:466, lines 391–95:

ne te indotatam dicas, quoi dos sit domi:
librorum eccillum habeo plenum soracum.
si hoc adcurassis lepide, cui rei operam damus,
dabuntur dotis tibi inde sescenti logi,
atque Attici omnes; nullum Siculum acceperis.

[You are not to say you have no dowry, when you have one at home. Why, look you! I have a whole hamper full of books. If you do a neat, careful piece of work on this job of ours, I'll give you a good six hundred witticisms out of 'em for a dowry, and all Attic ones, without a single Sicilian quip amongst 'em.]

I owe the idea of turning to the *Persa* for assistance with my argument to a fine lecture on the dramatist by Patricia Rosenmeyer.

2. Welsford, *The Fool*, pp. 138ff. See also, Sandra Billington, *A Social History of the Fool* (New York: St. Martin's Press, 1984).

3. In calling Diderot the "party leader" of the Enlightenment, I am using the term in a deliberately broad sense. The *philosophes* never constituted a single cohesive movement, and recent research has tended to emphasize the variety of their views. But there is no doubt that they did share a common sense of mission, and that, for all the diversity of their specific beliefs, a number of central tenets were accepted by the major figures associated with the *Encyclopédie*. These tenets included a demand for a lay system of education, a limitation on Church power and wealth, a commitment to basic civil and legal rights grounded on a theory of "natural" human equality, and an insistence on some form of work as the duty of every member of the community. Since the *philosophes* scorned idleness in any guise, whether among the monastic orders or the court aristocracy, a parasite like Jean-François Rameau would be regarded as a particularly reprehensible type, irrespective of his other actions. For a discussion of the heterogeneity of the *philosophes'* convictions on topics like property rights, taxation, systems of government, economic principles, etc., see John Lough's perceptive study, *The Philosophes and Post-Revolutionary France* (Oxford: Oxford University Press, 1982). Dena Goodman's *Criticism in Action: Enlightenment Experiments in Political Writing* (Ithaca: Cornell University Press, 1989) offers a reading of texts by Montesquieu, Rousseau, and Diderot that highlights their conception of writing as a conscious part of "the Enlightenment's civic project to change the common way of thinking" (p. 3). The best study of the publication and transmission of the *Encyclopédie* itself as a cultural document is Robert Darnton's *The Business of Enlightenment: A Publishing History of the Encyclopédie 1775–1800* (Cambridge: Harvard University Press, 1979).

4. Interestingly enough, the Café de la Régence was also where Marx had his first long conversation with Engels on August 28, 1844.

5. There is also a compelling depiction of Vertumnus in Ovid's *Metamorphoses* 14.641ff. In his successful wooing of Pomona, one of Vertumnus's ploys consists of boasting that he can take on any form he—or his beloved—might desire. The same instability that troubles Horace becomes, typically for Ovid, a positive force, the symbol of fruitful metamorphosis in the service of desire.

6. Ernst Robert Curtius, *European Literature and the Latin Middle Ages*, trans. Willard R. Trask (Princeton: Princeton University Press, 1967), pp. 573–83.

7. cf., Horace, *Satires* 2.7.8–14:

> saepe notatus
> cum tribus anellis, modo laeva Priscus inani,
> vixit inaequalis, clavum ut mutaret in horas,
> aedibus ex magnis subito se conderet, unde
> mundior exiret vix libertinus honeste;
> iam moechus Romae, iam mallet doctus Athenis
> vivere, Vertumnis, quotquot sunt, natus iniquis.

> [Passing from a stately mansion, he would bury himself in a den, from which a decent freedman could scarcely emerge without shame. Now he would choose to live in Rome as a rake, now as a sage in Athens—a man born when every single Vertumnus was out of sorts.]

8. Within the dialogue itself there are at least six direct, or closely paraphrased, "tags" transposed from the satirists Diderot most admired: Horace (p. 37), Juvenal (twice in a row, p. 38 and p. 44), Persius (p. 55), Horace again (p. 60) and Lucian (p. 67). The crucial point here is not so much the dense classical texturing of *Le Neveu de Rameau* but the fact that these citations are voiced by *Moi* and *Lui* equally, thereby establishing both characters' familiarity with the same exemplary works invoked by the author of the opening epigraph. Most of the Horatian tags are uttered by *Moi*, while *Lui*, not surprisingly, draws his stock of quotes primarily from Juvenal. At the end of the series just listed, there is a final quotation that is given entirely in Latin: "Vivat Mascarillus, fourbum Imperator [Long live Mascarillus, Emperor of cheats]" (p. 76). Significantly, this is the only time Molière is quoted directly (*L'Eturdi* 2.8). One reason why Diderot might have introduced Molière via a line in Latin is the structural as well as linguistic link thereby suggested between the French dramatist and the Romans—an attempt, perhaps, to hint that the best French satires, including, by implication, *Le Neveu de Rameau*, are the direct descendants of the classical models. For an intelligent discussion of Diderot's debt to both the Latin and the French satiric traditions, see Donal O'Gorman, *Diderot the Satirist* (Toronto: University of Toronto Press, 1971). For an interesting link between *Le Neveu de Rameau* and the tradition of medieval *sotties*, see Heather Arden, "Le Fou, la sottie et *Le Neveu de Rameau*," *Dix-Huitième Siècle* 7 (1975): 209–23. Arden makes the valuable point that Diderot's use of a fool as a legitimate satiric voice is highly unusual among Enlightenment authors, for most of whom any connection to the traditional court jester or buffoon was unwelcome, both because of a general resistance to medieval literary practices and because of a fundamental opposition to anything that seemed to privilege the irrational. But Arden's commitment to the medieval sources of *Le Neveu de Rameau* prevent her from seeing that it was only by recasting elements of the *sottie* as subordinate strands within the larger genre of the Saturnalian dialogue that Diderot could use them so productively in his own text.

9. For example, in Curtius's reading, the parallels of form and imagery lead directly to an equivalence of argument: "The basic theme—contrast between the fool enslaved by want, necessities, lust, and passions, and the self-sufficient and therefore only free man, the sage—is identical in the two works" (Curtius, *European Literature and the Latin Middle Ages*, p. 582). Yet an antithetical position, represented most succinctly by Herbert Dieckmann, insists that it is the differences between Horace-Davus and *Moi-Lui* which are decisive: "The *Moi* cannot possibly be identified with the stoic conception of the sage. The nephew, on the other hand, is undoubtedly the victim of desires, passions, and vices, but he has many redeeming features, not only thanks to Diderot's art, but also in Diderot's opinion. He is not a fool in the Stoic sense, but in a modern sense, which presupposes the Renaissance" (Herbert Dieckmann, "The Relationship between Diderot's *Satire I* and *Satire II*," *Romanic Review* 43 [1952]: 25). Essentially, traditional judgments on the meaning of *Le Neveu de Rameau* kept taking up one or another of these fundamental positions, while at the same time each was forced to acknowledge the absence of any conclusive evidence that would prove the opposing point of view untenable.

10. P. 5: "Ils m'arrêtent une fois l'an."

11. P. 5: "parce que leur caractere tranche avec celui des autres, et qu'ils rompent cette fastidieuse uniformité que notre education, nos conventions de société, nos bienseances d'usage ont introduite. S'il en paroit un dans une compagnie, c'est un grain de levain qui fermente et qui restitue a chacun une portion de son individualité naturelle. Il secoue, il agite; il fait aprouver ou blamer; il fait sortir la verité; il fait connoitre les gens de bien; il demasque les coquins; c'est alors que l'homme de bon sens ecoute, et démêle son monde." It is worth noting how closely *Moi*'s account summarizes the classical function of the parasite. See, for example, Michel Serres's richly elaborated study *The Parasite*: "His role is to animate the event. His is a social role, and thus, theatrical" (Serres, *The Parasite*, trans. L. R. Schehr [Baltimore: Johns Hopkins University Press, 1982], p. 190).

12. P. 5: "ces originaux la."

13. On the uses of paradox in Stoic logic and its connection to the Stoic conception of the Sage, see *The Stoics*, ed. John M. Rist. Rosalie Colie's *Paradoxia Epidemica* (Princeton: Princeton University Press, 1966), still one of the most useful general studies of the paradox in Renaissance philosophy and literature, is also worth consulting in this context.

14. Lorraine Daston, in *Classical Probability in the Enlightenment* (Princeton: Princeton University Press, 1989), shows the close connection between the eighteenth-century idea of probabilistic expectation and the *philosophes'* conception of reasonable behavior. Reasonable men, it was assumed, will regulate their actions according to calculably rational self-interest; so one reasonable man can calculate how another is likely to behave, whether on juries, in legislatures, or in the marketplace. Condorcet called such calculations "social mathematics" and thought of them as a crucial instrument in political, legal, and economic planning. Although these ideas were already criticized in their own time, they were clearly successful and widespread enough to form the basis for the kind of *bien pensant* liberal philosophy against which Dostoevsky's Underground Man rebels.

15. Stallybrass and White, *The Politics and Poetics of Transgression*, p. 98. The chief coffeehouse of the Encyclopédistes in Paris was the famous Le Procope, not *Le Neveu de Rameau*'s Café de la Régence.

16. Shakespeare again provides the major exception to the general rule. In *As You Like It*, for example, the "country wench" Audrey is wooed by, and finally married to, Touchstone. But although we see their wedding, we do *not* see any of her subsequent married life as the wife of a licensed fool. At the play's end, she is only a future "Mrs. Fool," and we never actually observe her in that capacity.

17. Bakhtin, *Rabelais and His World*, pp. 37ff.

18. Robert Darnton's *The Literary Underground of the Old Regime* (Cambridge: Harvard University Press, 1982) provides a glimpse into the daily life of poverty and deprivation endured by the marginal literary figures of the Enlightenment. Darnton finds numerous historical parallels to Jean-François Rameau's constant alterations of fortune and describes the Nephew as "a tormented man who suffered from the psychology of the *raté* as well as the pangs of hunger" (pp. 118–19). Darnton also mentions that during the last years of the *ancien régime*, the *salon* became the exclusive preserve of the successful writers and *philosophes*, who consequently abandoned the cafés in which they used to meet to the lower species of hack *littérateurs* (p. 23). Thus, the fact that Rameau has been expelled from a *salon*, even

if from so debased a one as Bertin's, and must conduct his activities in a café is a crucial index of his declining status.

19. For example, Elisabeth de Fontenay reminds us that Rameau's illness may be as responsible as his psychological instability for some of the eccentricities he manifests. See Elisabeth de Fontenay, *Diderot: Reason and Resonance*, trans. J. Mehlman (New York: Braziller, 1982), pp. 175–76: "We have not detected those symptoms of [the Nephew's] poor health, of chronic illness. . . : he is afflicted in the lungs . . . suffering from an illness that the nineteenth century and the beginning of the twentieth will associate with the hyperaesthesis of genius, but that, in the present case, only accentuates its impotence."

20. Rameau mentions Diderot in a list of the most distinguished thinkers of the day (p. 57) whom the circle supported by Bertin pretends to scorn. *Moi* says that he is proud to be mentioned in the same breath as so many gifted and virtuous men (p. 58: "tant d'habiles et honnetes gens").

21. For a series of fine essays that touch on this theme, see Pierre Nora, ed., *Les Lieux de mémoire* (Paris: Gallimard, 1986), vol. 1: *La République*; vol. 2, nos. 1–3: *La Nation*. In vol. 1, Mona Ozouf's essay "Le Panthéon" (pp. 139–66) traces the emergence and ideological significance of the veneration of *les grands hommes*. Daniel Milo's essay, "Le Nom des rues" (vol. 2, no. 3, pp. 283–315) points out that it was in eighteenth-century Paris that streets were first named after literary figures like Corneille, Racine, and Molière.

22. P. 59: "C'est, me repondit il, qu'on tire parti de la mauvaise compagnie, comme du libertinage. On est dedommagé de la perte de son innocence, par celle de ses prejugés. Dans la societé des mechants, ou le vice se montre a masque levé, on apprend a les connoitre"

23. Diderot's relationship with Catherine the Great brings into question the link between the duties of a philosopher and the obligations of a paid servant (officially an "adviser") of the powerful. Diderot was certainly not Catherine's parasite, but there is no doubt that her financial generosity made him temper his criticism of her autocratic rule. Arthur M. Wilson's biography, *Diderot* (New York: Oxford University Press, 1972), provides a detailed, if at times too unquestioningly sympathetic, account of Diderot's dealings with the Empress. Elisabeth de Fontenay asks what seems to me the right question here, seeing in the encounter between Catherine and Diderot "The tale of what happens to knowledge when it is summoned before power, and when that power, far from persecuting it, decides to protect it. The opposite of Galileo, in brief, and a greater danger still" (*Diderot: Reason and Resonance*, p. 84). In *Cataract: A Study in Diderot* (Middleton, Conn.: Wesleyan University Press, 1979), Jeffrey Mehlman devotes several interesting pages to Diderot's uneasy compromises with his Imperial patron (pp. 63ff.). Rameau's constant touching of a reluctant *Moi*, as a rather pathetic attempt to establish some kind of physical intimacy across the barriers of their differences, seems to echo the ways Diderot would reach out and grasp Catherine during their dialogues. He was so insistent upon a bodily correlative to speech that the Empress had to restrain her guards from arresting the *philosophe*, and then, when the practice became irritating to her, to insist upon meeting him only across a large wooden table. Readers of Horace and Virgil undoubtedly will be tempted to speculate about the family resemblance between the two poets'

friendship with the Emperor and the *philosophe*'s dealings with the absolute ruler of Russia.

24. P. 108: "ma pauvre petite femme etoit une espece de philosophe."

25. P. 4: "Mes pensées ce sont mes catins."

26. Pp. 59–61:

> LUI. . . . Et puis j'ai un peu lu.
> MOI. - Qu'avez-vous lu?
> LUI. -J'ai lu et je lis et relis sans cesse Theophraste, La Bruiere et Moliere. . . .
> Moi, j'y recueille tout ce qu'il faut faire, et tout ce qu'il ne faut pas dire. Ainsi
> quand je lis l'*Avare*, je me dis: Sois avare, si tu veux; mais garde toi de parler
> comme l'avare. Quand je lis le *Tartuffe*, je me dis: Sois hypocrite, si tu veux;
> mais ne parle pas comme l'hypocrite. Garde des vices qui te sont utiles; mais
> n'en aie ni le ton ni les apparences qui te rendroient ridicule. Pour se garantir
> de ce ton, de ces apparences, il faut les connoitre. Or ces auteurs en ont fait des
> peintures excellentes. . . . Je me rapelle alors tout ce que les autres ont dit, tout
> ce que j'ai lu, et j'y ajoute tout ce qui sort de mon fonds. . . .

27. Rameau's observations contain more than a share of truth, for in Molière's world the monomaniacs are not really punished for their vices, but rather for letting these become public knowledge. In many French comedies of the seventeenth and eighteenth centuries, the whole notion of a ludicrous character depends upon his not realizing that he is out of step with the rest of the world. Others see the mono-maniac's fixation and use their knowledge to mock and take advantage of him. (The same rule also holds in the Roman comedies of Terence and Plautus from whom the French derive much of their comic dramaturgy.) But when there is a character who senses his own obsessiveness and feels both pain and pride at his predicament, we move closer to the Romantic vision of the tragic hero. A characteristic instance of both aspects is found in Stendhal, whose figures are tragic in their moments of self-awareness, and ludicrous when they are blind to their situation.

28. P. 60: "l'amusement et l'instruction."

29. *Moi* is echoing lines 343–44 of Horace's *Ars Poetica*: "omne tulit punctum qui miscuit utile dulci, / lectorem delectando pariterque monendo. [He has won every vote who has blended profit and pleasure, / at once delighting and instructing the reader]." Until well into the nineteenth century, these verses were invoked with such frequency and so mechanically that they became little more than truisms. It is entirely appropriate that *Moi* should utter them to explain his happily unproblematic sense of the classical satirists, just before Rameau delivers his most subversive reading of their true significance.

30. Carol Blum, *Diderot: The Virtue of a Philosopher* (New York: Viking Press, 1974), p. 82.

31. For an extended discussion of how Diderot continually subverts the traditional philosophical dialogue, see Jay Caplan, *Framed Narratives: Diderot's Genealogy of the Beholder* (Minneapolis: University of Minnesota Press, 1985), pp. 64ff.

32. Carol Blum points out how significant a challenge *Le Neveu de Rameau* mounts to Diderot's own earlier faith in Shaftesbury: "*Lui* is endowed with exquisite taste in aesthetic matters but seems to be totally deprived of moral sense. The

very idea of such a person contradicts the basis of Shaftesbury's theory that aesthetic taste and moral discernment were inextricably wed in the human soul" (*Diderot: The Virtue of a Philosopher*, p. 80).

33. Pp. 39–40: "Vous croyez que le meme bonheur est fait pour tous. Quelle
etrange vision! . . . Vous decorez cette bizarrerie du nom de vertu; vous l'appelez
philosophie. Mais la vertu, la philosophie sont-elles faites pour tout le monde?"

34. P. 61: "Au reste, souvenez-vous que dans un sujet aussi variable que les
moeurs, il n'y a d'absolutement, d'essentiellement, de generalement vrai ou faux.
. . . Si par hazard la vertu avoit conduit a la fortune; ou j'aurois eté vertueux, ou
j'aurois simulé la vertu comme un autre. On m'a voulu ridicule, et je me le suis fait."

35. From the beginning, the most effective attack on the ideas of the Enlightenment proceeded by contesting their global pretensions. German writers like
Johann Georg Hamann initiated the attack by stressing the imaginative power of
local traditions and folk customs against what he saw as a sterile rationalist univer-
salism. Showing that the *Encyclopédistes* were really only speaking for a particular
and limited class or ideological group has been the central strategy of an astonishingly diverse group of critics, ranging from Marxists to defenders of the Catholic or
Russian Orthodox churches (e.g., Claudel and Dostoevsky), to theoreticians of the
Frankfurt School (e.g., Horkheimer and Adorno in *Dialektik der Aufklärung*).

36. In "Le Fou, la sottie et *Le Neveu de Rameau*" (p. 211, n. 2), Heather Arden
points out that the tradition of the court fool began to decline in both France and
England in the seventeenth century. France's last "fou en titre" to the monarch was
Louis XIV's celebrated Angely who was sufficiently famous in his own day to figure
in Boileau's *Satire 1*.

37. P. 40: "Tenez, vive la philosophie; vive la sagesse de Salomon: boire de bon
vin, se gorger de mets delicats; se rouler sur de jolies femmes; se reposer dans des
lits bien mollets. Excepté cela, le reste n'est que vanité."

38. Pp. 40–41: "Il n'y a plus de patrie. Je ne vois d'un pole a l'autre que des
tyrans et des esclaves. . . . Est ce qu'on a des amis? Quand on en auroit, faudroit-il
en faire des ingrats? . . . La reconnoissance est un fardeau; et tout fardeau est fait
pour etre secoué. . . . Remplir ses devoirs, a quoi cela mene-t-il? A la jalousie, a la
persecution. . . . Quoi qu'on fasse, on ne peut se deshonorer, quand on est riche."

39. P. 82: "Il y a de la raison, a peu près, dans tout ce que vous venez de dire."

40. P. 12: "Oh! vous voilà, vous autres! Si nous disons quelque chose de bien,
c'est comme des fous, ou des inspirés; par hasard. Il n'y a que vous autres qui vous
entendiez. Oui, monsieur le philosophe. Je m'entends; et je m'entends ainsi que
vous vous entendez."

41. G.W.F. Hegel, *The Phenomenology of Mind*, trans. J. B. Baillie (New York:
Harper and Row, 1967), p. 538.

42. Ibid., p. 539.

43. Ibid., pp. 543–44. Baillie's standard translation of this passage uses the
term *repudiation* rather than *abjection* to render the German "Vererfung." (See
G.W.F. Hegel, *Die Phänomenologie des Geistes*, ed. Georg Lasson [Leipzig:
Durrschen, 1907], pp. 339–40). In a book subtitled *The Abject Hero*, it would be
disingenuous of me to claim that my choice of words is entirely innocent, but it is
also fair to add that Hegel's own term, from the verb *verwerfen*, is remarkably close
to "abjection," both in its etymology ("to throw away from," "to discard"; cf. the

English word's derivation from the Latin *abject-us*, past participle of *abjicere*) and in its metaphoric resonance.

44. Henri Lefebvre, *Diderot* (Paris: Hier et aujourd'hui, 1949), p. 210: "la révolte intérieure, l'affranchissement complet du pauvre diable à travers son abjection et son déchirement."

45. For example, pp. 37–38: "Dans la nature, toutes les especes se devorent, toutes les conditions se devorent dans la société [In nature, all the species feed on one another; in society each class preys on the other]"; or the litany of "vanities" on pp. 40–41.

46. P. 38: "La voix de la conscience et de l'honneur, est bien foible, lorsque les boyaux crient." Fabre (p. 178, n. 134) points out how similar Rameau's thought here is to a famous passage in Juvenal's Seventh Satire, lines 59–62:

> neque enim cantare sub antro
> Pierio thyrsumque potest contingere maesta
> paupertas atque aeris inops, quo nocte dieque
> corpus eget: satur est cum dicit Horatius "euhoe!"

> [For how can unhappy Poverty sing songs in the Pierian cave and grasp the thyrsus when it is short of cash, which the body needs both night and day? Horace's stomach was well-filled when he shouted his "Evoe!"]

Juvenal's lines are particularly appropriate in this context since they show his resentment at the patronage enjoyed by his most famous predecessor in the satiric tradition. Just as Rameau sometimes believes that only lack of support has prevented him from being as brilliant a composer as his uncle, so Juvenal enjoys pretending that the differences between his poetry and Horace's are due to their contrasting social positions.

47. Michel Serres's description of the biological parasite offers a useful point of comparison to Rameau's behavior and values vis-à-vis those of his paymasters: "a parasite makes or secretes tissue identical to that of its host. . . . The parasite plays a game of mimicry. It does not play at being another; it plays at being the same" (*The Parasite*, p. 202).

48. I owe this description to Richard Sieburth, who read my manuscript for Princeton University Press, and am glad of the opportunity to acknowledge his numerous helpful comments and suggestions.

49. See, for example, de Fontenay, *Diderot: Reason and Resonance*, p. 241.

50. For an interesting discussion of the "ethics of mimesis or mimetic manipulation" in *Le Neveu de Rameau*, see Jack Undank, *Diderot: Inside, Outside & In-Between* (Madison: Coda, 1979), pp. 40–41.

51. Mimesis is also the key to Rameau's musical theory, as well as to his skill in pantomime, flattery, etc. *Moi's* dilemma, in part, is that he accepts the general category, but rejects all of the Nephew's specific interpretations and the uses to which *Lui* would put his gifts.

52. Juvenal, Satire 7.145, p. 148.

53. P. 56: "Il faut cependant que vous aiez peché une fois contre les principes de l'art et qu'il vous soit echappé par megarde quelques unes de ces verités ameres qui blessent."

54. Lionel Trilling, *Sincerity and Authenticity* (Cambridge: Harvard University Press, 1971), p. 29.

55. Rameau's contempt for the word *espèce* makes his designation of his wife that I quoted earlier ("ma pauvre petite femme etoit une espece de philosophe") even more sardonic in its judgment about the significance of *philosophes*.

56. P. 14: "Le meilleur ordre des choses, a mon avis, est celui ou j'en devois etre."

57. P. 51: "Songez que. . . . Songez que. . . . Songez que. . . ." Most English translations, including Leonard Tanock's in the 1966 Penguin Classics series, dilute the formulaic regularity of Rameau's narrative by translating the phrase differently each of the three times it occurs: "Remember that. . . . Bear in mind that. . . . Think that . . ." (*Rameau's Nephew/D'Alembert's Dream*, p. 75).

58. P. 73: "Trop d'ardeur pouvoit faire echouer son project."

59. *Moi* also offers a narrative intended to present his solution to the issues raised by the Nephew's tales. But *Moi's* moralistic parable of the noble *Frère-Cadet* (pp. 42–43) is the least convincing exemplum of all. The story of a hero with no name, country, or historical epoch is too schematic, its characters too narrowly located by their social/familial functions, to engage one's interest. The bare recitation of virtuous actions, without sufficient attention to the shaping of the narrative, is insufficient to generate a persuasive counter-instance. My discussion here is influenced by a thoughtful essay, "*Homo Ardens* in Horace and Diderot," written by David Fishelov for a seminar I taught at U.C. Berkeley in 1984.

60. Wilda Anderson, *Diderot's Dream* (Baltimore: Johns Hopkins University Press, 1990), p. 217: "The personal powerlessness of the jester allowed him to serve as the social safeguard: the king without a fool was a tyrant, a person using public power to further private ends. But the king was equally important to the fool's having a real social function, for a fool without a king is a madman." Anderson's analysis of Rameau's dismissal (pp. 214–22) is among the best recent interpretations of this episode.

61. P. 46: "Je veux bien etre abject, mais je veux que ce soit sans contrainte."

62. P. 21: "dignité attachée a la nature de l'homme."

63. The two most interesting discussions of *Le Paradoxe sur le Comédien* that I know are from radically different theoretical perspectives. The first is Philippe Lacoue-Labarthe's essay "Le Paradoxe et la *mimesis*" in his collection *L'Imitation des modernes* (Paris: Galilée, 1986), pp. 15–36; the second is Richard Wollheim's piece "Imagination and Identification," in *On Art and the Mind* (Cambridge: Harvard University Press, 1974), pp. 54–83, esp. pp. 60–63.

64. It is fascinating to observe how closely some of Diderot's comments on pantomime were echoed a century later by Charles Baudelaire. In the prose poem "Une Mort Héroïque" (Number 27 of *Le Spleen de Paris*) Baudelaire's example of a great actor is the royal buffoon and mime Fancioulle, and in the essay "De l'essence du rire," he recalls the enormous power of the first English pantomime he saw in Paris. The memory of that performance inspires Baudelaire to declare: "La pantomime est l'épuration de la comédie; c'en est la quintessence; c'est l'élément comique pur, dégagé et concentré [Pantomime is the purification of comedy; it is the quintessence of comedy; it is the basic element of comedy in its pure form, freed and concentrated]." See Baudelaire, "De l'essence du rire" in *Curiosités ésthétiques et L'art romantique*, ed. H. Lemaitre (Paris: Garnier, 1962), pp. 241–63; the sentence quoted appears on p. 259 of the essay. On Baudelaire and Diderot, see Yoichi

Sumi, *Le Neveu de Rameau: Caprices et logiques du jeu* (Tokyo: France Tosho, 1975).

65. Denis Diderot, "Entretiens sur *Le Fils naturel*," in *Oeuvres ésthétiques*, ed. Paul Vernière (Paris: Garnier, 1965), p. 100: "La pantomime si negligée parmi nous, est employée dans cette scène; et vous avez éprouvé vous-même avec quel succés! Nous parlons trop dans nos drames; et conséquemment, nos acteurs n'y jouent pas assez. Nous avons perdu un art, dont les anciens conaissaient bien les ressources. [Pantomime, which is so neglected in our theatre, is used in this scene, and you yourself have felt its force! We talk too much in our plays, and as a result our actors do not act enough. We've lost an art whose resources the ancient authors understood well]."

66. Bakhtin, *Rabelais and His World*, pp. 10–11.

67. During agricultural ceremonies the Romans used to offer each god a collection of diverse first fruits of the harvest, randomly piled up together on a large platter. This was called a *lanx satura*, or simply *satura*, the feminine form of the adjective *satur*, meaning "repletion." Moreover, a law passed *per saturam* was one with numerous clauses relating to various, often quite distinct, situations. See Ulrich Knoche, *Roman Satire*, trans. E. S. Ramage (Bloomington: Indiana University Press, 1975) and Michael Coffey, *Roman Satire* (London: Methuen, 1976) for a more extensive discussion of the origin of the term *satura*.

68. De Fontenay, *Diderot: Reason and Resonance*, pp. 203–4.

69. P. 102: "il designoit son extreme besoin, par le geste d'un doigt dirigé vers sa bouche entrouverte [he showed his extreme need by pointing a finger at his half-open mouth]."

70. P. 104: "Le pis, c'est la posture contrainte ou nous tient le besoin. L'homme necessiteux ne marche pas comme un autre; il saute, il rampe, il se tortille, il se traine; il passe sa vie a prendre et a executer des positions."

71. P. 83: "Lui n'apercevoit rien; il continuoit, saisi d'une alienation d'esprit, d'un enthousiasme si voisin de la folie, qu'il est incertain qu'il en revienne; s'il ne faudra pas le jetter dans un fiacre, et le mener droit aux Petites Maisons."

72. For a very different and, I think, fundamentally unconvincing interpretation of the Nephew's pantomime, in which *Lui*'s extravagance is seen as "a controlled state of passion . . . [that] created a spellbinding, absorptive group attentiveness," see Anderson, *Diderot's Dream*, pp. 242–43. For Anderson, there is no link between Rameau and the mediocre actor of the *Paradoxe sur le comédien*, and even his total physical collapse is interpreted as a brilliantly conceived theatrical/pedagogic gesture.

73. Starobinski, *1789: The Emblems of Reason*, pp. 236–37.

74. Michèle Duchet comments perceptively on this point: "le jeu gestuel se voit réduit au rôle de catalyseur pour ainsi dire, puisque *Moi* l'englobe dans sa propre réflexion. . . . C'est au philosophe qu'il revient de découvrir et d'affirmer la portée universelle de la pantomime. Il domine en ceci que la pantomime n'est plus que l'origine de la réflexion de *Moi*-philosophe sur la pantomime. Celle-ci donc, de création grandiose qu'elle était, et bien qu'elle ait gagné une sorte de profondeur morale, en est réduite au rôle de *spectacle*; Rameau de créateur tout-puissant, artiste génial, au rôle d'histrion [The gesture is seen reduced to the role of a catalyst, since *Moi* enfolds it into his own reflections. . . . It is once again up to the philosopher to discover and assert the universal significance of pantomime. He dominates because

pantomime is only the origin of the philosopher's meditation on pantomime. Thus, pantomime, from the grandiose creation that it was [at the dialogue's outset] and in spite of having gained a kind of moral profundity, is reduced to the status of a *spectacle*, and Rameau, from all-powerful creator and inspired artist, to a histrionic clown]" (M. Duchet and M. Launay, *Entretiens sur "Le Neveu de Rameau"* [Paris: Nizet, 1967], pp. 99–100).

75. P. 106: "le philosophe qui n'a rien et qui ne demande rien."

76. P. 18: "une liberté que je prenois sans consequence; car moi, je suis sans consequence." The whole tradition of the licensed jester makes clear that to be a real person, to have one's words heeded, means to be *punishable* for them. In *King Lear*, for example, because Kent is a man whose words matter, he is banished for saying no more than does the Fool, none of whose early speeches are heard as significant. When Lear's daughters threaten to punish the Fool, it shows that they have fallen so low as to ignore their proper roles as the Fool's royal (and royally indifferent) audience.

77. Pp. 39 and 52: "Mais je crois que vous vous moquez de moi; monsieur le philosophe, vous ne scavez pas a qui vous vous jouez; vous ne vous doutez pas que dans ce moment je represente la partie la plus importante de la ville et de la cour. . . . Mais je suis trop bon. Vous etes un profane qui ne merite pas d'etre instruit de miracles qui s'operent a coté de vous."

78. P. 65: "Cent fous comme moi! Monsieur le philosophe, ils ne sont pas si communs. Oui, des plats fous. On est plus difficile en sottise qu'en talent ou en vertu. Je suis rare dans mon espece, oui, tres rare."

79. It is important to stress that all of these attributes must be present for a character to be considered an Abject Hero. Thus, for example, a figure like Tristram Shandy, although clearly a self-conscious descendant of the "wise fool," is far too exuberant and playful for an Abject Hero. Although there are elements in the Abject Hero's discourse that draw upon the rhetorical tropes and psychological attitudes familiar to us as "Romantic irony," both the growing sense of *ressentiment* and the agony of belatedness under which the Abject Hero suffers serve to distinguish him from the romantic ironist.

80. P. 109: "Rira bien qui rira le dernier."

Chapter Four
Lacerations: The Novels of Fyodor Dostoevsky

1. Fyodor Dostoevsky, *The Brothers Karamazov*, ed. R. E. Matlaw, trans. Constance Garnett and R. E. Matlaw (New York: Norton, 1976), p. 34. Future references to *The Brothers Karamazov* will be from this edition. In Victor Terras, *A Karamazov Companion: Commentary on the Genesis, Language, and Style of Dostoevsky's Novel* (Madison: University of Wisconsin Press, 1981), we learn that the anecdote about this meeting was actually reported, although in an obviously less ridiculous form, by Platon's biographer, I. M. Snegiriov (p. 145, n. 37).

2. On the theme of paradox and parody in the novel, and especially on Smerdyakov as a consummate paradoxialist, see Gary Saul Morson's essay, "Verbal Pollution in *The Brothers Karamazov*," *PTL: A Journal for Descriptive Poetics and Theory of Literature* 3 (1978): 223–33.

3. The need to account for Karamazov's growing wealth sounds the first of what will be a whole network of anti-Semitic motifs throughout the novel. It was to Odessa, a city with one of Russia's most prominent Jewish communities, that Fyodor Karamazov went after his second wife's death. While there, he spent his time among "a lot of low Jews, Jewesses, and Jewkins" and began to develop "a peculiar faculty for making and hoarding money" (p. 16). Upon his return to Skotoprigonevsk, he put those lessons to good use by becoming both a money-lender and the owner of a large number of taverns, two occupations traditionally held responsible for the plight of the peasantry and linked to Jews in Russian anti-Semitic polemics. On Dostoevsky's hatred for Jews see, David I. Goldstein, *Dostoevsky and the Jews* (Austin: University of Texas Press, 1981). On the failure of most commentators, including Goldstein, to confront this theme with sufficient intellectual honesty or rigor, see Gary Saul Morson, "Dostoevsky's Anti-Semitism and the Critics," *Slavic and East European Journal* 27, no. 3 (1983): 302–17.

4. Bakhtin, *Rabelais and His World*, p. 11.

5. Fyodor Dostoevsky, *Notes from Underground*, in *Notes from Underground and "The Grand Inquisitor,"* trans. R. E. Matlaw (New York: Dutton, 1960), pp. 13–14. Future references to *Notes from Underground* will be from this edition.

6. Bakhtin comments usefully on the confession/toothache parallel in *Notes from Underground*. See Mikhail Bakhtin, *Problems of Dostoevsky's Poetics*, ed. and trans. Caryl Emerson (Minneapolis: University of Minnesota Press, 1984), pp. 233–34. In *The Failure of the Word: The Protagonist as Lawyer in Modern Fiction* (New Haven: Yale University Press, 1984), Richard H. Weisberg suggests that the Russian adjective *zloi* (spiteful), which figures so centrally in the opening pages of *Notes from Underground*, is remarkably akin to Nietzsche's *ressentiment* in its implications.

7. Or, in a more psychologically nuanced reading, one may conclude that Father Zosima's acknowledgment is itself a kind of "noble lie." In this view, Father Zosima, like Prince Myshkin of *The Idiot*, knows that most of the people he encounters are frauds but deliberately chooses to tell them they are not, so that they may acquire the urge to live up to his higher image of them. In general, as Caryl Emerson suggested to me, one can distinguish at least two kinds of confessions. In the first kind one speaks to God or some other absolutely superior and unbendable interlocutor. Here, the situation is not fundamentally dialogical. One does not so much want to "talk it over," explain motives, probe psychology, or suggest extenuating circumstances; one is driven, rather, by the need to get to the point of saying the sin out loud, of no longer getting away with it, of creating a witness to one's evil. In the second kind of confession, there really is a full dialogue with an equal who will tell one, "You're not like that, you don't really mean that, you [and your story] have another side as well; you'll *change* and become better." This is a listener who will be changed by listening to the confession and whose listening, in turn, will change the sinner.

8. It is exactly to mark Zosima's freedom from the abjection of theatricality that his body must stink of decay after his death. He is the one character who is entirely uninfected by what the novel teaches us to recognize as "the Karamazov principle": the performance of the self. Zosima will not perform himself, he will not use himself as a spectacle or act out his ethics as a public drama. Hence, he will also not "perform" the saint's miracle/gesture of manifesting no bodily "corruption."

9. Robert L. Belknap, *The Structure of The Brothers Karamazov* (The Hague: Mouton, 1967), p. 46.

10. Fyodor Dostoevsky, *Winter Notes on Summer Impressions*, trans. Richard Renfield (New York: McGraw-Hill, 1965), p. 63; cf., the Underground Man's description of the capital as "the most abstract and intentional city in the whole world" in *Notes from Underground*, p. 6.

11. Bakhtin, *Problems of Dostoevsky's Poetics*, p. 143.

12. Ibid.

13. Fyodor Dostoevsky, "Bobok," in *The Gambler/Bobok/A Nasty Story*, trans. Jessie Coulson (Baltimore: Penguin, 1966), p. 178.

14. It may be salutary, moreover, to remember that an earlier, and more acute, reader than Bakhtin already noticed the link between Dostoevskian buffoons and classical drama. In *La Prisonnière*, Marcel explains to Albertine, who has been devouring Dostoevsky's novels, that figures like Lebedev and Fyodor Karamazov are more like "personnages de la comédie antique" than like ordinary novelistic characters (Marcel Proust, *A la recherche du temps perdu*, 3 vols. [Paris: Pléiade, 1954], 3:380). I have benefited from a fine paper on this topic by Dalya M. Sachs, a graduate student at U.C. Berkeley.

15. George Steiner, *Tolstoy or Dostoevsky: An Essay in the Old Criticism* (New York: Knopf, 1959), p. 226.

16. Ivan Turgenev, *Diary of a Superfluous Man*, trans. David Patterson (New York: W. W. Norton, 1984), p. 77.

17. Ibid., p. 8.

18. George Steiner was, I believe, the first critic to have noticed a connection between the Underground Man and earlier characters like Homer's Thersites, the parasites of Roman satire and comedy, the legendary Diogenes, the figures of Lucan's dialogues, Shakespeare's Apemantus and Thersites, as well as Rameau's Nephew (*Tolstoy or Dostoevsky*, pp. 216–21). But Steiner undermines the force of his own insight by extending the network of affiliations beyond any real theoretical or practical coherence. A list that can add, to the figures already cited, names like Sancho Panza, Don Juan's Leporello, Faust's Wagner, the Fool in *King Lear*, and François Villon is simply too amorphous to be of significant critical assistance. In *Dostoevsky: The Stir of Liberation 1860–1865* (Princeton: Princeton University Press, 1986), Joseph Frank also mentions the echoes of *Le Neveu de Rameau* in *Notes from Underground* and goes on to comment that "considering the intrinsic interest of the question there has been astonishingly little written about the relationship between *Notes from Underground* and *Le Neveu de Rameau*" (p. 311).

19. It is clear that some Dostoevskian abject buffoons like Captain Snegiriov and Lebedyev are motivated by economic misery, but such compulsions need not be present, and indeed, in many instances, the characters are men of substantial independent means.

20. Fyodor Dostoevsky, *The Notebooks for "A Raw Youth,"* ed. Edward Wasiolek, trans. Victor Terras (Chicago: University of Chicago Press, 1969), pp. 425–26.

21. Ibid., p. 426.

22. Michael Ignatieff, "Paradigm Lost," *Times Literary Supplement*, September 4, 1987, p. 939.

23. Ibid.

24. For a discussion of this point with specific reference to *Notes from Underground*, see Richard I. Sugarman, *Rancor Against Time: The Phenomenology of Ressentiment* (Hamburg: Felix Meiner Verlag, 1980), pp. 12ff.

25. Steiner, *Tolstoy or Dostoevsky*, p. 219.

26. How easy it is to become so fascinated by the text's arguments as to misread the plot is amusingly demonstrated by Dominick LaCapra's "Notes on Dostoevsky's *Notes from Underground*," in *History, Politics, and the Novel* (Ithaca: Cornell University Press, 1987), pp. 35–55. LaCapra tells us that "one sign of displacement and distortion is the fact that the servant who appears as an unnamed woman in Part One becomes a man—Apollon—in Part Two. The sex of the servant is reversed as one moves from part to part, and as a male he acquires a name—a name that recalls Apollo" (p. 41). In fact, the two servants are kept entirely distinct, and the Underground Man explicitly tells us that after "seven whole years" Apollon left his services to "read the Psalms over the dead, and at the same time he kills rats and makes shoe polish" (*Notes from Underground*, p. 100). Apollon's career change is sufficiently bizarre on its own terms without requiring the further addition of a sexual transformation.

27. Wendy Lesser's, *The Life Below the Ground: A Study of the Subterranean in Literature and History* (Boston: Faber and Faber, 1987), shows the metaphor's power over its explicators. She assumes that the narrator of the *Notes from Underground* "lives in a mental and physical basement" (p. 110), as though dwelling in the former necessarily entailed the latter.

28. Donald Fanger, *Dostoevsky and Romantic Realism* (Cambridge: Harvard University Press, 1965), p. 112.

29. Friedrich Nietzsche, *Selected Letters*, ed. and trans. C. Middleton (Chicago: University of Chicago Press, 1969), p. 327. The comment is in a letter of November 20, 1888 to Georg Brandes. See also, Nietzsche's letter to Franz Overbeck of February 23, 1887 (pp. 260–62) in which he describes his initial excitement at discovering Dostoevsky's *L'Esprit souterrain* (*Notes from Underground*) in "a recent French translation." A subsequent letter of March 7, 1887 to Heinrich Köselitz (wrongly identified in Middleton's English edition as having been sent to Peter Gast) continues Nietzsche's enthusiasm for Dostoevsky's work and shows him having now read *The House of the Dead* and *The Insulted and Injured*. See Friedrich Nietzsche, *Sämtliche Briefe: Kritische Studienausgabe*, ed. Giorgio Colli and Mazzino Montinari, 8 vols. (Munich: Walter de Gruyter and Co., 1975–84).

30. Friedrich Nietzsche, *Götzen-Dämmerung, oder: Wie Man mit dem Hammer philosophiert*, vol. 4 of *Werke in sechs Bänden*, ed. Karl Schlechta (Munich: Carl Hanser Verlag, 1980), sec. 9, no. 45, p. 1021.

31. Nietzsche, *Zur Genealogie der Moral*, vol. 4 of *Werke in sechs Bänden*, pt. 1, sec. 10, p. 782. The English version cited is by Walter Kaufmann, *On The Genealogy of Morals and Ecce Homo* (New York: Vintage Books, 1969), p. 36.

32. Given the prevalence of *ressentiment* in modern thinking and its power as a political spur, it is surprising that except for Nietzsche, so few thinkers have chosen to engage the problem directly. *Ressentiment* remains one of the last taboos of contemporary self-consciousness, a motive for ideas, values, and actions that, unlike sexuality, we are still reluctant to confront. Max Scheler's classic study, "Über

Ressentiment und moralische Werturteile" (first published in 1912 and revised as "Das Ressentiment im Aufbau der Moralen" in 1915), is still the only post-Nietzschean account to have attained a significant stature in its own right. Scheler's work is wildly uneven and in places unintentionally comic in its eccentricity, but it also contains a number of remarkable insights. An English version of Scheler's book is available as *Ressentiment*, ed. Lewis Coser, trans. William Holdheim (New York: Free Press of Glencoe, 1961). Richard Ira Sugarman's *Rancor Against Time: The Phenomenology of "Ressentiment"* (Hamburg: Felix Meiner Verlag, 1980), offers a competent summary and critique of Nietzsche, Scheler, and Heidegger, but its own analysis is rather pedestrian. Richard H. Weisberg's *The Failure of the Word: The Protagonist as Lawyer in Modern Fiction* (New Haven: Yale University Press, 1984) recapitulates both Nietzsche and Scheler and then attempts to apply the idea of *ressentiment* to a whole range of fictional texts in which issues of legality are central, including works by Dostoevsky, Flaubert, Melville, and Camus, but his specific readings are often disappointingly thin. Among the specialized studies of *ressentiment* in Nietzsche, see Amandus Altmann, *Friedrich Nietzsche: Das Ressentiment und seine Überwindung* (Bonn: Bouvier Verlag, 1977). The most searching treatment of the problem in modern philosophy is found in the pages Heidegger devotes to Nietzsche's concept of revenge and temporality in *Was heisst Denken* (Tübingen: Max Niemeyer Verlag, 1954), translated by J. G. Gray as *What Is Called Thinking* (New York: Harper and Row, 1968). My own engagement with the whole question of *ressentiment* has been greatly influenced by Heidegger's comments.

33. Nietzsche, *Zur Genealogie der Moral*, vol. 4 of *Werke in sechs Bänden*, pt. 3, sec. 15, p. 869: "'Ich leide: daran muß irgend jemand schuld sein.'"

34. For this formulation from part 1, section 4, I have preferred Serge Shishkoff's translation, originally published by Thomas Y. Crowell Co. and reprinted by the University Press of America, in Fyodor Dostoevsky, *Notes from Underground*, ed. R. G. Durgy, trans. S. Shishkoff (Lanham, Md. and London: University Press of America, 1969), p. 14.

35. Bakhtin, *Problems of Dostoevsky's Poetics*, pp. 232–33.

36. For a comparative literature graduate course on the Abject Hero that I taught in the Fall 1988 semester at Berkeley, Jennifer Beachey wrote a fine essay on the theme of debtorship in *Notes from Underground*, and I am glad of the chance to acknowledge how much I learned from her contributions to the seminar, as well as from those of the other participants.

37. The Underground Man's denial of temporality, and thus of predictability, crystallizes how thoroughgoing is his rejection of the whole ethos of the Enlightenment. As I remarked in the previous chapter, the eighteenth-century idea of probabilistic, calculable expectations and its conception of a reasonable man were closely linked, in both moral and economic theory.

38. See, for example, the characteristic account of this development in Alex de Jonge, *Dostoevsky and The Age of Intensity* (London: Secker and Warburg, 1975), pp. 12–14.

39. On this theme, see Gary Saul Morson, *The Boundaries of Genre: Dostoevsky's Diary of a Writer and the Traditions of Literary Utopia* (Austin: University of Texas Press, 1981).

40. See, for example, the description of St. Petersburg as "a reflection of all the architectures of the world, of all periods and all fashions" in Fyodor Dostoevsky, *The Diary of a Writer*, trans. Boris Brasol (Salt Lake City: Peregrine Smith Books, 1979) pp. 120–21.

41. The motif of St. Petersburg as an "unreal city" is prominent throughout nineteenth-century Russian literature, finding powerful expression in works as diverse as Pushkin's famous poem "The Bronze Horseman" and Gogol's tales. Geoffrey Kabat's *Ideology and Imagination: The Image of Society in Dostoevsky* (New York: Columbia University Press, 1978) contains a good analysis of Dostoevsky's response to the theme. For a more general and chronologically arranged discussion of the dilemma, see the chapter "Petersburg: The Modernism of Underdevelopment," in Marshall Berman's *All That Is Solid Melts into Air: The Experience of Modernity* (New York: Simon and Schuster, 1982), pp. 173–286.

42. Here, I am paraphrasing Marshall Berman's argument about St. Petersburg in *All That Is Solid Melts into Air*, p. 245. Berman adds the valuable point that the Underground Man "is wrong, of course, about Paxton's crystal palace, at which thousands of genteel and cultivated tongues were stuck out, but right about Chernyshevsky; wrong, in other words, about the Western reality of modernization, which is full of dissonance and conflict, but right about the Russian fantasy of modernization as an end to dissonance and conflict."

43. This point is forcefully made in one of the best essays on the novel, Tzvetan Todorov's, "Notes d'un souterrain," *Les Genres Du Discours* (Paris: Seuil, 1978), pp. 135–60.

44. Emile Littré, *Dictionnaire de la langue française* (Paris: Gallimard, 1961), 6:1447. Cf., the following typical usage of the term in classical French theatre:

BÉRÉNICE: Tandis qu'autour de moi votre cour assemblée
Retentit des bienfaits dont vous m'avez comblée,
Est-il juste, Seigneur, que seule en ce moment
Je demeure sans voix et sans ressentiment?

(Racine, *Bérénice* [Paris: Pléiade, 1950], 2.4.2–5, p. 487)

45. Friedrich Nietzsche, *Also sprach Zarathustra*, pt. 2,"Von der Erlösung," in *Werke in sechs Bänden* 3:394: "'Es war': also heißt des Willens Zähneknirschen und einsamste Trübsal. Ohnmächtig gegen das, was getan ist—ist er allem Vergangenen ein böser Zuschauer. . . . Dies, ja dies allein ist *Rache* selber: des Willens Widerwille gegen die Zeit und ihr 'Es war.'" I have modified R.J. Hollingdale's English version, *Thus Spoke Zarathustra* (Baltimore: Penguin, 1961), pp. 161–62 for my quotation.

46. Karl Marx, *The Eighteenth Brumaire of Louis Bonaparte*, p. 15.

47. See the useful article by Nicolas Moravcevich, "The Romantization of the Prostitute in Dostoevskij's Fiction," *Russian Literature* 4, no. 3 (July 1976): 299–307, for a detailed discussion of this theme. Moravcevich outlines the long history of sentimentalizing the prostitute in Russian literature and shows how powerfully the writings of the French Romantics contributed to this tradition. Not only did Nekrasov's 1845 poem "When from thy error, dark, degrading" derive from Hugo's 1835 lyric "Oh! n'insultez jamais une femme qui tombe!," but such figures as Paquette in *Notre Dame de Paris* (1831) and Fantine in *Les Misérables* (1862)

both had a profound effect upon Russian authors. All of these sentimental texts are as vital a part of the context for *Notes from Underground* as the more commonly discussed sources, such as Chernyshevsky's treatment of the theme of the redeemed whore in *What Is to Be Done?* For the French context for many of these issues, see Charles Bernheimer, *Figures of Ill Repute: Representing Prostitution in Nineteenth-Century France* (Cambridge: Harvard University Press, 1989).

48. Leo Tolstoy, *Resurrection*, trans. V. Traill (New York: Signet, 1961), chap. 48, p. 164. I was alerted to this echo by George Siegel's, "The Fallen Woman in Nineteenth Century Russian Literature," *Harvard Slavic Studies* 5 (1970): 81–107.

49. Anton Chekhov, "An Attack of Nerves," in *The Portable Chekhov*, ed. A. Yarmolinsky (New York: Viking, 1985), pp. 242–43.

50. Cf., Joseph Frank, *Dostoevsky: The Stir of Liberation 1860–1865* (Princeton: Princeton University Press, 1986); Tzvetan Todorov, "Notes d'un souterrain"; Robert Louis Jackson, *The Art of Dostoevsky: Deliriums and Nocturnes* (Princeton: Princeton University Press, 1981); Michael Holquist, *Dostoevsky and the Novel* (Princeton: Princeton University Press, 1977). These examples could be multiplied almost ad infinitum, but the following quotation from Jackson's *The Art of Dostoevsky* can serve as a typical instance of the "positive" reading of the Liza episode: "In the embrace of the Underground Man and Liza, all walls of ego and pride are dissolved. It is a moment of revelation of higher truth, an epiphany, a pietà. The fundamental problem of freedom posed in *Notes* is not resolved here; it is dissolved. It is not twice two is four, not twice two is five, but reciprocal love that is the way out of the underground" (p. 180).

51. For this episode from part 2, section 6, I have again preferred Serge Shishkoff's translation (p. 93).

52. Here I have also preferred Shishkoff's translation (p. 120).

53. Gary Saul Morson, "A Response to Robbins and Bernstein" (Paper read at the Northwestern University Conference on Narrative, May 1987).

54. Cf. the earlier discussion of plagiarism between Ivan and Alyosha, which powerfully, if indirectly, echoes throughout the chapters "Rebellion" and "The Grand Inquisitor." When Ivan finishes his "Legend of the Grand Inquisitor," Alyosha responds by kissing him, just as Christ had kissed the Inquisitor: "'That's plagiarism,' cried Ivan, highly delighted. 'You stole that from my poem. Thank you though'" (p. 244). All the later, more elaborate treatments of plagiarism and citationality will hearken back to this scene and develop its implications.

55. Fyodor Dostoevsky, *Selected Letters*, ed. Joseph Frank and David Goldstein, trans. A. R. MacAndrew (New Brunswick, N.J.: Rutgers University Press, 1987), p. 486. The letter to Pobedonostsev is dated August 25, 1879.

56. Ibid., p. 486.

57. Here it is important to stress that Ivan justifies his rebellion against God by citing the Divine silence in a world where small children are made to suffer. As Geoffrey C. Kabat rightly argues, a chapter like "Rebellion" needs to be understood not only in the context of the novel as a whole but, more centrally still, in light of who is telling it. Ivan was himself an abused child who now gathers *faits divers* about tormented children in order to prove his claim that "everything is permitted." That Ivan narrates his horrible stories with a mixture of ghoulish and latently sadistic pleasure, masochistic identification, and abstract intellectual dis-

tancing is an index of his emotional confusion and a warning not to take his out-burst as the expression of a strictly philosophical or moral argument. See Geoffrey C. Kabat, *Ideology and Imagination: The Image of Society in Dostoevsky* (New York: Columbia University Press, 1978), pp. 142–62.

58. Kabat, *Ideology and Imagination*, p. 154.

59. For a more detailed discussion of these particular links between Ivan's Devil and his father, see Belknap, *The Structure of The Brothers Karamazov*, pp. 41–45, and Kabat, *Ideology and Imagination*, pp. 154–57.

60. Shakespeare, *Twelfth Night* 5.1.367.

61. For a good discussion of this theme, see Kabat, *Ideology and Imagination*, p. 112 and pp. 125–26. My argument in the two sentences here follows closely Kabat's reading of the function of the "intelligent protagonist" in Dostoevsky's novels.

62. Bakhtin, *Rabelais and His World*, p. 37.

63. In "Notes d'un souterrain," pp. 142–43, Todorov points out that the dense network of references to other works already creates a *they* with whom the Underground Man is in dialogue, but along side this *they* there is a *you* who is constantly and explicitly addressed, so that the dialogue is doubled and redoubled from the outset. Moreover, the *you* changes in the course of the book. In the first six chapters, the *you* is the typical, everyday man of the world. From chapters 7 to 10, though, the *you* begins to be less passive and replies at great length to the narrator. The *you* begins to merge with the *they* (Chernyshevsky, etc.) who are the Underground Man's ideological opponents. Richard Peace, in *Dostoevsky: An Examination of the Major Novels* (Cambridge: Cambridge University Press, 1971), p. 13, notices that "the disturbing thing is that his reader has been conceived in his own image as a man who sneers and jeers at the arguments of the Underground Man in much the same way as he ridicules the ideas of his adversaries."

Chapter Five
L'Apocalypse à Crédit: Louis-Ferdinand Céline's War Trilogy

1. Dostoevsky, *The Brothers Karamazov*, p. 120.

2. Louis-Ferdinand Céline, *D'un château l'autre*, *Nord*, et *Rigodon* in vol. 2 of *Romans II*, ed. Henri Godard (Paris: Bibliothèque de la Pléiade, 1974). All references to the trilogy are to Godard's invaluable edition and will be acknowledged in the body of the text. For the English translations, I have used Ralph Manheim's versions, published in 1976 by Penguin Books as *Castle to Castle*, *North*, and *Rigadoon*. I have, however, regularly modified Manheim's formulations when the French seemed to me to require such a change. Source citations for the trilogy will use a letter (*C* for *D'un château l'autre*; *N* for *Nord*; and *R* for *Rigodon*), in each case followed first by the page number in Godard's edition and then by the page number in Manheim's translation. The French text will be found in the notes.

Since Céline's three dots are an integral part of his rhythm, I will retain them in all my quotations and indicate any elisions by placing the dots within square brackets.

3. These letters have been reprinted in Louis-Ferdinand Céline, *Lettres de guerre 1941–1945*. No doubt for copyright reasons, the book lists neither publisher nor

date of publication, but it was readily available in Paris bookstores when I bought it in 1980. The demand for a "Racisme fanatique total" appeared in *Je suis partout* on November 22, 1941.

4. Diderot, *Le Neveu de Rameau*, p. 76: "Je ne scavois, moi, si je devois rester ou fuir, rire ou m'indigner."

5. The term *féerie* designates a particular French sub-genre full of spectacular scenic effects and supernatural characters, including sorcerers and demons. In the devastation of whole cities caused by the saturation bombing raids of World War II, Céline saw a thoroughly modern and all-too-real enactment of the fantasy havoc of the *féerie*.

6. Miguel de Cervantes, *The Adventures of Don Quixote*, trans. J. M. Cohen (New York: Penguin, 1950), pt. 1, chap. 7, p. 66.

7. Ibid.

8. Ibid., pt. 2, chap. 45, p. 754.

9. The best history of the French presence in Sigmaringen is Henry Rousso's *Un Château en Allemagne: La France de Pétain en exil, Sigmaringen 1944–1945* (Paris: Ramsay, 1980). Céline gives the number of Frenchmen in Sigmaringen as 1,142 (*C* 105/127), a count that is probably fairly accurate. In any case, the population kept changing as new refugees arrived while others fled Sigmaringen to seek shelter elsewhere. Rousso (p. 59) estimates the maximum number of Collaborators and their dependents in Sigmaringen at any one time at around 1,500. It is worth pointing out that in Sigmaringen both Pétain and Laval took on the role of "passifs," claiming that they had been taken there against their will and refusing to fulfill any further official functions. In every important detail, life at Sigmaringen was controlled by the Germans, but some old leaders of the Collaboration, like Fernand de Brinon, Marcel Déat, Joseph Darnand, and Jean Luchaire, kept up the illusion that they would soon be returning to France as conquerors and spent their days conspiring against one another and making elaborate plans for how they would settle old scores as soon as they were back in power.

10. In their careful and extraordinarily sad book, *Vichy France and the Jews* (New York: Basic Books, 1981), Michael R. Marrus and Robert O. Paxton show that by the end of 1944 over seventy-five thousand Jews were deported of whom only about twenty-five hundred (i.e., 3%) survived. This happened largely because the anti-Semitism of the Vichy government not only collaborated with, but habitually enacted and enforced, far stricter anti-Jewish decrees than the Nazis had expected to obtain. In Marrus's and Paxton's words, "Vichy mounted a competitive or rival antisemitism [to that of Germany] not a tandem one" (p. 12). For a more recent study that takes into account work done since the ground-breaking labor of Marrus and Paxton, see Paul Webster's *Pétain's Crime: The Full Story of French Collaboration in the Holocaust* (London: Macmillan, 1990).

11. The studies of Vichy France that I have found most helpful in understanding the period include Robert Aron, *L'Histoire de Vichy* (Paris: Fayard, 1954); Jean-Pierre Azéma, *De Munich à la Libération, 1938–1944* (Paris: Editions du Seuil, 1979); Yves Durand, *Vichy (1940–1944)* (Paris: Bordas, 1972); Marc Ferro, *Pétain* (Paris: Fayard, 1987); Pascal Fouché, *L'Édition française sous l'Occupation: 1940–1944*, 2 vols. (Paris: Bibliothèque de la Littérature Française Contemporaine de l'Université de Paris VII, 1988); Bertram M. Gordon, *Collaborationism in*

France during the Second World War (Ithaca: Cornell University Press, 1980); Gerhard Heller, *Un Allemand à Paris 1940–1944* (Paris: Editions du Seuil, 1981); Eberhard Jäckel, *La France dans l'Europe de Hitler*, trans. Denise Meunier (Paris: Fayard, 1968); Herbert R. Lottman, *Pétain, Hero or Traitor: The Unknown Story* (New York: William Morrow, 1985); Michael R. Marrus and Robert O. Paxton, *Vichy France and the Jews* (New York: Schocken Books, 1983); Robert O. Paxton, *Vichy France: Old Guard and New Order 1940–1944* (New York: Knopf, 1972); Pascal Ory, *Les Collaborateurs, 1940–1944* (Paris: Editions du Seuil, 1976); Pascal Ory, *La France allemande 1933–1945: Paroles du collaborationnisme français* (Paris: Gallimard/Julliard, 1977); David Pryce-Jones, *Paris In The Third Reich: A History of the German Occupation, 1940–1944* (New York: Holt, Rinehart and Winston, 1981); John F. Sweets, *Choices in Vichy France: The French under Nazi Occupation*, (Oxford: Oxford University Press, 1986); Richard Cobb, *French and Germans, Germans and French: A Personal History of France under Two Occupations, 1914–1918/1940–1944* (Hanover: Brandeis University Press, 1983); H. R. Kedward, *Occupied France: Collaboration and Resistance, 1940–1944* (Oxford: Basil Blackwell, 1985); Roderick Kedward and Roger Austin, *Vichy France and the Resistance: Culture and Ideology* (London: Croom Helm, 1985); Dominique Veillon, *La Collaboration: Textes et débats* (Paris: Livre de Poche, 1984). For a more general study of collaboration in a number of different countries, see David Littlejohn's *Patriotic Traitors: A History of Collaboration in German-Occupied Europe, 1940–1945* (London: Heinemann, 1972).

12. "Combien ces princes ducs et gangsters, avaient pioché de trous, cachettes, oubliettes? . . . dans la vase, dans les sables, dans le roc? quatorze siècles d'Hohenzollern! [. . .] tout l'afur était sous le Château, les doublons, les rivaux occis, pendus, étranglés racornis . . . les hauts, le visible, formidable toc, trompe-l'oeil, tourelles, beffrois, cloches . . . pour le vent! miroir aux alouettes! . . . et tout dessous: l'or de la famille! . . . et les squelettes des kidnappés [. . .] trésors des marchands florentins [. . .] quatorze siècles d'oubliettes . . . "

13. According to Henri Rousso, *Un Château en Allemagne: La France de Pétain en exil, Sigmaringen 1944–1945*, p. 70, Laval actually rather liked Céline.

14. "un escroc, un capable-de-tout, un traître, et un juif!"

15. "le Casino 'Tout-va' de l'Histoire."

16. In fact, Laval did try unsuccessfully to take cyanide a few hours before his execution by a firing squad. The scene in Céline's novel, is, so far as we know, fictitious, but it is likely that the details of Laval's suicide attempt gave the novelist the idea for the episode. Laval's last words were indeed "Vive la France!" as Céline correctly reports (*C* 32/35).

17. "peut-être on contestera mes titres? . . . que j'ai pas Saint-Pierre et Miquelon! . . . d'abord, que Laval est mort! . . . et que Bichelonne a rien laissé, rien écrit! . . . qu'on ne trouve rien aux 'Colonies!' et que ma parole suffit pas!"

18. I have preferred to use the correct name for the Danish prison, rather than Céline's spelling of Vesterfangsel. But the fact that he misspells both ends of his journey, the Castle-Fortress and the Castle-Prison, is worth remarking. Neither the setting nor the characters are intended to be quite the same in his fiction as they were in his life.

19. Since *Rigodon* was only published in 1969, eight years after Céline's death on July 1, 1961, it really did become his *Mémoire d'Outre-tombe*. The novel forced

the whole question of Céline's reputation, and of the Collaboration in general, back into the French literary consciousness.

20. For a fine discussion of the *tempérament du droit* and its use as a descriptive-analytic category by Jacques Maritain, see Robert Speaight, *Georges Bernanos* (London: Collins and Harville Press, 1973), pp. 36ff. Although Speaight does not discuss Céline, what he writes about the French right wing makes it clear how different Céline's ideas and style were from anything Maurras would have found tolerable. William D. Irvine's *French Conservatism in Crisis* (Baton Rouge: Louisiana State University Press, 1979) indirectly reveals just how marginal a figure Céline was in the French political scene by never mentioning him at all, even though writers like Drieu la Rochelle and Robert Brasillach do figure, if only in passing, in his study.

21. I do not want these distinctions to suggest that Céline's position had no political resonance in the internecine struggles of the French Right throughout the 1930s. In *Reproductions of Banality: Fascism, Literature, and French Intellectual Life* (Minneapolis: University of Minnesota Press, 1986), Alice Yaeger Kaplan shrewdly suggests that "what Céline is offering to the fascist right . . . is a chance to differentiate itself" from the aristocratic snobbism of the Action Française, and to embrace a populist vitalism and earthiness that is simultaneously imbued with the prestige of the "culturally avant-garde" (p. 120). Yet, Kaplan also admits that we have little evidence of "the extent to which the right took him up on his offer," and nothing that I have yet read suggests that such evidence is likely to be forthcoming.

22. Here, the difference between Céline and more conventional Collaborators and Fascist writers like Drieu la Rochelle, who sought an explanation for France's defeat in the nation's democratic and racially tolerant institutions, is particularly striking. For an illuminating analysis of Drieu's career from this perspective, see Marie Balvet, *Itinéraire d'un intellectuel vers le fascisme: Drieu la Rochelle* (Paris: Presses Universitaires de France, 1984).

23. Lucien Rebatet, "D'un Céline l'autre" in *Cahiers de l'Herne*, nos. 3 and 5 (Paris, 1972), p. 232.

24. Ibid.

25. "l'Hitler, semi-tout, mage du Brandebourg, bâtard de César, hémi-peintre, hémi-brichanteau, crédule con marle, semi-pédé, et gaffeur comme!"

26. "tenez pour les Juifs, combien était appointés à la Chancellerie? . . . et tout proches d'Adolf? . . . "

27. Patrick McCarthy, *Céline: A Biography* (New York: Penguin, 1977), p. 301. What is curious is how ready McCarthy is to see absurd motifs like this as a sign that Céline "loves to make fun of the master race theory." For McCarthy, "on one level this is comic, on another Céline is deadly serious: the Nazis show their brutality by trying to exterminate the cat, the creature who understands, as among humans only Lili the dancer can understand, what life and beauty are all about" (p. 301). One might have thought that Céline had other examples at hand of the Nazis' brutality, but even on his own terms, it is clear that he does not reproach the Germans for their "master race theory" as such, but for their refusal to apply it with sufficient consistency. Céline's humor is too problematic to permit one to see it as a way of expressing some conventionally positive content, and although in cases like this he clearly intends to mock the Nazis, it is hardly from the vantage-point of a late convert to humanistic values. *Rigodon* is dedicated "aux animaux." Céline never

denied that he valued animals far above people, and he insisted throughout his writings that he had extremely good grounds for such a choice.

28. "vous allez là, voir [. . .] mystique nationale-socialiste! les assassins au commandement!"

29. "la haine des Allemands, soit dit en passant, s'est surtout vraiment exercée contre les 'collaborateurs' . . . pas tellement contre les Juifs."

30. "les Chinois, les vrais, les Chinois de choc, ceux qui viendront nous occuper [. . .] il en viendra d'autres! bien d'autres! d'à travers les steppes . . . de ces hordes [. . .] l'important le sang!. . . le sang seul est sérieux! tous 'sang dominant.'"

31. In Lucien Rebatet's memoir, "D'un Céline l'autre," there is a story that shows just how unreliable an ally Céline could be. Rebatet tells about the inaugural meeting of the "Institute des Questions Juives" in Nazi-occupied Paris. Céline attended incognito and after listening to several speeches warning the audience about the "tyrannie judéo-marxiste" stood up to ask why no one ever mentioned the "blatant stupidity of the Aryans": "Et la connerie aryenne, dis, t'en causes pas? [But what about how dumb-ass the Aryans are? How come you never talk about that?]" (p. 234). Céline was immediately accused of being a Jew himself and a near-riot ensued that interrupted the whole meeting. I do not believe this anecdote in any way mitigates Céline's anti-Semitism, which no one, not even his most apolitical academic admirers, has ever really questioned, but it does show that he never felt like belonging to any organized movement for very long.

32. David Pryce-Jones, *Paris in The Third Reich: A History of the German Occupation, 1940–1944* (New York: Holt, Rinehart and Winston, 1981), p. 201.

33. "une bombe de concentration! de foi! [. . .] une terrible bombe morale!"; "la plus colossale statue, Charlemagne en bronze en haut de l'avenue de La Défense [. . .] Charlemagne et ses preux . . .Goebbels en Roland."

34. Benjamin discusses the *culte de la blague* in *Charles Baudelaire: A Lyric Poet in an Age of High Capitalism* (London: New Left Books, 1973). The parallel between Benjamin's account and Céline's practice was brought to my attention by Nicholas Hewitt's *The Golden Age of Louis-Ferdinand Céline* (Leamington Spa: Oswald Wolff Books, 1987), p. 198.

35. Henri Godard's annotations to the Pléiade edition of the trilogy contain a useful account of contemporary critical reactions in the French press to each of the books as it appeared. He discusses the Cousteau review on p. 1016.

36. Diderot, *Le Neveu de Rameau*, p. 46: "Je veux bien etre abject, mais je veux que ce soit sans contrainte."

37. "le vrai rideau de fer c'est entre riches et les miteux . . . les questions d'idées sont vétilles entre égales fortunes."

38. Letter of March 2, 1935, printed in *Cahiers de l'Herne*, nos. 3 and 5, p. 75: "Le malheur en tout ceci c'est qu'il n'y a pas de 'peuple' au sens touchant où vous l'entendez, il n'y a que les exploiteurs et les exploités, et chaque exploité ne demande qu'à devenir exploiteur [. . . .] Le prolétariat héroïque égalitaire n'existe pas. [. . .] Le prolétaire est un bourgeois qui n'a pas réussi."

39. "dix ans de vacheries, dont deux de cellule . . . eux là, eux autres, Racine, Loukoum, Tartre, Schweitzer, faisaient la quête de ci . . . de là . . . ramassaient les ronds et Nobel! . . . magots énormes! pâmés, bouffis, comme Goering, Churchill, Bouddha! . . . Commissars pléthores super-pâmés!"

40. "on pourra dire tout ce qu'on voudra, je peux en parler à mon aise puisqu'il me détestait, Pétain fut notre dernier roi de France. 'Philippe le Dernier' . . . la stature, la majesté, tout! . . . et il y croyait! . . . d'abord comme vainqueur de Verdun . . . puis à soixante-dix ans et mèche promu Souverain! qui résisterait? . . . raide comme! 'Oh, que vous incarnez la France, Monsieur le Maréchale!' le coup d'incarner' est magique! [. . .] Pétain qu'il incarnait la France il a godé à plus savoir [. . .] vous pouviez lui couper la tête: il incarnait! [. . .] Charlot fusillant Brasillach! aux anges aussi! il incarnait!"

41. "avait trouvé pour les Français de Siegmaringen une certaine façon d'exister, ni absolument fictive, ni absolument réele [. . .] statut fictif, 'mi-Quarantaine-mi-opérette.'"

42. The trilogy functions largely through such unexpected merging of genres, and as Céline reminds us in *Nord*, there was a time when the experience of war itself was narrated as a kind of picaresque tale called, in an image of singular pertinence, the travels of the nations: "[les] voyages des peuples" (*N* 311/11). By the time he wrote trilogy, Céline had clearly decided to become the "chroniqueur" (*N* 304/4) of the *Voyage au bout de la nuit* of his whole continent.

43. "vous êtes méprisé? faites-y-vous!"; "cette malédiction générale n'est pas sans vous apporter certains avantages . . . notamment à vous dispenser une fois pour toutes d'être aimable avec qui que ce soit . . . rien de plus émollient, avachissant, émasculant que la manie de plaire . . . pas aimable, violà c'est fini, bravo!"

44. One such echo to the *Quixote* occurs towards the end of *Nord*, when the senile old Rittmeister, armed only with his World War I sabre, rides away from Zornhof on his thin nag, the mare Bleuette, to attack the advancing Russian tank columns (*N* 580/301). The analogy to Cervantes's knight attacking the windmills or the troops of soldiers is, I think, both unmistakable and deliberate.

Henri Godard, in *Poétique de Céline* (Paris: Gallimard, 1985, pp. 335–36), is the only other critic I know of who has taken seriously the link between Céline's trilogy and *Don Quixote*. He does not mention the common motif of the governorship in both novels, but shrewdly links the incomplete narrative of each of the three books, its refusal of closure, to the episode in part 1, chapter 22 of the *Quixote* where the knight rescues a group of men condemned to serve as galley-slaves. One of these, Gines de Pasamonte, is himself the author of *The Life of Gines de Pasamonte*. When Quixote asks him if the work is finished, he answers "How can it be finished . . . if my life isn't?" He goes on to add that he does not mind going to the galleys, "for I shall have a chance there to finish my book" (*Don Quixote*, pp. 176–77). Godard's insight would only be strengthened if he had added that the image of a galley-slave was one of Céline's favorite metaphors for the labor involved in writing, from *Voyage au bout de la nuit* through the trilogy, where he constantly describes himself as a slave wearily rowing in Gallimard's ship. What makes the situation particularly abject is that he originally *chose* to be an author, rather than having it forced upon him: "'Taisez-vous! . . . ils avaient déjà aux galères, dix pour cent de 'volontaires,' vous êtes de ceux!' [Shut up! . . . even among the galley slaves there were ten percent of volunteers. You're one of them!]" (*N* 303/1). As my earlier comparison of Céline's to Sancho Panza's longing for a governorship also makes clear, Céline freely draws on whatever aspect of *Don Quixote* he needs for his immediate purposes, and if he increasingly resembles the haggard knight in appearance, his skepticism about abstract ideals and emphasis on the priority of physical survival maintain a link with the squire as well.

45. André Gide, "Les Juifs, Céline et Maritain," originally published in *Nouvelle Revue Française* 295 (April 1938); reprinted in *Cahier de l'Herne*, nos. 3 and 5, pp. 468–70.

46. Julia Kristeva, *Powers of Horror*, p. 180. The strategy of phrasing an obviously false or highly dubious assertion as a question, so as to introduce it without taking real responsibility for it (a literary version of what was called the principle of "plausible denial," used when a government's covert operations seemed especially damaging to its reputation), seems to me unhappily characteristic of much recent criticism.

47. Barthes's description is quoted in a list of observations about Céline, some favorable, others hostile, gathered by Frédéric Vitoux in his study *Céline* (Paris: Pierre Belfond, 1978), pp. 243–44: "Il [i.e., Céline] s'est trompé seulement parce qu'il portait un regard littéraire sur la réalité. Il transformait la réalité avec son langage."

48. "je vis encore plus de haine que de nouilles! . . . mais la juste haine! pas 'l'à peu près'!"

49. For a more extended discussion of this argument rejecting the aestheticizing "defenses" of a different author equally compromised by his anti-Semitism and Fascist allegiances, see my *The Tale of the Tribe: Ezra Pound and the Modern Verse Epic* (Princeton: Princeton University Press, 1980).

50. Hewitt, *The Golden Age of Louis-Ferdinand Céline*, p. 190.

51. For a characteristically intense advocacy of this position, and an unusual defense of Lucien Rebatet's *Les deux étendards* over Céline's novels, see George Steiner's essay "Cry Havoc," in *Extra-Territorial: Papers on Literature and the Language Revolution* (New York: Atheneum, 1976), pp. 35–46.

52. Alice Yaeger Kaplan, *Relevé des sources et citations dans "Bagatelles pour un massacre"* (Tusson, Charente: Du Lérot, 1987). Although no such study exists for the other pamphlets, I suspect that if *L'Ecole des cadavres* were examined with the same textual attentiveness, the findings would be quite similar. Because of their greater historical specificity (Céline's trip to the U.S.S.R. in one case, the French defeat by Germany in the other), *Mea culpa* and *Les beaux draps* are unlikely to have been composed as farragoes of racist commonplaces, although both of these works certainly exhibit an analogous reliance upon the most shabby second-hand topoi of their genre.

53. For a fascinating history of this text's composition, circulation, and regular reemergence as the foundation of many of the anti-Semitic clichés writers like Céline relied upon, see Norman Cohn's *Warrant for Genocide: the Myth of the Jewish World Conspiracy and the Protocols of the Elders of Zion* (New York: Harper and Row, 1967).

54. Critics have often been surprised that Céline could so quickly propound in his own name the same ideas he had ridiculed as part of Auguste's self-pitying paranoia in *Mort à crédit*. But I think such astonishment betrays a misreading of *Mort à crédit*, because although there is no doubt that Auguste is a thoroughly unappealing character, Ferdinand is far closer to his father in temperament than either he—or most of the novel's readers—have been willing to recognize. Nicolas

Hewitt's *The Golden Age of Louis-Ferdinand Céline* is one of the few studies I know that carefully pursues the numerous parallels between Ferdinand and Auguste throughout the novel (see especially pp. 117–22).

55. Merlin Thomas' *Louis-Ferdinand Céline* (London: Faber and Faber, 1979) has the most helpful discussion in English on Céline's language, especially in the pamphlets (pp. 79–183). Some of the most telling examples Thomas analyzes (pp. 97–100) are from the first half-page of *Bagatelles pour un massacre*. Céline delights in verbal forms like "enculagailler," an intensifier of the standard slang term for "to sodomize" (*enculer*) with the addition of the pejorative termination *-ailler*, which also indicates repeated action; "cocoriquer," from the onomatapoetic noun *cocorico* (the crow of a rooster, like our cock-a-doodle-do), to mimic the preening of celebrities; or, from *Les beaux draps*, the noun "vachardise" (from *la vache*, or cow), to indicate sluggishness, cowardice, and indolent passivity. Not surprisingly, Céline's lexical inventiveness is stimulated most by the drive to insult and attack.

56. I owe this phrase to Gary Saul Morson.

57. For a fascinating early response to the *Bagatelles pour un massacre*, see Hanns-Erich Kaminsky's counter-pamphlet, *Céline en chemise brune* (originally published in Paris in 1938 by Nouvelles Editions Excelsior and reprinted in 1983 by Editions Champs Libre). Steiner's phrase is from "Cry Havoc," in *Extraterritorial: Papers on Literature and the Language Revolution*, p. 39.

58. See especially Robert Brasillach's review of *L'école des cadavres* in the February, 17, 1939 issue of *Je suis partout*.

59. Céline, *L'école des cadavres* (Paris: Editions Denoël, 1938), p. 189: "Le latinisme est un lien lycéen, un lien de narcissime académique. [. . .] Il peut pas quitter le lycée. [. . .] C'est un lycéen enragé. [Latinism [in one's style] is a high school bond, a bond of academic narcissism. [. . .] He can't leave high school behind. [. . .] He's a furious schoolboy]." Although I have often deviated from his suggestions, I want to register my thanks to Christophe Lamiot, a graduate student in the French department at the University of California, Berkeley, for assisting me with the translations from Céline's pamphlets in this chapter.

60. Céline, *L'école des cadavres*, pp. 133, 144, etc.: "Nos redresseurs nationaux, les hommes comme La Rocque, comme Doriot, Maurras, Bailby, Marin, la suite [. . . .] C'est en somme des complices de Juifs, des empoisonneurs, des traîtres. [. . .] Et le style [de Maurras]! le fameux Style! Liquoreux, ânanonant, tendancieux, faux-témoin, juif [Our national saviors, men like La Rocque, like Doriot, Maurras, Bailby, Marin, and all the rest [. . . .] They are in fact bosom pals with the Jews, poisoners, traitors. [. . .] And [Maurras's] style! the so-called Style! Sugary, st-st-stuttering, tendencious, bought, Jewish]."

61. Céline, *L'école des cadavres*, p. 126: "Badriotes! Tous devant moi! Bedain! Ça va? Je suis derrière vous tous! moi Bedain! Tout pour les yites de partout! Pour la Badrie des cadavres! [. . .] Je vous retrouve aux Nécropoles! Je veux que ça soit le plus gigantesque cimetière! mon cimetière Bedin! Le plus énorme! [Badriots! Line up in front of me! I'm Bétain, OK?! I'm standing behind all of you! me, Bédain! I'll do everything for all the kikes the world over! For the l-l-land of the corpses! [. . .] I'll see all of you at the Necropolis. I want it to be the most enormous cemetery, my Bédian cemetery! The biggest one of all!]"

62. Emmanuel Berl, *Interrogatoire par Patrick Modiano suivi de "Il fait beau, allons au Cimetière"* (Paris: Gallimard, 1976), pp. 126–27: "Il dit que tout espèce d'individu qui a été au lycée, est par là même juif. Que pour lui, les prototypes du juif, c'est Mallarmé et Racine. . . . Il est très violent, mais on ne sait plus très bien contre quoi, parce que, finalement, était juif quiconque ne parlait pas l'argot. Tout académicien, etc. . . . Il restait à peu près seul à ne pas être juif."

63. Such images are traditional topoi of anti-Semitic literature at least since the Middle Ages, and Hitler's *Mein Kampf* incorporates as many as possible into a single book. During the Third Reich, German girls in the BDM (*Bund deutscher Mädchen*, the female equivalent of the boys' Hitler Youth) were told that one of the fundamental religious commandments every male Jew had to fulfill was to impregnate an Aryan woman.

64. Louis-Ferdinand Céline, *Bagatelles pour un Massacre* (Paris: Denoël, 1937), pp. 197–98: "Regarde comme ils sont heureux tes 'Français de race' d'avoir si bien reçu les Romains . . . d'avoir si bien tâté leur trique . . . si bien rampé sous les fourches . . . si bien orienté leurs miches . . . si bien avachi leurs endosses. Ils s'en congratulent encore à 18 siècles de distance! . . . Toute la Sorbonne en jubile! . . . Ils en font tout leur bachot de cette merveilleuse enculade! Ils reluisent rien qu'au souvenir! . . . d'avoir si bien pris leur pied . . . avec les centurions bourrus . . . d'avoir si bien pompé César [. . . .] Puisque c'est le destin des Français de se faire miser dans le cours des âges . . . puisqu'ils passent d'un siècle à l'autre . . . d'une bite d'étrusque sur une bite maure . . . sur un polard de ritain . . . Une youtre gaule ou une saxonne? . . . Ça fait pas beaucoup de différence! [. . .] Regarde un peu toutes les mignonnes, les Aryennes [. . . .] Elles foncent toutes, remarque, littéralement sur le Juif, sur le crépu, sur le 'toucan.' [See how they're so happy, your "purebred French people" to have welcomed the Romans so . . . to have felt their rod so well . . . crawled under the pricks so well . . . offered their ass so well . . . groveled so well. They are still congratulating one another about it all, after eighteen long centuries! . . . All the Sorbonne's in ecstasy over it! . . . They've turned this wonderful ass-fucking into an institution! They brighten merely at remembering it! . . . to have had so much pleasure . . . with the boorish centurions . . . to have pumped Caesar so skillfully [. . . .] Since it's the Frenchman's fate to be fucked through the ages . . . since they go from one century to the next . . . from an Etruscan cock to a Moorish cock . . . on a pig's pillow . . . A Gaulish Yid or a Saxon one? . . . Doesn't make that much difference! [. . .] See all the cute ones, the Aryan girls [. . . .] Notice how they all literally throw themselves at the Yid, the hairy one, the large-beaked toucan]."

65. Céline, *Bagatelles pour un massacre*, p. 198: "A présent que c'est le tour des youtres, leur suprême triomphe, ils vont finir raides comme des passes . . . Mais plus on se fait foutre . . . plus on demande . . . Et puis voilà qu'on leur promet aux Français, des bourreaux tartares! . . . C'est pas des choses à résister . . . Mais c'est une affriolance! [. . .] Après on aura les kirghizes . . . C'est au programme! . . . Ah! c'est promis! . . . Et puis des Mongols! . . . encore plus haineux! . . . plus bridés! [Right now it's the Yids' turn, their supreme triumph, they are going to die stone broke . . . But the more you're fucked . . . the more you ask for it . . . Now the French they're told they're going to get Tartar torturers! . . . That's not something that can be turned down . . . It's all so titillating [. . .] Then Kirghizes . . . It's on

the menu! . . . Ah! it's guaranteed! . . . Then Mongols! . . . still more ghastly . . .
more slit-eyed!]"

66. Ibid., p. 193.

67. Ibid., p. 14 and pp. 127–28.

68. Louis-Ferdinand Céline, *Mort à crédit*, in *Romans*, vol. 1 (Paris: Bibliothèque de la Pléiade, 1981), p. 570: "On empestait la campagne. . ."

69. I offer these lines without any pretense at originality or great confidence in
their explanatory value, but they seem to me basically accurate, even if limited in
scope. My work on anti-Semitism has convinced me that any global explanation
will be similarly deficient, and that each situation seems to bring forth a different
configuration of circumstances requiring specific and detailed study. Even then, I
fear, we are unlikely to understand its persistence across such different cultures,
historical eras, and social conditions. Jean-Pierre Richard's *Nausée de Céline* (Paris:
Fata Morgana, 1980) provides a lucid phenomenological interpretation of Céline's
consciousness, which is valuable even for those who, like me, do not share many of
Richard's methodological assumptions. Philippe Alméras, *Les Idées de Céline* (Paris:
Bibliothèque de Littérature Française Contemporaine de l'Université de Paris 7,
1987) and Jacqueline Morand's *Les Idées politiques de Louis-Ferdinand Céline* (Paris:
Librairie Générale de Droit et de Jurisprudence, 1972) contain more detailed discussions of Céline's shifting positions, although their treatment of his anti-Semitism is not particularly enlightening.

70. See Thomas Pynchon, *Gravity's Rainbow* (New York: Viking, 1973), p.
638: "Of course a well-developed They system is necessary—but it's only half the
story. For every They there ought to be a We. . . . Creative paranoia means devel-
oping at least as thorough a We-system as a They-system."

71. Céline, *Bagatelles pour un massacre*, p. 48: "D'ailleurs, il faut bien l'avouer
. . . mes frères de race [. . .] se montreront, c'est certain, cent mille fois plus abjects
que n'importe quels youtres. [Furthermore, one has to admit . . . my racial brothers
[. . .] have shown themselves without a doubt one hundred thousand times more
abject than any kikes]."

72. Even before the War, Céline's letters to correspondents who did not share
his political views were full of declarations like "Je ne suis qu'un ouvrier vous savez
d'une certaine musique. Je cherche n'importe où mes notes—où je les trouve—dans
les clairs et dans les ténèbres. Ce ne sont que des notes. En elles-mêmes elles ne
s'intéressent pas. . . . Je ne suis qu'un ouvrier d'une certaine musique et c'est tout et
tout le reste est infiniment indifférent, incompréhensible, paniquement ennuyeux
[I'm just a craftsman of a certain music. I look anywhere for my notes—wherever
I find them—in the light and in the darkness. They are just notes. They don't
interest me in themselves. . . . I'm just a craftsman of a certain music and that's all
and all the rest is infinitely lifeless, incomprehensible, suffocatingly boring]" (letter
to Evelyne Pollet, May 31, 1938). After his arrest in Denmark, this argument begins to dominate his tone with the outside world, especially in his exchange of
letters with Milton Hindus. E.g., "je suis beaucoup plus poète que prosateur et je
n'écris que pour transposer [I am much more a poet than a prose writer and I write
only to transpose [my materials]]," and "Le fait que vous me trouviez styliste me
fait plaisir—je suis cela avant tout—point penseur nom de Dieu! ni gr[and] écrivain
mais styliste je crois l'être [That you think of me as a stylist pleases me—that's what

I am above all—not a thinker damn it! nor a gr[eat] writer, but a stylist, that I really think I am]" (letters of March 30, 1947 and April 16, 1947, in *Cahiers de L'Herne*, nos. 3 and 5, pp. 89, 110, 111). Céline continued to stress the point in his 1957 recording "Louis-Ferdinand Céline vous parle": "Les idées, rien n'est plus vulgaire. [. . .] Je ne suis pas un homme à messages. Je ne suis pas un homme à idées. Je suis un homme à style [Ideas, nothing is more vulgar than ideas. [. . .] I have no message to deliver. I am not an idea man. I am a style man]" (*Romans* 2:934). Similarly, he was extremely fond of the comparison between his technique and that of the great avant-garde painters: "les peintres ne s'occupent pas spécialement de la pomme. La pomme de Cézanne, le miroir de Renoir, ou la bonne femme de Picasso, ou la chaumière de Vlaminck, ils sont le style qu'ils lui donnent [Painters are not especially concerned with apples. Cézanne's apple, Renoir's mirror, or Picasso's women, or Vlaminck's cottage, they are the style that their painters give them]" ("Entretien avec Albert Zbinden," in *Romans* 2:937). Needless to say, quotes such as these have played a major role in critical studies intent on "sanitizing" Céline for academic consumption by pretending that his content was a matter of no real significance.

73. See, for example, his justification for *Bagatelles* and his claim that his racist ideas have yet to be "disproved" in the interview with Albert Zbinden, most readily available in the Pléiade edition of the trilogy, pp. 936–45.

74. There is a fascinating compilation of most of these publicity efforts in Jean-Pierre Dauphin's and Henri Godard's "Le Lancement de *D'un château l'autre* (Juin–Octobre 1957)," in *Cahiers Céline* (Paris: Gallimard, 1976), 2:11–90.

75. In the trilogy itself, Céline offers a quite different and more unusual analogy, one critics have rarely mentioned. Toward the end of *D'un château l'autre*, Céline compares his writing technique to the efficient assassination method of Horace Restif, the political killer: Celine's language, like Restif's way of swiftly cutting his victim's throat, is "pratique, expéditif! . . . c'est tout! [practical and expeditious! no more, no less!]" (*C* 266/309).

76. "tous intellectuels bien sérieux! . . . c'est-à-dire pas gratuits! verbaux! du tout! non! . . .payants! l'article 75 bien au trouf! bien viandes à poteaux! [. . .] crevant bien de faim, de froid, et de gale."

Throughout the trilogy, Céline refers to himself and the other Collaborators having to flee France from assassination by the Resistance or post-War legal execution under "Article 75." Part of the "Décret-loi" of July 29, 1939, this article of book 3, chapter 1 of the French penal code specifies five kinds of treasonable actions, each of which carries the death penalty. These include (1) bearing arms against France; (2) entering into a relationship with a foreign power to encourage it to engage in hostilities against France or to assist it once such hostilities have begun; (3) delivering any French troops, territories, cities, fortresses, etc., to a foreign power; (4) encouraging French troops to defect to a foreign power during wartime, or recruiting directly for such a foreign power; and (5) entering into a relationship with a foreign power during a time of war in such a way as to assist that power in any way whatsoever. There is obviously a considerable degree of overlap in these categories, and Céline can be excused for believing that if he had been accused on any one charge he would be found guilty of them all. The complete text of Article 75 is given on p. 1063 of the Pléiade edition of the trilogy.

77. "le petit succès de mon existence c'est d'avoir tout de même réussi ce tour de force qu'ils se trouvent tous d'accord, un instant, droit, gauche, centre, sacristies, loges, cellules, charniers, [. . .] que je suis le plus grand ordure vivant."

78. From an undated letter to Galtier-Boissière reprinted in *Cahiers de l'Herne*, nos. 3 and 5, p. 193: "Je peux me flatter d'avoir fait pendant la période la plus enragée de l'Histoire de France, l'unanimité des Français au moins sur un point: mon assassinat." We have already seen in the instance of Laval's supposed dislike of Céline, that Céline has no hesitation about changing historical facts when it suits his novelistic intentions. Presenting himself as detested by the Vichy leaders serves three essential functions: (1) it furthers his claim to be an innocent victim of the War, rather than an important Collaborator; (2) it maintains the worm's-eye perspective of the story of one "ordinary" Frenchman trapped in Sigmaringen by forces beyond his comprehension; and (3) it endows his judgments on various political figures with a greater authority, since individual loyalties do not figure in his comments. Typical of Céline, he is sure that loathing is a far likelier guarantor of honesty than affection. Thus, before giving an example of Pétain's personal courage, he is careful to preface the anecdote with the comment: "I want to set things straight . . . I can be fair, because he really hated my guts [. . .] I can speak without prejudice, he detested me [je peux rétablir la vérité, je peux dire moi qu'il détestait, je parle en parfaite indépendance [. . .] je peux parler de lui bien librement, il m'exécrait]" (*C* 135/161).

79. In France, as Henri Thomas points out, most accounts of the Second World War were either written by professional historians or as memoirs by generals and leading political figures, whether successful like Charles de Gaulle, whose three volume *Mémoire de guerre* was published in 1954, or defeated like General Weygand, who wrote various books of self-vindication beginning in 1949. See Henri Thomas, "A propos *D'un château l'autre*," in *Cahiers de l'Herne*, nos. 3 and 5, p. 415. The War and the Occupation generated few accounts by ordinary French citizens, and although Céline's fame made him anything but "typical," the *literary* narration of his experiences, especially in the trilogy, is always pitched at the level of the ordinary, bewildered French victim, with no affection for either side in the struggle. At the beginning of *Nord*, Céline links the twin themes of himself as the neglected voice of the lowly citizen and his emphasis on the economic hazards of authorship. What serves as the glue binding the themes is, not surprisingly, *ressentiment*. Céline is wildly jealous of the "milliards" de Gaulle earned in royalties from his memoirs, while his own texts brought in a mere pittance—"quelque 'cent francs' lourds . . ." (*N* 311/11).

80. One of the first essays to focus upon the similarity between Céline and Dostoevsky was Irving Howe's fine piece "The Sod Beneath the Skin," originally published in *The New Republic* in 1963. The essay is reprinted in William K. Buckley, ed., *Critical Essays on Louis-Ferdinand Céline* (Boston: G. K. Hall and Co., 1989), pp. 53–63.

81. See the Pléiade edition of the trilogy, pp. 955–61, for a helpful calendar of events, and a discussion of Céline's distortions of the real historical sequence. For more detailed historical documentation, the best source is François Gibault's three volume biography of Céline: *Le Temps des espérances: 1894–1932*; *Délires et Persécutions 1932–1944*; and *Le Cavalier de l'Apocalypse: 1944–1961* (Paris: Mercure de France, 1977–85).

82. In reality, by the time Céline and Lily passed through Hamburg in March 1945, the bombing raids had become much less intense, if only because the cities no longer had any significant targets left standing. According to Sir Arthur Harris, *Bomber Offensive* (London: Collins, 1947) and Martin Middlebrook, *The Battle of Hamburg* (New York: Scribner's, 1980), Hamburg suffered its worst raids in July and August 1943. As so often in the trilogy, Céline's description, for all its vivid immediacy, is heavily fictionalized and dependent more upon his literary inventiveness than upon a reporter's accuracy. Céline's skill, of course, is precisely in making us believe he was an eyewitness to events he is now merely remembering. The discrepancy between Céline's account and the actual dates of the main bombing raids was first noticed by Catherine A. Clark, a student in one of my graduate seminars on Céline at U.C. Berkeley.

83. In this context, it is useful to stress Ian Noble's observation: "there are whole 'chapters' or series of chapters which are not concerned with narrating the events of 1944–5. The proportion of such passages differs widely from novel to novel: in *D'un Château l'autre* they amount to nearly 40 per cent, in *Nord* to a mere 3.5 per cent, and in *Rigodon* to 15 per cent, of the total number of pages. They are concerned mostly with events contemporary with the time of narration . . . [and] contribute to a powerful presence of the narrator in the text, and to a corresponding distancing from the wartime events he recalls" (Ian Noble, *Language and Narration in Céline's Writings: The Challenge of Disorder* [London: Macmillan, 1987], p. 138). Although Noble significantly overstates the degree to which we are ever allowed to forget Céline's wartime experiences—it is these very experiences that, as Céline keeps insisting, have determined the texture and pattern of his whole life and status in the narrative present—he is right to say that it is the narrator's *contemporary* tone and perspective that is decisive in orchestrating our reactions.

84. Louis-Ferdinand Céline, *Entretiens avec le professeur Y* (Paris: Gallimard, 1955), p. 70: "personne aime le 'je' d'autrui."

85. Blaise Pascal, *Pensées* (Paris: Garnier, 1964), nos. 451 and 455, p. 190: "Tous les hommes se haïssent naturellement l'un l'autre"; "Le *moi* est haïssable."

86. Céline, *Entretiens avec le professeur Y*, p. 98: "Je suis un type dans le genre de Pascal . . ."

87. Louis-Ferdinand Céline, *Mort à crédit* in *Romans* 1:536: "Elle a couru derrière moi, la folie . . . tant et plus pendant vingt-deux ans. [. . .] Elle a essayé quinze cents bruits, un vacarme immense, mais j'ai déliré plus vite qu'elle."

88. In *L'école des cadavres*, Céline describes European history as a blind staggering "d'un abattoir dans un autre [from one slaughterhouse to another]" (p. 206).

89. "'Mais non, Céline! . . . vous êtes tout d'attaque, au contraire! . . . le plus bel âge . . . Cervantès! [. . .] 81 ans! Don Quichotte!' Le truc de tous les éditeurs pour stimuler leurs vieux carcans . . . que Cervantès était tout gamin! 81 berges! 'Et plus mutilé que vous . . .Céline!'"

90. "je vais vous ennuyer peut-être . . . du plus drôle? . . . plus piquant? [. . .] vous connaissez mon souci! affriolez-vous! [. . .] le seul récit de nos avatars peut vous paraître monotone . . . quand vous avez tant de choses à faire ou simplement à vous asseoir, boire . . . vedettes, télévisions, pancraces, chirurgie du coeur, des nichons, des entre-fesses, des chiens à deux têtes [. . .] que je vienne moi en plus vous demander de vous procurer mon pensum d'une façon d'une autre! . . . je vois mal!"

91. "l'armée Leclerc à Stasbourg! . . . et ses Sénégalais coupe-coupe!" General Jacques Leclerc (1902–47) was Commander of the Free French forces in French Equatorial Africa, and later of the French Second Armored Division. It was Leclerc, at the head of his Free French forces, who entered Paris first at the Liberation. He then went on to capture Strasbourg. Céline's lines are a characteristic example of his complicated tone. Both Nazi and Vichy propaganda stressed the presence of so-called "inferior races" (Slavs, blacks, Jews, etc.) in the Allied armies. Since Senegalese troops, loyal to the anti-Vichy movement, served in Leclerc's armies, Fascist propaganda regularly described them as a wild horde of savages out to destroy European civilization. Céline records the real fear of the Collaborators in Sigmaringen, but gives it a racist tinge by fantasizing the African weapons the Senegalese supposedly will use upon them. So bizarre is his image that it is unclear whom he is satirizing: Leclerc's armies, the nightmares of the Collaborators, or the racist propaganda that has encouraged just such fears. My guess is that he meant the image as an accurate description of the Senegalese, but that the manically comic tone of the whole novel shifts the valence of such phrases toward the slapstick, irrespective of his underlying intention. At the same time, that original intention is still sufficiently registered to make the statement one more instance of Céline's racism continuing undiminished throughout the post-War years. It is also worth speculating whether the *Schwarzkommando* armies of Thomas Pynchon's *Gravity's Rainbow* do not owe at least part of their existence to Céline's fantasy of the "chop-chop Senegalese."

92. "c'est bien dix poubelles qu'on me barbote [. . .] on m'appelle plus 'Docteur' . . . seulement 'Monsieur' . . . bientôt ils m'appelleront vieille cloche! [. . .] un médecin sans bonne, sans femme de ménage, sans auto, et qui porte lui-même ses ordures [. . .] vous pouvez un peu réfléchir! . . . En attendant, réfléchissant, si vous m'achetiez un livre ou deux vous m'aideriez . . . "

The motif of the garbage cans, which occurs throughout the first sections of *D'un château l'autre* is one of the most comically successful of Céline's obsessions, and it owes its success to the maniacal insistence with which he keeps reverting to it as the sign of his utter public degradation. I have often wondered whether Céline has not also embedded a kind of witty pun on his own past as a literary hero of the Left in the motif. One of the first and most famous reviews of *Voyage au bout de la nuit* was by Leon Trotsky, who opened his praise of the novel with the wonderful sentence: "Louis-Ferdinand Céline est entré dans la grande littérature comme d'autres pénètrent dans leur propre maison [Céline has entered world literature like other men walk into their own houses]" (reprinted in *Cahiers de l'Herne*, nos. 3 and 5, p. 434). Trotsky made regular use of the Marxist phrase that anyone who disagreed with him belonged in the "garbage-can [or on the ash heap] of history." Since Céline's ignominy in Meudon is due to the hatred of the Left, the recurrent use of the garbage-can theme may be his way of mocking his enemies by reminding them (1) of how much they had once lauded him and (2) that their own current heroes could just as quickly be disgraced, as Trotsky himself was after losing his position in the Party to Stalin. If such a connection seems unlikely, and I offer it only speculatively, it is worth recalling how often in the trilogy Céline deliberately reminds his readers how *Voyage au bout de la nuit* was translated into Russian by Elsa Triolet with the aid of Louis Aragon, and that his novel was an enormous success in the USSR.

93. In a letter of March 8, 1952 to Albert Paraz, printed in *Cahiers de l'Herne*, nos. 3 and 5, p. 174: "tu trouves le truc du Temps [. . .] mais la musique du Temps change et n'est jamais la même d'un siècle à l'autre—seulement c'est la mort qui donne cette musique et elle seulement—*il faut payer*—c'est atroce et triste." For the best brief discussion of these themes in Proust, see Leo Bersani, "'The Culture of Redemption': Marcel Proust and Melanie Klein," *Critical Inquiry* 12, no. 2 (Winter 1986): 399–421, and his "1922, 18 November, Death of Marcel Proust: Death and Literary Authority," in Denis Hollier, ed., *A New History of French Literature* (Cambridge: Harvard University Press, 1989), pp. 861–66.

94. The connection between Céline and Proust is at last beginning to figure importantly in Céline criticism, but in spite of its centrality, no full study has yet been devoted to the issue. Henri Godard's *Poétique de Céline* (Paris: Gallimard, 1985) contains some of the most useful discussion of the Céline-Proust affinities that I have read. Specific parallels are also addressed in Nicolas Hewitt, *The Golden Age of Louis-Ferdinand Celine*, although neither of these books shows the connection extending into the trilogy. A useful bibliography of research on the subject can be found in Jean-Pierre Dauphin's "Répertoire," printed in succeeding issues of *Louis-Ferdinand Céline* in *La Revue des lettres modernes* beginning in 1974.

95. The sentence "Proust est un grand écrivain, c'est le dernier. . . C'est le grand écrivain de notre génération" is quoted in Jean Guénot, "Voyages au bout de la parole" in *Cahiers de L'Herne*, nos. 3 and 5, p. 356.

96. "que je les retrouve tous chez Caron, ennemis, amis, toutes leurs boyasses autour du cou!"

97. Henri Thomas shrewdly points out how very Parisian, in the specific sense initiated by Baudelaire's *Tableaux parisiens*, Céline's image of the *bateau mouche* really is (Thomas, "A propos *d'un château l'autre*," in *Cahiers de l'Herne*, nos. 3 and 5, p. 415). The whole encounter at the quai, with its swirling fog and sordid, tortured ghosts, with whom the narrator is soon embroiled in a violent exchange of insults, owes a great deal to *Les Fleurs du mal* and perhaps still more to *Le Spleen de Paris*. The relationship between Céline and Baudelaire, like so many of Céline's literary affiliations, still requires far more detailed study than it has yet received.

98. "cette lanterne magique."

99. "les gens s'attendaient que je provoque, que je bouffe encore du Palestin, que je refonce au gniouf! et pour le compte!" I have substituted "Jews" for Manheim's literal translation, "Palestinians," because it is clear whom Céline means, and Manheim's version only risks needlessly confusing readers.

100. "tout va! n'importe quoi vous est permis sitôt que vous êtes bien reconnu clown! que vous êtes certainement d'un Cirque! . . . vous êtes pas? malheur! pas de Chapiteau? billot! la hache!"

Chapter Six
These Children That Come at You with Knives:
Charles Manson and the Modern Saturnalia

1. Dostoevsky, *The Brothers Karamazov*, p. 651.

2. Ibid., p. 551.

3. Diderot, *Le Neveu de Rameau*, p. 95: "*Moi*: Si le petit sauvage etoit abandonné a lui meme; qu'il conservat toute son imbecillité et qu'il reunit au peu de

raison de l'enfant au berceau, la violence des passions de l'homme de trente ans, il tordroit le col a son pere, et coucheroit avec sa mere."

4. Dostoevsky, *Selected Letters*, p. 221. The passage I am quoting, from Dostoevsky's famous letter of September 1865 to M. N. Katkov announcing his plans for *Crime and Punishment*, was, it is only fair to note, written before Dostoevsky began serious work on the novel and as such represents only its initial germ, not its final realization. Nonetheless, I think it accurately summarizes Dostoevsky's view of the "strange, incomplete ideas . . . floating in the air" of his epoch, the kind of ideas to which the powerless and ambitious are regularly drawn.

5. Actually, as Gary Saul Morson remarked to me in a letter, the *Diary of A Writer* is about revolutionaries from two different eras. The first is the late 1840s, the epoch of the Petrashevtsy circle to which Dostoevsky himself belonged and for which he was sentenced to Siberia. The second is the time of the *Diary*'s publication, the mid- to late 1870s. The first group are treated as misguided but fundamentally decent idealists, motivated more by noble, but dangerously false, ideas than by *ressentiment*. The later revolutionaries, in Dostoevsky's view, are the century's Gadarene swine.

6. William Shakespeare, *Twelfth Night* 1.3.105–6, p. 58. No doubt the fact that Sir Toby Belch and Sir Andrew Aguecheek are both nobles, while Malvolio is an upstart, makes him a particularly tempting target for the "sport" of his social betters. My discussion here is greatly indebted to Stephen Booth's three essays, "*Twelfth Night*: I.i: The Audience as Malvolio," in *Shakespeare's "Rough Magic": Renaissance Essays in Honor of C. L. Barber*, ed. Coppélia Kahn (Newark: University of Delaware Press, 1985), pp. 149–67, "Getting Into the Spirit of *Twelfth Night*," and "The Last Few Minutes of *Twelfth Night*," both of which the author was kind enough to let me read in manuscript, as well as to Ralph Berry's fine discussion "Twelfth Night: The Experience of the Audience," *Shakespeare Survey* 34 (1981): 111–19.

7. This description helps account for the distinct strain of *ressentiment* in the writings of such champions of tradition and hierarchy as Allan Bloom, and of many of the writers associated with journals like *The New Criterion* and *Commentary*. It has always struck me as curious that their tone is so at odds with the supposed direction of their arguments, as though they did not realize that it is impossible to defend the claims of reason and order convincingly while oneself exhibiting the shrillness of injured vanity.

8. Fyodor Dostoevsky, *The Possessed*, trans. Constance Garnett (New York: Dell, 1961), p. 533.

9. In *The Brothers Karamazov*, Dostoevsky explicitly states that the future revolution will be made by the Smerdyakovs. In the chapter "Over the Brandy," for example, Ivan tells his father that Smerdyakov is "a prime candidate" to initiate a revolutionary uprising (p. 120).

10. Diderot, *Le Neveu de Rameau*, p. 109: "Rira bien qui rira le dernier."

11. I owe this description to Gary Saul Morson, "Genre and Hero/*Fathers and Sons*: Inter-generic Dialogues, Generic Refugees, and the Hidden Prosaic," an unpublished essay the author kindly showed me in February 1990. The phrase about seeing reality with "the eyes of the genre" is from P. N. Medvedev and M. M. Bakhtin, *The Formal Method in Literary Scholarship*, trans. A. J. Wehrle (Baltimore: Johns Hopkins University Press, 1978), p. 134. For a more detailed discussion of

these issues, see also Gary Saul Morson and Caryl Emerson, *Bakhtin: Creation of a Prosaics* (Stanford: Stanford University Press, 1990).

12. An exception to this point might be found in Céline's fascination with medieval legends, and especially in his own composition of the story of "Le Roi Krogold." But even that fable deals with death and betrayal, as much as with the dream-like loveliness Céline sometimes associates with Celtic mythology. Moreover, although the "Roi Krogold" figures throughout Céline's *oeuvre* in one form or another, after *Mort à crédit* it is never explicitly described again, and even in *Mort à crédit*, when the narrator does offer at least a synopsis of the legend, the only result in the actual world of the novel is Ferdinand's disgrace and the loss of his job.

13. Bernhard's novel *Wittgensteins Neffe* (Frankfurt: Suhrkamp, 1982), in particular, could serve as a telling example of the continuing vitality of the tradition I have traced here. In all of its central aspects it hearkens back to *Le Neveu de Rameau*, whose title it deliberately invokes. In Bernhard, as in Diderot, the roles of fool, philosopher, and artist are held up to question in an irresistible cascade of anger, wit and "vituperative abjection," as the narrator describes his lengthy friendship with Paul Wittgenstein, the eccentric nephew of the equally eccentric great philosopher. Bernhard's unmistakably autobiographical narrator asks which of the three—Ludwig, Paul, or he himself—lived the "much madder madness" ("die viel verrücktere Verrücktheit," p. 36), and which Wittgenstein—Ludwig or Paul—was the more deeply committed philosopher (pp. 44–45). But for all his skill at invective, as well as his readiness to accuse himself along with the horde of Austrian poseurs and time-servers who are his principal targets, Bernhard is too incensed by the stupidity and smugness of *others*, too authentically Juvenalian, to have the genuine *self*-loathing and compulsive theatricalization of his own feelings that form the constituent characteristics of an Abject Hero. I owe the suggestion to link *Wittgensteins Neffe* with my study, as well as the description of Bernhard's style as one of "vituperative abjection," to Richard Sieburth. (Bernhard's novel is translated into English by Ewald Osers as *Wittgenstein's Nephew* [London: Quartet Books, 1986]).

14. Albert Camus, *La Chute* (Paris: Gallimard, Collection Folio, 1956), p. 123: "prophète vide pour temps médiocres." I have used Justin O'Brien's English translation, published as *The Fall* (New York: Vintage Books, 1956), p. 117. Rima Drell Reck, in *Literature and Responsibility: The French Novelist in the Twentieth Century* (Baton Rouge: Louisiana State University Press, 1969), p. 81, n. 137, notices that Jean-Baptiste Clamence has the same first name Céline gave to Sartre in his vicious pamphlet-attack, *A L'agité du bocal*. Since so much of *La Chute* takes up issues from the famous quarrel between Camus and Sartre, Reck's point about the name is entirely plausible.

15. The French title, "Les Juges intègres" (p. 134), would probably be translated more accurately as "The Incorruptible Judges," but O'Brien's "The Just Judges" (p. 128) seems to me a fine decision, fully in keeping with the lexical patterns of *La Chute*.

16. Camus, *La Chute*, p. 70 (English ed., p. 65): "Songez pourtant à votre vie, mon cher compatriote! Creusez votre mémoire, peut-être y trouverez-vous quelque histoire semblable, que vous me conterez plus tard."

17. Horace, *Satires Epistles and Ars Poetica* 2.6.21–22, p. 226: "Non dices hodie, quorsum haec tam putida tendant, / furcifer? 'ad te, inquam' [Are you to take all day, you scape-gallows, in telling me the point of such rot? 'Tis you I say']."

18. The theme of refusing to help a suicide, or a person in desperate need, is itself a prominent theme in Dostoevsky. One thinks of Ippolit's suicide in *The Idiot*, or the story of the man who would not help the anguished little girl in "The Dream of a Ridiculous Man."

19. Dostoevsky, *Notes from Underground*, pp. 50–51.

20. Camus, *La Chute*, p. 151 (English ed., p. 145): "Regardez, la neige tombe! . . . Amsterdam endormie dans la nuit blanche, les caneaux de jade sombre sous les petits ponts neigeux, les rues désertes, mes pas étouffés." What is so amusing about Camus's indebtedness here, is that in Russian literature St. Petersburg itself was regularly called "the Amsterdam of the north," both because of its canals and because of Peter the Great's obsession with Holland.

21. Camus, *La Chute*, pp. 143–46 (English ed., pp. 138–40): "Puisqu'on ne pouvait condamner les autres sans aussitôt se juger, il faut s'accabler soi-même pour avoir le droit de juger les autres. Puisque tout juge finit un jour pénitent, il fallait prendre la route en sens inverse et faire métier de pénitent pour pouvoir en finir juge. . . . Plus je m'accuse et plus j'ai le droit de vous juger. Mieux, je vous provoque à vous juger vous-même, ce qui me soulage d'autant."

22. Camus, *La Chute*, p. 18 (English ed., p. 14): "Avez-vous remarqué que les caneaux concentriques d'Amsterdam ressemblent aux cercles de l'enfer?"

23. Camus, *La Chute*, p. 15 (English ed., p. 11): "Moi, j'habite le quartier juif . . . sur les lieux d'un des plus grands crimes de l'histoire."

24. For a contrary view, see Richard H. Weisberg's *The Failure of the Word: The Protagonist as Lawyer in Modern Fiction*. Weisberg recognizes how much Clamence owes to the Underground Man but finds that setting the novel in the shadow of the Holocaust endows *La Chute* with an exemplary authenticity in which "Clamence's 'fall' is that of a full generation of Europeans" who did not resist the Nazis (p. 128).

25. Camus, *La Chute*, p. 88 (English ed., p. 83): "nous nous confions rarement à ceux qui sont meilleurs que nous . . . nous nous confessons à ceux qui nous ressemblent et qui partagent nos faiblesses."

26. A character like McMurphy is clearly not an Abject Hero in the sense that I have defined the concept. But *One Flew Over the Cuckoo's Nest* depends heavily on the Saturnalian tradition in its most optimistic and celebratory sense. Although the Abject Hero could only arise out of the tradition of the Saturnalian dialogue, neither the classical Saturnalia nor a modern, theoretical construct of it like Bakhtin's privilege abjection, but rather the positive vigor of the briefly dominant underling. What Kesey's novel shows us, though, is how vitiated the idealization of the Saturnalia is today, and how it both vulgarizes its own literary heritage and manipulates the least challenging fantasies of its audience.

27. Vincent Bugliosi (with Curt Gentry), *Helter Skelter: The True Story of The Manson Murders* (New York: Bantam Books, 1975). An abridged text of Manson's speech is reproduced on pp. 524–31 of Bugliosi's book. A very different version of his testimony can be found in Nikolas Schreck, ed., *The Manson File* (New York: Amok Press, 1988), pp. 37–65. Schreck's compilation also contains numerous other texts by Manson, including short stories, songs and poems written in jail

since his arrest. For additional information, see also John Gilmore and Ron Kenner, *The Garbage People* (Los Angeles: Omega Press, 1971); Ed Sanders, *The Family: The Manson Group and Its Aftermath*, revised and updated edition (New York: Signet Books/New American Library, 1989); Nuel Emmons, *Manson in His Own Words as Told to Nuel Emmons* (New York: Grove Press, 1986); Susan Atkins (with Bob Slosser), *Child of Satan, Child of God* (Plainfield, N.J.: Logos International, 1977); Tex Watson (as told to Chaplain Ray), *Will You Die for Me?* (Dallas: International Prison Ministry/Cross Roads Publications, 1978).

28. Another popular candidate for this role was the rock concert at Altamont, California on December 6, 1969, where one of the spectators, Meredith Hunter, was murdered in the crowd, probably by a member of the Hell's Angels who had been hired as "event security." The general climate of violence at Altamont caused the concert to figure as a kind of "anti-Woodstock" in the popular press, but unlike the Manson killings, its significance never extended far beyond those specifically interested in the world of hippies and rock music culture.

29. David Felton and David Dalton, "Year of the Fork, Night of the Hunter," *Rolling Stone*, June 25, 1970, pp. 25–26. The issue features a picture of Charles Manson on the cover with the heading "A Special Report: Charles Manson, The Incredible Story of the Most Dangerous Man Alive."

30. "The Adventures of Ozzie and Harriet" ran on ABC from 1952 to 1966; "Make Room for Daddy: The Danny Thomas Show" was on various networks from 1953 to 1965, and "Father Knows Best" from 1954 until 1960. Later, post-"Helter Skelter" programs like "The Brady Bunch" (1969–74) and "The Partridge Family" (1970–74) managed, in the face of all contrary evidence, to maintain the same saccharine view of the American family throughout a period of often intense and unyielding generational struggles. Today, "The Cosby Show" has revived the genre with spectacular commercial success. In *Vineland*, Thomas Pynchon repeatedly invokes these kinds of programs, especially "The Brady Bunch," as icons of addictive and literally stupefying narratives. For additional information on this theme, see David Marc, *Comic Vision: Television Comedy and American Culture* (Boston: Unwin Hyman, 1989).

31. My discussion of figures like Charles Manson or Ira Einhorn is not meant to elide the distinction between the anarchic and the politically revolutionary strains in the ideologies of the sixties. An anarchic "counter-culture" movement and a would-be revolutionary rebellion can differ in a number of crucial ways, including divergent attitudes toward organized and disciplined group actions, questions of individualistic choice versus collective policy, etc. Concretely, one could sketch a descriptive model in which the activists of SDS (Students for a Democratic Society) and the "flower children" occupied antithetical poles. In today's climate, for example, the demand for "politically correct" behavior on university campuses is obviously not an anarchic, but a functionally conformist (although supposedly "revolutionary") criterion that a rebellious temperament might oppose because of its very dominance. But from the perspective of prosaic, anti-Utopian thinking, the two oppositional strains have more often proved identical in their disdain for the present order, their willingness to sacrifice themselves, or, more frequently, others, in order to rectify social ills. Both proceed from an abstract, theoretical model of a better world, in whose name long-established com-

munal habits, customs, and practices are to be discarded. The fact that the imagined new world orders envisaged by the two tendencies are incompatible is irrelevant from the vantage-point of the presently existing society. The movements are not essentially different in their *negative* force, even if the shape of the future order for which they articulate their critiques is fundamentally different.

32. Dostoevsky, *Notes from Underground*, p. 6.

33. My argument here is essentially identical to the point made by the opening "Editor's Note" that frames *Notes from Underground*: "such persons as the writer of these notes, not only may, but positively must, exist in our society, considering those circumstances under which our society was in general formed" (p. 3).

34. Dostoevsky, *The Brothers Karamazov*, p. 680.

35. Thomas Mann, *Dr. Faustus*, trans. H. T. Lowe Porter (New York: Modern Library, 1966), p. 25.

36. Thomas Mann, *Dr. Faustus*, p. 236. It is worth pointing out that these lines are actually spoken by Leverkühn's Devil in a long encounter that precisely duplicates, and is intended as a comment upon, the dialogue between Ivan and the Devil in *The Brothers Karamazov*. I am not convinced that Mann's taking up the challenge of Dostoevsky's prior examples succeeds without a certain embarrassment at his obvious strain, but the sections certainly rehearse the whole panoply of platitudes about the artist as daemonic victim/perpetrator.

37. Charles Lindholm's *Charisma* (Oxford and Boston: Basil Blackwell, 1990) takes Jim Jones, Charles Manson, and Adolf Hitler and their respective followers as three case studies in the phenomenon of charisma. He is especially interested in the disciples of charismatic leaders and, in an argument eerily reminiscent of *Notes from Underground*, uses the prevalence of charismatic cults to challenge any theory of human nature that maintains all human beings are "rational calculators," who first determine what they want and then use "instrumental reason" to get it. The total and often self-destructive fidelity of followers to their cult leaders points to a serious limitation in the model of a purely prudential, or even functional, explanation of human conduct.

38. Bugliosi, *Helter Skelter*, p. 531.

39. It is instructive to see how often writers who continue to glamorize Manson and see him as the inspired martyr-madman of our era draw upon Foucault for what they regard as the intellectual support his writings lend their positions. For example, Nikolas Schreck's collection, *The Manson File*, opens with an extended quotation from *Madness and Civilization* in which Foucault is discussing de Sade's *Les 120 journées de Sodome*: "The madness of desire, insane murders, the most unreasonable passions—are all wisdom since they are a part of the order of nature. Everything that morality and religion, everything that a clumsy society has stifled in man, revives in the castle of murders. There man is finally attuned to his own nature" (*The Manson File*, p. 7; *Madness and Civilization*, p. 282). Of course, Foucault is not responsible for the (mis-)use others make of his thinking, but the ease with which such appropriations take place and the regularity of their occurrence ought perhaps to make one skeptical, if not so much about Foucault himself then about his epigoni, whose invocation of, and dependence upon, the more lurid exempla in his writings is just as facile in academic journals as in the pages of Amok Press.

40. See *Rolling Stone*, June 25, 1970, p. 26.

41. This may, however, be an overly optimistic assessment. The ineradicable fascination of certain intellectuals and writers for the "emotional directness" and supposed insight into society's contradictions possessed by violent criminals is strikingly exemplified by the relationship between Norman Mailer and Jack Henry Abbott. Abbott, who by then had been a prisoner for nearly twenty-five years, began to write to Mailer about surviving in America's penal system. These letters became the basis for Abbott's book, *In the Belly of the Beast* (New York: Random House, 1981), published with a glowing preface by Mailer, and helped secure Abbott's parole. His brief season as a literary celebrity was abbreviated more decisively than most when, six weeks after his release, Abbott stabbed to death a waiter/actor/playwright in a Lower East Side Restaurant over the use of the men's room. When he was asked for his reaction, Mailer reportedly said, "It's a tragedy all around." Jean-Paul Sartre's complex idealization/re-creation of Jean Genet is a not dissimilar instance, even though Genet is a far more gifted writer than Abbott and made less lethal use of his freedom.

42. "A Ghost of Manson Reappears in the East," *New York Times*, Dec. 5, 1989, p. A11.

43. Dostoevsky, *The Brothers Karamazov*, p. 651. I have, of course, added the part in square brackets to amend Ivan's speech to my purpose here. I have felt justified in doing so since the passage is correctly quoted in its original context on page 157 of this chapter.

44. Allan Kozinn, "Manson Massacre as Myth," a preview of *The Manson Family* in the *New York Times*, July 17, 1990, p. B2.

45. Allan Kozinn, "Manson Massacre as Myth," p. B2. The initial, and more interesting, title of Moran's piece was *The Manson Family: Helter Five-O*. The composer intended to replace Manson's actual prosecutor, Vincent Bugliosi, with Steve McGarrett, the main detective on the long-running television show "Hawaii Five-O." I find such an idea particularly interesting because the actor Jack Lord portrayed Steve McGarrett as an authority figure of such stiff, unbending rectitude and moral certainty that his character often appeared unintentionally comical. However, CBS, which owns "Hawaii Five-O," protested, and Moran changed the name to Steve X and deleted any explicit references to the television series. For all the decisive differences, *Moi* and *Lui* nonetheless might have recognized their distant and rather dreadful descendants in these two icons of the sixties' popular imagination. But imagining such a fictional encounter is really unnecessary since Manson's actual courtroom opponent, Vincent Bugliosi, is sufficiently enamored of himself and his skill as both a prosecuting attorney and an investigator to make his dialogues with Manson already read like a grotesque metamorphosis of the mutual recriminations exchanged between Dostoevsky's "gentlemen readers" and the Underground Man. Manson is far crazier and more dangerous than Rameau, but Bugliosi is also far more vain, self-satisfied and fame-obsessed than the *philosophe*. In Robert Hendrickson's fascinating 1973 film, *Manson*, which could not have been shot without Bugliosi's extensive cooperation, the attorney is described (essentially by himself, although he has the words put into others' mouths) as: "Vincent T. Bugliosi was selected from 450 lawyers to prosecute Charles Manson and his co-defendants. He went far beyond the traditional role of a prosecutor, personally gathering much of the evidence. Colleagues, judges, the press, and even Charles Manson have called Bugliosi a judicial genius."

46. Frank Rich, "A Cast of Killers Made in America Sings Sondheim," *New York Times*, January 28, 1991, pp. B1 and B4.

47. Heiner Müller, "Die Hamletmaschine," in *Mauser* (Berlin: Rotbuch Verlag, 1978), p. 97: "Wenn sie mit Fleischmessern durch eure Schlafzimmer geht, werdet ihr die Wahrheit wissen."

48. Charles Manson, *Manson in His Own Words*, p. 12. The television program "Charlie's Angels" ran on ABC from September 1976 until 1981. See Les Brown, *Les Brown's Encyclopedia of Television* (New York: New York Zoetrope Books, 1982).

49. Joseph Conrad, *Lord Jim* (New York: Bantam Books, 1958), p. 138.

50. Jacques Lacan, *Le Moi dans la théorie de Freud et dans la technique de la psychanalyse*, livre II, 1954–55, séminaire du 25 mai 1955 (Paris: Seuil, 1978), p. 288: "que l'analyste ne soit pas un miroir vivant, mais un miroir vide."

51. Primo Levi, *I Sommersi e i Salvati* in *Opere* (Torino: Einaudi, 1987), 1:685: "non so, e mi interessa poco sapere, se nel mio profondo si annidi un assassino, ma so che vittima incolpevole sono stato ed assassino no; so che gli assassini sono esistiti, non solo in Germania, e ancora esistono, a riposo o in servizio, e che confonderli con le loro vittime è una malattia morale o un vezzo estetistico o un sinistro segnale di complicità; sopratutto, è un prezioso servigio reso (volutamente o no) ai negatori della verità." This work was translated by Raymond Rosenthal as *The Drowned and the Saved* (New York: Vintage Books, 1989); see pp. 48–49.

52. As a painfully apposite example, consider Shoshana Felman's yoking together of Primo Levi's writings about his concentration camp experience and Paul de Man's silence about his contributions to the Belgian Collaborationist newspaper *Le Soir* ("Paul de Man's Silence," *Critical Inquiry* 15, no. 4 (Summer 1989): 704–44). For Felman, Levi and de Man are in morally analogous positions, both wrestling with the difficulty of "bearing witness" to the Holocaust—a judgment about which I can say little beyond registering a certain numbness at how far intelligent critics are willing to go to justify their local gods.

53. Theodor Adorno, *Minima Moralia: Reflexions from Damaged Life*, p. 60.

54. Thomas Mann, *Dr. Faustus*, p. 357. I have somewhat modified the translation for clarity.

55. Roy Porter, *A Social History of Madness: The World through the Eyes of the Insane* (New York: Weidenfeld and Nicolson, 1987), p. 5.

56. This is obviously not the place to specify in more detail the contours of a principled defense of the quotidian, prosaic world. But it is not only considerations of space and immediate emphasis that make me resist the impulse to begin such a description here. How I understand the issues at stake would be contradicted by the kind of global and abstract formulation that could be included at this stage in the discussion. The texture and rhythm of our daily routines and decisions are too particular, too closely interwoven with changing context and circumstances, to be caught up and adequately accounted for by universal categories. The kind of ethics for which I am contending can better be enacted than formalized. Any adequate description must itself contain sufficient local depth and resonance to make vivid the lived world in which particular actions take place. That is why the novel is such a powerful repository of the kinds of exempla my position requires; instead of a series of moral imperatives, it is more pertinent to point to books like *The Golden Bowl*, *Anna Karenina*, *Shirley*, *Middlemarch*, etc., to prose meditations/memoirs like

Se Quest'è Un'Uomo, or indeed to the other texts already mentioned in the course of this book, for both positive and negative instances of a vital moral debate. It is notoriously difficult to articulate moral concerns without falling into a restrictive moralism. But one important distinction, to appropriate some of Michael Oakeshott's more explicitly political formulations, is that an ethical critique should not presume to offer a foundation for human practice but should express a distillation of practice itself. In opposition to much of what is considered "advanced" thinking in contemporary criticism, I believe that the role of theory should only be to illuminate practice, never to dictate it.

57. It is this uncertainty that marks the limit of my agreement with, or, perhaps more accurately, confidence in, the otherwise compelling notion of "prosaics" as developed by Gary Saul Morson in *Hidden in Plain View: Narrative and Creative Potentials in "War and Peace"* (Stanford: Stanford University Press, 1987) and in his "Prosaics: An Approach to the Humanities," *The American Scholar* (Autumn 1988): 515–28, as well as by Caryl Emerson and Gary Saul Morson in *Bakhtin: Creation of a Prosaics* (Stanford: Stanford University Press, 1990). For them, prosaics cannot be identified with the position of the *philosophe* or the "gentlemen readers": it rejects the whole Saturnalian dialogue, rejects, that is, both sides of the debate. But I remain concerned about how easily their prosaics, in less careful analyses, could begin to sound uncomfortably like the moralistic voices they explicitly do *not* accept as models. However, I have learned a great deal from my ongoing dialogue with their works, and our areas of shared concern outweigh the differences in our understanding of what a prosaic ethics entails.

58. See, for example, Emmanuel Le Roy Ladurie, *Carnival in Romans*, trans. Mary Feeney (New York: George Braziller, 1979); Norman Cohn, *The Pursuit of the Millennium* (London: Secker and Warburg, 1957). On millenarianism in general, see Kenelm Burridge, *New Heaven, New Earth: A Study of Millenarian Activities* (Oxford: Basil Blackwell, 1969); Sylvia L. Thrupp, ed., *Millennial Dreams in Action* (New York: Schocken, 1970).

59. Fyodor Dostoevsky, *The Idiot*, trans. Constance Garnett (New York: Dell, 1959), p. 348.

Index

Abbott, Jack Henry, 232n.41
Abetz, Otto, 128
Abject Hero, 6, 15; compulsion of, to perform, 22, 30–31, 51, 54–55, 73–76, 93, 106, 117; and crisis of citation, 30–31, 51, 73–75; definitions of, 15, 18–19, 27–32, 93–99, 155, 184; dialogism of, 10, 18, 22–23, 27, 50–51, 54–55, 94–97, 100–101, 116–17, 130, 143, 154, 167, 176, 182; distinguished from outlaw and monster, 27, 119–20, 171–72; history of, 116–17; and intelligentsia, 96; and licensed fool, 23, 30, 81; and monster, 26–27, 30–33, 118–19, 147; novelization of, 81–82, 93–99, 116–17, 130, 162–63; and *ressentiment*, 9, 19, 27–33, 54–55, 82–83, 89–90, 102–6, 120–21, 154–55; and self-consciousness, 15, 22, 30–31, 73, 82, 94–96, 106, 162; and vanity, 32, 51–52, 80
abjection: and citationality, 112, 163; and compulsion to perform, 88–96, 98, 119, 121; definitions of, 9, 18, 26–29, 70, 88, 97; and dialogism, 29, 70, 89–90, 95, 112, 117, 142, 147, 155; distinguished from suffering, 28, 70–74, 80, 92; and lack of glamor, 27–29, 72, 80, 88–89, 105, 112–16, 121–22; and rebellion, 80, 88–90, 98, 107–8, 126–29, 181; and *ressentiment*, 9–10, 27–28, 103–12, 120, 153–54, 171, 179, 183; and Saturnalia, 18, 23, 100, 184; and spectacle, 17, 23, 106; as state of mind, 28–29, 88, 101
Adams, Henry, 131
Adorno, Theodor, 8, 26, 180, 201n.35
Alexander III (czar), 114
Alméras, Philippe, 221n.69
Altamont concert (California), 230n.28
Amichai, Yehuda, 153
Anderson, Wilda, 75, 203n.60, 204n.72
Anderson, William S., 192n.33
Angely (fool of Louis XIV), 201n.36
anti-Semitism, 9; citationality in, 136–37, 218n.53, 221n.69; in Dostoevsky,

206n.3; *Protocols of the Elders of Zion*, 134; Russian, 206n.3; and Vichy France, 213n.10. *See also* Céline: racism in; *Je suis partout*; Vichy France
Apocalypse, 8, 39, 160; in Céline, 122; and Manson, 171. *See also* carnival; intelligentsia; Saturnalia
Aragon, Louis, 225n.92
Arden, Heather, 197n.8, 201n.36
Aristophanes, 34
Aristotle, 38
Aron, Robert, 214n.11
arriviste: in Dostoevsky, 115; in Shakespeare, 15, 115. *See also* Horace; parasite
Article 75, 140. *See also* Céline, Louis-Ferdinand
Ashanti, the: *Apo* festival of, 36, 37
Auschwitz, 29
Austin, Roger, 214n.11
authenticity, 132, glamorization of, 7, 8
Azéma, Jean-Pierre, 213n.11

Bailey, D. R. Shackleton, 192n.34, 194n.48
Bakhtin, Mikhail: and carnival laughter, 17, 34; on confession, 94, 206n.6; on dialogism, 77, 81, 105, 113, 116–17; on genre memory, 94, 162–63, 178–79; his theories of carnival, 17–18, 23, 35–39, 63, 81, 117, 190n.11, 227n.11 (Bakhtin and Medvedev)
Balvet, Marie, 215n.22
Balzac, Honoré de, 106, 111
Barthes, Roland, 132, 218n.47
Baudelaire, Charles, 203n.64; and Céline, 226n.97
Beachey, Jennifer, 209n.36
Beatles, The, 171
Beckett, Samuel, 80, 121
Belknap, Robert L., 92, 212n.59
Benjamin, Walter, 26, 128, 186n.2, 191n.21
Bergson, Henri, 139
Berl, Emmanuel, 220n.62
Berman, Marshall, 210n.42